CHILDREN OF HIROSHIMA

By Mrs Toshiko Akamatsu

children of hiroshima

HARPER COLOPHON BOOKS
Harper & Row, Publishers
New York, Cambridge, Philadelphia, San Francisco
London, Mexico City, São Paulo, Sydney

55337

This work was first published in the United States by Oelgeschlager, Gunn & Hain, Inc., in 1982. It is here reprinted by permission.

88 - 164 14

First HARPER COLOPHON edition published 1982.
Library of Congress Catalogue Card Number 82-47906

ISBN: 0-06-090965-X   (previously ISBN: 0-89946-128-X *cloth*)
                                              0-89946-129-9 *paper*)

82 83 84 85 10 9 8 7 6 5 4 3 2 1

Blood

While taking down classroom notes,
My head bent intently,
All of a sudden
A drop of blood fell on my pencil.

Without ceasing,
The nose-bleed went on without ceasing,
Coloring the words, turning them red.
Death,
That is raising its head
From some corner of my heart, awaiting its chance.

Death!
But I do not want to die,
Because of the atom bomb.
I do not want to die without speaking a word.
Is it right that the Bomb,
May drop and take away the people's lives,
Anywhere in the world?
May force such miserable creatures as I,
To bear a fate like mine,
Anywhere in the world?

I do not want to die!

I steal a glance at my arm, under the sleeve —
Death's spot is not there yet.

Koichi Tokuno
11th grade boy (5th grade at the time)

ARATA OSADA, Litt.D.,
Ph.D. (1887–1961) – Born
1 February 1887. A grad-
uate from the Department
of Philosophy (pedagogy)
at Kyoto University in 1918. Received a doctorate in literature in 1919
for his research work on Johann Heinrich Pestalozzi (1746–1827), a Swiss
educator. Experienced the atom bombing of Hiroshima 6 August 1945.
Appointed president of the Hiroshima University of Humanities and Science and dean of the Hiroshima Higher Normal School 6 December 1945.
Designated president of the Japan Association of Pedagogy in 1947. Elect-
ed a number of the Japan Council of Science in December 1948. Retired
from the presidency of the Hiroshima University of Humanities and Science
30 June 1949. Published *Children of Hiroshima: Appeals from the Boys
and Girls of Hiroshima* in October 1951. Gave a lecture on Pestalozzi at
the Universität Zürich and received a doctorate in philosophy 29 April
1960. Died 17 April 1961. Part of his remains have been buried next to
Pestalozzi's grave.

from editor

I

Children of Hiroshima: An Appeal from the Children of Hiroshima was compiled by Dr. Arata Osada and published thirty years ago, and still remains an indispensable classic of relevance to the problem of nuclear weapons. The reason for issuing this English translation after the passage of thirty years is that we feel very strongly the need for it to be read afresh by the people of the present day.

The original book was written six years after the atom bomb was dropped on Hiroshima. Now it is hard to imagine just how difficult it was to talk about the atom bomb in the years immediately following the Hiroshima bombing of August, 1945.

The San Francisco Peace Treaty and the U.S.-Japan Security Treaty came into effect in April 1952. Bringing up the subject of the atom bomb during the allied occupation was considered to be related to anti-Americanism because of the extremely inhumane nature of the weapon and so any such discussion was strongly restricted. A Hiroshima primary school teacher wrote the following, in August 1951.

"I was always one of those who wanted peace. Because of this I did not ask the children about the atom bomb and I didn't teach them anything about it directly .... I don't want to give a clumsy interpretation of the atom bombing, or of war, or peace, or put a good face on everything. In fact, as far as possible I tried not to touch on such things .... One thing was that I thought that for the children of Hiroshima talking about the atom bomb or about war would be too cruel."

In Japan, it was only after the 'Bikini incident' in March, 1954, two years after the end of the occupation, when a Japanese fishing vessel was contaminated by fallout from a nuclear test, that the subject of the atom bomb could be discussed in ordinary society. It was from that point that, at long last, the anti-bomb movement arose; a campaign to collect signatures was launched and in August, 1955, the first Ban-the-Atom-Bomb World Conference was held in Hiroshima.

II

How many people died in Hiroshima? Even now, there are no clear figures on this. A number of scholars have been conducting studies on this subject in recent years, but deciding the figure is by no means easy. Perhaps the figures given in the children's accounts in this book may be found unsatisfactory, because they are very approximate. However, in the period following the bombing, studies to clarify the figures were taboo. And now, at the present day, it is very difficult to clarify the situation of those days.

Also tabooed were surveys and research into the effects of the atom bombing on the human body. Readers may often note in the children's accounts references to 'poison' being inhaled, and this is because in 1951 that was about the general level of comprehension regarding the effects of radiation.

After the Bikini incident of 1954 some victims of the atom bombing finally came forward and demanded treatment, but in the nine years prior to that the tens of thousands of bomb victims who were worried about after-effects were given no care whatsoever. Perhaps the state of things in those days may be judged to some extent by the fact that even now, thirty-five years after the bomb was dropped, no proper relief or compensation laws have been enacted. Just how difficult were the conditions under which *Children of Hiroshima* was compiled, and how much courage did it require for the children to write of such things? Atom bomb victims were feared as if they were the carriers of a contagious disease and it was a major obstacle to their finding employment or getting married, something that we hope readers will discern by reading between the lines of the accounts.

At least one victim of the bomb has been heard to say that for him there was no joy in life until after the first Ban-the-Atom-Bomb World Conference in 1955.

From what has been written here, it is possible to see this book as one of the starting points of the debate on the problems of nuclear weapons. Also, it is necessary to add a note of explanation concerning the time at which the book was published.

III

The peace treaty, which I have already mentioned, was signed on September 8, 1951, in San Francisco. This treaty, which did not include Russia, was strongly opposed by Japanese scholars and intellectuals. At the time this treaty was being debated by the Japan Science Council, Dr. Osada was one of the central figures opposing it as being a unilateral treaty.

In the period of the Cold War, after 1946, the American Government began intervening on a major scale here in order to rebuild the economy and social structure, so as to form Japan into a bulwark of defense against communism. What is termed the "Red Purge" started in 1949, with many activists being driven from their workplaces. Then, on June 25, 1950, war broke out on the Korean Peninsula. This is why some of the accounts in this book contain references to the Korean War. At the same time, it is probable that Dr. Osada felt that there was a considerable risk of nuclear weapons being used in Korea, and this possibility was most likely part of his motivation in compiling the book. In connection with this, Dr. Osada stated in the preface to the original edition his wish that the book be used as a text for education in peace studies. But having people write such accounts is in itself an education in peace, and is a statement that the moral education, of which the Japanese Government has begun to speak, has to be, in content, peace education.

IV

The original Japanese edition of *Children of Hiroshima* (*Gembaku no Ko* in Japanese) is still on sale even now, and partial translations have already been published. Unfortunately, however, up to now there has been no complete translation

which included Dr. Osada's preface, and one undeniable reason
for this was that his strong devotion in the pursuit of peace
would not allow him to make any compromise toward realizing
the publication of a complete translated version. However, with
last year, 1979, being designated the International Year of the
Child, talk began about translating and publishing the work. The
result was the formation of an association to gain wide support
and cooperation and promote the translation and publication of
the book, with the participation of Ms. Setsuko Hani, President
of the Japan Association for the Protection of Children, Ms.
Fuki Kushida, President of the Federation of Japanese Women's
Organizations, and Mr. Motobumi Makieda, Chairman of the
General Council of Trade Unions of Japan, plus Mr. Ichiro
Moritaki, Professor Emeritus of Hiroshima University, and Mr.
Takeshi Shinmura, Professor Emeritus of Nagoya University. I,
as Vice-President of the Japan Association for the Protection of
Children, was given the responsibility of coordinating the pro-
ject.

There were many difficulties, but with the thoughtful
cooperation of all quarters, the task was brought to completion,
and for this we would like to express our deep gratitude. As
touched on in the biographical note on Dr. Osada, he was elect-
ed president of the Japan Association for the Protection of Children upon its inception, and remained in that post for many
years. It also gives us pleasure to be able to publish the work
of one who had such a long and close affiliation with the Association.

The original translation, which was done by Dr. Osada
himself, has been edited completely by IEC Inc.

As can be imagined, the translation involved many difficulties. To begin with the writers were children, and their accounts sometimes contain contradictions, inconsistencies and
expressions in the local Hiroshima dialect, and in places the

children's intended meaning is difficult to follow. It is also very difficult to reproduce in English the same tone, that is, the words and sentences that reflect those used by the children in their original Japanese. In this respect, it may be necessary to gradually make improvements in the English as they are found to be necessary.

Be that as it may, I think that at this point the important thing is to bring out this complete translation.

With regard to Dr. Osada's preface, the translation of the first three sections is as faithful as we can make it, while I have replaced sections four, five and six with an explanatory note. I welcome comments on whether this was best or not. I do not feel, however, that anything of Dr. Osada's original intention has been lost.

We have not given detailed explanations every time an object or custom peculiar to Japan is mentioned. Some of these are simple and straightforward; others, if the attempt were made, would require an explanation encompassing Japanese traditions. Since World War II, there have been wide-ranging and rapid changes in Japanese customs and way of life, it may be that this also requires explanation in some parts. However, in nearly all cases we have dispensed with any explanatory notes or comments. We welcome any comments readers may have on this point.

V

What the publishers of this book want most, of course, is for it to be read by as many people as possible, and in accordance with Dr. Osada's strong desire, for it to form one step toward the banning of nuclear bombs and the establishment of world peace.

At the beginning of his preface, Dr. Osada refers to a branch of the Osaka Bank, on the stone steps of which was the imprint of a human form. This has now disappeared completely, but the powerful impression it left on anyone who saw it can never be erased. The imprint may be gone, but the impression it made on the hearts of men will never fade. It must never disappear until the day comes when people everywhere are truly at peace.

Many people assisted in the work of issuing this English translation, too many to mention here individually. Needless to say, if it had not been for the enthusiasm shown by Dr. Osada's family, the project would never have got off the ground. Many also cooperated by providing contributions. With regard to the composition of the book, the format and other such points, advice was received in particular from Mr. Nobuo Kusano, Ms. Yuhko Yamaguchi and Mr. Shoichiro Kawasaki. A student of Dr. Osada's, Mr. Yutaka Okihara, conducted various surveys and we also received the cooperation not only of people of Hiroshima, but also that of citizens of Nagasaki. The members of the press also were warmly cooperative in publicizing this work.

Mr. Hajime Yukimune carried out much detailed work on the book, while Mr. Richard Foster and others of the firm of IEC showed the greatest conscientiousness in the task of editing and partially translating the book. Thanks for the work involved in the printing must go to the Asahi Evening News, especially to Ms. Kiyoko Mizukoshi for doing the proofreading. Finally, I would like to express my gratitude to Iwanami Shoten, the publishers of the original Japanese edition of *Children of Hiroshima*, for their unconditional permission to carry out the translation.

One point that still troubles my mind concerns the writers (some of whom are now dead) of the accounts: should I have spoken to each of them about this translation? In the intervening years they must have experienced many things.

I also feel responsibility for the many (several thousand) accounts not included. I really do not know what is best. But I do believe that this book will help to banish nuclear weapons and establish peace around the world, and I therefore ask the forgiveness of all for any shortcomings I may have displayed in carrying out my task.

June 1980

Yoichi Fukushima

prof. osada's preface

Preface to the Original Edition in 1951
(As abridged by the editor of this book)

I

Six years have passed since that most tragic moment in the history of the human race—fifteen minutes past eight on the morning of August 6, 1945—which was said to be the beginning, or else the end, of the world. That day, on which the first atom bomb ever dropped on the earth exploded above Hiroshima City, has come around once again. By that single explosion, the entire city was reduced to ashes and 247,000 lives, or well over half the population of the city (400,000), were wiped out.

The city of Hiroshima lies on the delta of the Ohta River, which has its source in the Chugoku Mountain Range and separates into six streams as it flows through the valleys toward the Seto Inland Sea. Now, six years after the disaster, in this river which was once practically filled with scorched corpses, clear water flows silently, reflecting the green trees along its banks. Makeshift shops built along the streets are among the meager indications of reconstruction. If you walk a few steps to the other side of the main street, you will find fallen tombstones, rusty iron scraps and pieces of brick scattered here and there about the open spaces covered with thriving weeds. The streets, once busy and illuminated with many electric lights, are now dark and dreary at night. Though the city has revived to a small extent, the life of the people is still at a low-water mark, still desolate. It is brought home to you that conditions in Hiroshima are totally beyond comparison with those of other war-damaged cities in the world. Certain journalists may comment favorably on the state of rehabilitation in Hiroshima. But, if you continue your walk along the city's streets, you cannot miss the large number of crude, makeshift shacks roofed with galvanized iron sheets and patched with pieces of wooden board. Some former residences like the wooden houses on the outskirts of the city, for example, survived the bomb though losing parts of their walls; they still stand, after a fashion, with their supporting pillars knocked askew by the blast. A few imposing ferroconcrete public buildings are still prominent on the scene, but their interiors are totally gutted. None of this makes for a harmonious landscape.

No less than two-thirds of the people living in the city moved there after the catastrophe. Most of those who were in the city at the time of the blast and barely escaped with their lives have dispersed either to the rural areas or to other districts. The number of those who have been able to return to their old homes is therefore only a third of the present population of about 290,000. Many of the returnees were once wealthy merchants with big stores on the main streets; now, in order to earn a minimum livelihood, they dispense their scanty wares in tiny stalls along the back streets.

There is a branch office of the Osaka Bank (at the time of the blast, it was called the Sumitomo Bank) about five hundred yards away from the center of the explosion. A simple wooden framework is constructed on one side of the stone steps leading up to the main entrance. If you look at it, you will find it encloses a dark silhouette of a man printed on the stone wall and the steps. Upon these steps at the moment of the blast, a man must have been sitting, perhaps with an elbow on one knee and one hand supporting his chin, in an attitude of deep thought. The powerful action of the radioactive waves "printed" the outline of this man on the wall, marking the moment of his death. The dark silhouette is gradually disappearing and, as time passes, memories of that tragic time will gradually be forgotten. But the shadows will never lift from the hearts of the people of Hiroshima who lost their parents, brothers and sisters and friends. Though they smile cheerfully in answer to inquiries after them from sympathizers and even appear carefree at times, the agony remains profound and lasting.

I should like to discuss here some of the atom bomb-induced injuries and diseases. Most of the survivors of the disaster have scars on their skin. Those who are able to conceal these under their clothes are comparatively fortunate. But many who have ugly scars on their faces or hands, especially girls of marriageable age, are filled with secret anxieties. A seventh-grade girl, Chieko Sakamoto, says in her account, "The only treatment given us at the first-aid station was a smear of mercurochrome. If I had been given adequate medical aid at that time, no scar would have remained. When I think about this, I can't keep from crying. My mother's eyes are full of tears when she tells me, 'You're a lucky girl, Chieko, to have survived. We thought you would die.' My mother's tears make me feel sadder and I cry silently for a long time."

Etsuko Fujioka, a girl in the eleventh grade, writes, "I'll have the scar on my face as long as I live. Why am I so conscious of this scar? Because people began to tease and taunt me about it saying it was a *pikadon* [an onomatopoeic term for 'flash' and 'boom,' referring to the bomb] scar. Thinking that it could all be worse, I stayed quiet and did not say anything about it to my father or mother . . . . I came back to Hiroshima. Even there I was teased and made fun of by neighbors and classmates, even by students in the lower grades. After I entered [middle school], I became more unhappy . . . . But the thought of the future terrifies me." (p. 182)

The injuries are not limited to the skin surface, however. They penetrate deep into the body. According to the *Effects of the Atom Bomb* jointly compiled by the American Atomic Bomb Commission, the U.S. War Department and the Los Alamos Scientific Research Institute, "temporary sterility can occur with smaller doses, however, as happened among Japanese men and women, and the vast majority of these have since returned to normal." The term "majority" may be interpreted in different ways. It is an undeniable fact that there are quite a few victims of the bombing who have not recovered from their sterility. A young woman, who at the time of the bombing was a schoolgirl, related that she was unable to bear children; this strongly shocked me making me feel that the world had been plunged into darkness. I could not but be deeply moved, however, to know that she had not lost hope and, with her parents' encouragement, struggled to follow her ideals and, in some way, lead a meaningful life.

The gamma rays and neutrons produced by the atomic explosion penetrated deep into the marrow of human bones. Many people who had no external wound and looked healthy began to be affected, some of them in a few days, others in a few weeks and, still others, after a few months. Their hair began to fall, their gums began to bleed, diarrhea occurred for no obvious reason, dark purple spots appeared on their skin and the frequent vomiting of blood commenced. Eventually they died, having been fully aware all the while of what was happening to them. But these occurrences decreased in number as the months went by and with the passing of October we hoped that they had come to an end. On the contrary, however, today, six years after, the disease will suddenly attack a girl who might be playing happily with her friends or an apparently perfectly healthy man at work. Ikuko Wakasa, a fifth-grade girl, writes, "Only six months ago [January, 1951], a ten-year-old girl lost all her hair from radiation sickness. The Red Cross Hospital doctors did their best to help her, but she vomited blood and died in twenty days. I was shocked to hear such a sad story of death after six years and it reminded me of that day again." (p. 13)

When I was in the middle of writing this preface, a young man of Aki County, Hiroshima Prefecture, came to see me. He told me that his father, who had been in Hiroshima at the time the atom bomb fell, had since seemed well and worked in the fields as usual. In July this year, he fell ill from some unknown cause and had to be confined to bed. After giving him a careful examination, the doctor said that his white blood corpuscles had greatly decreased in number and that he was obviously a victim of radiation sickness, for which no adequate treatment was yet available. The deeply grieving family could only sit around and watch the sick man, not knowing what to do. In spite of the fact that six years have gone by since the atomic catastrophe, similar stories are still heard in and around Hiroshima.

Moreover, even the offspring of those exposed to radioactivity are affected. Not knowing anything myself of the laws of heredity, I cannot say how true this is. But, according to a Reuter report, the distinguished English scientist, Dr. Julian Huxley, announced a new theory on the biological effects of atom bombs. It was his premise that radioactivity could affect human heredity by causing generally harmful mutations in the hereditary factors. The effects would not, of course, appear immediately, but only after two generations. Furthermore, the effect might vary according to various influences exercised upon the hereditary factor and the degree of mental shock afflicting the person concerned. For this reason, in Hiroshima, whenever parents see children at their innocent games, they are greatly saddened at the thought of the future miseries that face these children, the children that come after them and, in fact, all children born after the disaster.

The destructive power of the atom bomb has greatly affected the human body, but what it has done to the minds and hearts of the people and to relationships among human beings is even greater. Some of the children who were under school age at the time the bomb fell are now in the upper grades in primary school; others have finished primary school and are now in middle school. They were too young to know the meaning of death. Many of them cannot remember the faces of the parents they lost. But they have now grown old enough to realize their loss, and that their parents did not die from illness as they thought. Keiko Sasaki, a sixth-grader, writes:

"At the time of the bombing, I was living in the country with my grandmother . . . . When she came back [from Hiroshima] after a week I asked, 'Where's Mother?'

" 'I brought her on my back,' was the answer.

"I was very happy and shouted, 'Mummy!' But when I looked closely I saw she was carrying only a rucksack. I was disappointed. My sister and our neighbors began to cry. I couldn't understand why. Then my grandma put the rucksack down and took some bones out of it and showed them to everybody. There were my mother's gold teeth and a piece of her elbow bone. I still didn't understand. A year passed, and then another year, but my mother didn't come home. Three years later I was a second grader. Then I understood that my mother died. Since then I miss her very much and I visit her grave every day." (p. 39)

Similar sentiments were voiced by Kazuo Mori, a boy in the ninth grade who lost his father in the atomic disaster: "It was not before I finished primary school that I began to think about my father. I got more and more sad over his death whenever I saw my friends whose fathers were alive." (p. 114) Thus were the seeds of grief implanted in the hearts of innocent children.

It is my purpose here to present to the public a collection of essays written by boys and girls who were living in Hiroshima at the time the atom bomb fell. The essays are accounts relating their personal experiences at the time.

We know that the bomb's power and its deadly effect upon human and other living organisms continue to be important areas for intensive investigation and study in the fields of the physical and medical sciences, both in Japan and abroad. At the same time, it is necessary to consider its psychological effect upon not only the adult population but also upon the guileless and sensitive boys and girls who were of preschool age or going to primary school at the time of the bombing. It is important that educators, religious bodies, political figures and people in all walks of life understand what these children thought and felt at the time, and how they are now.

Many works have already appeared on the subject, notably John Hersey's *Hiroshima*, published in the United States. A few novels have appeared in which details of the disaster appear as part of the background of the story. For this publication, I made up my mind to collect and classify the accounts written by boys and girls whose thought, at the time they underwent that tragic experience, had not yet been tinted with any specific political ideology or view of the world. It is my hope that these accounts will forever serve as material for 'instruction' in the ways of peace, so important for the 'education' of the world, and as reference material for studies in the cultural history of the human race.

As I went on, though, I found that the task was not as easy as I had expected. For one thing, having lost their houses and families, those who had survived the disaster had dispersed to different places. Despite this and other difficult conditions, school principals, for example, and teachers and, in particular, the children themselves who wrote of their experiences understood the aim of my project and were unsparing of their cooperation. Manuscripts arrived one after another and were piled high on my desk. Again and again, I could not help being astonished at the profound miseries described therein. I was more than sixty years old and had, I thought, gone through all the hardships life had to offer; but I had to close the manuscripts many times to wipe away the tears that ran down my cheeks when I read these frank and matter-of-fact descriptions of the day of doom. These children, who had survived only by the merest of chances, had seen their parents, brothers and sisters, teachers or dear friends dying, crushed by the timbers of a fallen house, or being burned alive, enshrouded by flames. Words uttered by the dying were quoted in their compositions. A certain schoolgirl was the only survivor out of a class of over forty pupils who, when the bomb fell, were engaged in compulsory labor enforced under wartime government policies. She wrote, "I some-times encourage myself with the thought that the souls of the more than forty I knew who died are protecting me. When I'm feeling better, I feel ashamed that I have not gotten more done in the life I have been allowed to continue. Above everything else, I realize that I must be determined and work hard to be worthy of my forty classmates." (p. 233) Surely, it is not stretching the imagination too much to hear in this the last message from those who will never come back to life, expressed through the voice of the living.

Having read through these precious accounts, I could not bring myself to simply keep them as a private source for mere research on my part. I took it to be my duty as well as my privilege to publish the material, or at least part of it, just as it is and as soon as possible, so that it might be read by conscientious persons in all walks of life, not only in Japan but all over the world.

I may add that these records of personal experiences are too forceful in their truth and too grave in import for them to be considered simply as 'compositions' or reports by schoolchildren. Kikuko Nagara, a ninth-grade girl of the Suzugamine Institute, writes, "Each time I began to write, re-collections of the disaster rose up in my mind, one after another. It was a hard job for me to write them down; I faltered several times because the pain was so sharp, as if I had touched a hardly healed wound. I resolved to write this, however, hoping that what I wrote would be a tribute to my father, sister, uncle, many friends and hundreds of thousands of peo-ple, who lost their lives." As this passage indicates, it took a great deal of effort for these young children to write these papers. They were upset at having to recollect the deaths of their fathers and mothers, and often discouraged at the sometimes halting progress of their pens. The results of their labors are the crystallizations of their tears and blood. Their writings symbolize an anger against a war that deprived them of their blood relations, and are also an expression of their earnest and sincere prayers and appeals for efforts toward permanent peace. It is hoped that those of you who read these essays will do so not out of mere curiosity or a passing interest, but from a shared desire for peace and goodwill among men, along with the children who wrote them.

Chiefly on account of the limited space, it has not been possible to include all of the accounts. A few were, for one reason or another, felt to be unsuitable for publication. When there were a number of accounts involving the same point, only one was selected, however well composed

xxii Children of Hiroshima

the others were. Some were chosen for inclusion not for their literary value but because of the significance of their contents. I have deliberately preserved the simple and unpolished styles of the originals in order to maintain objectivity. The writers are not grown-ups but boys and girls in the course of learning; thus it is inevitable that certain immature or mis-construed observations occasionally turn up. As it is, however, they record a turning point in world history, the cry of the atom bomb-affected child. Should you once read these essays, the hitherto plausible-sounding cries of the prewar militarists calling for "armament for the sake of peace" or "war for peace" will no longer deceive you. We may well ask whether indeed there are any so foolish as to still dream of gaining world peace by means of destructive wars. Who can now imagine the establishment of peace on a war-devastated earth, destined to be a graveyard for the casualties of war?

II

In the preamble to the Japanese Constitution, at present the only basis for formulating national policies in Japan, there occurs the following paragraph: "We, the Japanese people, desire peace for all time and are deeply conscious of the high ideals controlling human relationship, and we have determined to preserve our security and existence, trusting in the justice and faith of the peace-loving peoples of the world. We desire to occupy an honored place in an international society striving for the preservation of peace, and the banishment of tyranny and slavery, oppression and intolerance for all time from the earth. We recognize that all peoples of the world have the right to live in peace, free from fear and want."

From the declaration of these intentions, Chapter 2 of the Constitution goes on to announce its renunciation of war: "Aspiring sincerely to an international peace based on justice and order, the Japanese people forever renounce war as a sovereign right of the nation and the threat or use of force as a means of settling international disputes.

"In order to accomplish the aim of the preceding paragraph, land, sea, and air forces, as well as other war potential, will never be maintained. The right of belligerency of the state will not be recognized."

The Japanese people accepted the Potsdam Declaration in a spirit of repentance for all the destruction and misery inflicted upon a large number of the human race by the militaristic Japan of the war years. They approved, through the Diet, the new Constitution that completely renounced war and advocated permanent peace for the world, something that had never been done before in the history of mankind. The new Japanese Constitution thus embodies the ideals and the ultimate aims of the Japanese nation. The spirit of the absolute peace of Christianity which tells us that "He maketh wars to cease unto the end of the earth; he breaketh the bow, and cutteth the spear in sunder; he burneth the chariots in the fire." (Psalm 46), has thus been first realized in the bold and grave statements in the Constitution of Japan, and not in the constitutions of the Christian states of the West.

The Constitution was not made by foreign powers but by the Japanese people themselves. The terms of unconditional surrender did not permit Japan to establish a constitution on her own authority. The course to be pursued by postwar Japan was, at this stage, determined within the framework of the Potsdam Declaration and the wishes of the Allied Powers. Nevertheless, it stands for a fact that the Allied Powers to whom Japan was responsible for her fulfillment of the terms of the Potsdam Declaration did not object to it. Furthermore, the Japanese nation was not forced by other countries into establishing a constitution that declared Japan's renunciation of war. What lay behind this renunciation was the repentance on the part of the Japanese people for the sins they had committed before the whole human race. The new Constitution renounced war in the spirit of "trusting in the justice and faith of the peace-loving peoples of the world . . . in an international society striving for the preservation of peace, and the banishment of tyranny and slavery, oppression and intolerance for all time from the earth." Therefore, the renunciation of war is a duty, no less, that the Japanese people owe to the whole human race.

Seen in this light, has not the situation imposed on the Allied Powers, in their turn, a duty—at least a moral one—to the Japanese people with their new resolves, "trusting in the justice and faith of the peace-loving peoples of the world," to extend help and encouragement to the defeated?

There are problems, of course. For example, a large number of Japanese people deeply sympathize with the Korean people who are now involved in unnecessary conflict. But there are some who would have it that the Korean War is a "divine wind"* because it works to the economic advantage of Japan, which is now bereft of its former colonial resources and prewar prosperity.

Dr. Yoshishige Abe, President of Gakushuin Institute (the former

---

*During the war, some Japanese believed a "divine wind" was something that could, for example, actually destroy enemy ships at the last crucial moment.

Peers' School) says, in his book called *Desire for Peace* (Iwanami, 1951), "It is an amazing fact that among the Japanese people there are some who do not realize that war has brought upon them such great damage and misery. Forgetting the racial and national tragedy in which several hundred thousands of people in Hiroshima and Nagasaki were used as animals in a testing of the first atom bomb in the world, they propose to make use of the breaking out of another war for the purpose of ridding themselves of their postwar destitution and economic depression. It must be clearly borne in mind by every Japanese that, if these people persist in fishing in troubled waters, resorting to petty tricks and taking advantage of the discord between the United States and Soviet Russia, they will, without an atom of doubt, plunge an already defeated Japan into complete chaos.

"The proper policy for an unarmed Japan is one of neutrality that will call for her to stand aloof from international conflicts, whether cold or hot. In view of the present realities, however, and the international situation in which Japan is involved, some may say that a neutral stand is hardly possible. If that were true, then, what would be the use of renouncing war? Could it be reasonable for a state that has renounced war to participate in the war of another country? Were this sort of reasoning merely theoretical, we might be able to tolerate or ignore it. But it is obviously more than theory and there is a strong possibility that Japan will eventually be involved in the battle. Consequently, the horrors of war will again be inflicted upon the people, the Constitution will be ignored, and the moral and physical bases of the Japanese nation will be demolished. This being so, at all costs the Japanese people must refrain from cooperation with or participation in war in any sense of the word."

After all, man is not a mere product of the environment. Man is creating history and, at the same time, is being created by history. As it is man who has repeatedly started wars, it must be man who eliminates them. Future history must include the fact that man is capable of avoiding war. But when we look at the world as a whole, in spite of the fact that a few ambitious people, as few as one in a million, are trying very hard to propagate the inevitability of war, do we discover that human beings are proving that war can indeed be avoided? Yes and, in fact, they are actually eliminating it. Humanity has reached the stage where it is able to exterminate war by exerting its will and reason. The establishment of the Japanese Constitution demonstrates that absolute and lasting peace, once thought to be an unrealizable dream, has now become a practical proposition.

In the preamble to the UNESCO charter, it is stated that, "Since wars begin in the minds of men, it is in the minds of men that the defenses of peace must be constructed." The origins of a war, whatever they might be, lie in man; whence it develops, fostering a certain psychological state of mind conducive to warlike hostilities. Therefore, education, whose object is to train the spirit of man, is the very first step toward permanent peace in the world. It is not incidental that UNESCO places education side by side with science and culture, in order that it might play an active part in the peace movement. In view of the historical fact that prewar militarists utilized, both in public and in secret, scholastic education, newspapers, magazines and the radio for indoctrination and propaganda purposes in order to justify war, we heartily concur with UNESCO's intentions to construct the defenses of peace in the minds of men. The pacifist movement, which entirely disapproves of fraudulent and deceptive slogans such as 'Armament for the Sake of Peace,' or 'War for Peace,' and which denies that problems cannot be solved through peaceful means, is nothing less than an educational movement, in the broadest sense of the word. It is right and wise that the Preamble to the Japanese Fundamental Law of Education, in the anticipation that education will help in realizing the ideal of lasting peace in the world and the proper welfare of mankind, stipulates as follows: "Having established the Constitution of Japan, we have shown our resolution to contribute to the peace of the world and welfare of humanity by building a democratic and cultural state. The realization of this shall depend fundamentally on the power of education.

"We shall esteem individual dignity and endeavor to bring up people who love truth and peace, while education which aims at the creation of culture, general and rich in individuality, shall be spread far and wide."

This is reinforced by the feeling held by educators in Japan and their unspoken thought: 'We have suffered every hardship imaginable that can be brought on by war. We do not want to let war break out again on earth. We shall see that our children shall be kept from involvement in war by every means in our power.' At the time of the atom bomb disaster, many teachers tried to rescue hundreds of their pupils from under the crushed and burning buildings, until they themselves were caught in the fires and burned to death. What did they cry out in their dying moments? Many of their dying words are faithfully recorded in the accounts written by the children who survived them. It was their wish that every child, without exception, become the kind of person who would help to build a peaceful community, and who would hold the establishment of peace on earth to be the highest morality of a human being. We should make the most of their sacrifice, so that they shall not have died for nothing.

III

A report introducing the Educational Conference for the Improvement of International Understanding (a peace movement) was made public by Iwao Nishimura, director of the Public Relations and UNESCO Division, Secretariat of the Minister of Education. In it, a practical plan for the development of "international understanding" was presented as follows:

"If education for 'international understanding' is to be considered a subject of study in parallel with other subjects, we shall propose the following points. The items enumerated should be referred to when dealing with all subjects of study, including social study. Education in international understanding should not be an independent subject, but should be involved in all subjects in order to bring the point home to every child.

"1. Since wars begin in the minds of men, the defenses for peace must be constructed in the minds of men.

"2. If troubles are not solved through peaceful means, great harm will be done to civilization.

"3. Our daily life is closely related with the world, both physically and morally.

"4. The advancement in the sciences and technology has brought every country on earth into closer relationship.

"5. The fruits of scientific research must be used for the promotion of international fellowship and goodwill.

"6. There are various differences among the racial groups of the world. But no science has ever proved those differences to be the basis for an innate superiority or inferiority in any one of these groups.

"7. For the promotion of peace, it is essential for people to have a thorough understanding of other peoples, irrespective of race, sex, language or creed.

"8. Much effort has been made in order to establish peace in the world.

"9. We as students are able to make contributions in many ways for the sake of international amity."

Let us look under the heading, "A Plan for the Solving of the Problem," with specific reference to item No. 2, which states that "if troubles are not solved through peaceful means, great harm will be done to civilization." (This section is applicable to Middle School.)

Grade	Teaching Method
(Social Study) 7th grade; Unit I	Have the pupils draw graphs comparing the results of physical examinations conducted immediately after the Pacific War and during the present time with the results of examinations made prior to the war. Have the pupils describe how their home life was affected by the war. Consider problems related to daily living. Discussion should be carried out in class with attempts being made to find solutions to the problems. Have the students report to school the results of their investigations into the conditions of those who suffered in the war —evacuees, war orphans and repatriates.
8th grade; Unit 2	Discussions on crime statistics of before and after the war.
9th grade; Unit 5	Discuss personal experiences during the Pacific War. Have the pupils draw graphs showing the damage caused by modern wars, and hold discussions on the subject.
(Mathematics) Actually, this section is to be chiefly utilized during the sessions on statistical graphs, in the 8th grade.	Investigate war damage in modern history, relative to statistical graphs.
(Physical Education) The theory of physical education and international athletic contests.	Investigations into the cause of the decline of the ancient Olympic games.

(Science)	Investigations into the fact that recent advancements in science have made war impossible.
(Painting and Manual Arts)	Promote the study of the fine arts of Japan and the West. Guide the students in investigations into the ways in which civilization has been hampered by wars, and what measures have been taken by the belligerents to protect works of art.
(Special activities in education)	Have the pupils draw graphs showing the damage inflicted on the human race by past wars, and discuss them.

As Mr. Nishimura has pointed out, if all and sundry agree that the essential mission of education is to help all children learn to be willing to work for the realization of lasting world peace, education in ethics, so recently advocated in Japan, must take this proposition into account. Fostering "people for peace" is the proper aim of moral education. Moral codes are created as part of the process of solving historical or social problems pertaining to a specific social condition in a specific age. We should also remind ourselves, however, that if too much emphasis is placed upon fragmental ethical aspects, good manners or discipline, for example, this would only result in an unwelcome resuscitation of the old and detestable formalist type of education, far removed from the goals we seek.

Summary of the Other Sections

In the original edition compiled by Dr. Osada, the foregoing three sections were followed by a further three sections. Section four dealt mainly with the proposition that it was not necessary to drop the atom bomb in order to force Japan to surrender, and included arguments on this subject put forward by numerous people.

It has to be pointed out that at the time, 1951, the mere putting forth of such a proposition had a historical significance; but there has been a considerable amount of research undertaken into this subject in the intervening years and we do not consider that Dr. Osada's thesis, if presented just as it was, would necessarily have a strong appeal to today's readers, and we therefore decided to omit this section. But I think it is necessary to mention here that Dr. Osada tried to protest the use of the atom bomb, and in doing so was forced to use data and documents published abroad because of the situation under the occupation at that time.

In section five, Dr. Osada emphasizes that the atom bombing was a surprise attack, and that this resulted in increased casualties. To back this up, Dr. Osada quotes from the accounts of more than 80 children, showing that it was the dropping of the atom bomb just after an air-raid warning alert had been called off that resulted in such a heavy casualty figure, as the people had returned to their normal, everyday life. At the same time, he used the accounts of the 80-odd children to recreate Hiroshima as it was at that point in time. However, this is brought out in most of the accounts in the book, so that the reader will be able to fully appreciate the state of things at the time without these extracts, and so we have decided to omit this section, too, except for one part near the beginning which we include out of respect for Dr. Osada's intention.

At 8:15 on the morning of August 6, the Enola Gay flew into the sky above Hiroshima. Tetsuo Miyata, who at that time was living in the suburbs of Hiroshima City, and who is now a student majoring in chemistry at the Hiroshima University of Science and Literature, witnessed its flight and writes of his impressions as follows:

"Suddenly far overhead in the sky the roar of B-29 engines! Probably just one, or maybe two. The alarm hasn't sounded; no need to worry. It had probably just come to check on the effect of last night's air raid. Thus were we so used to B-29 reconnaissance flights that we didn't think much about it at first. Suddenly, though, the roar changed to a high howl and we looked up without thinking. A single B-29, its huge fuselage gleaming in the direct rays of the midsummer sun, was turning sharply and tearing up into the blue, leaving a trail of vapor in the sky." (p. 320)

At this very moment, the fate of Hiroshima was decreed and a scene of sheer hell was about to be staged. At 7:30 that morning, the air-raid warning had been sounded, but the all-clear had been given soon after. Then the fateful bomb exploded right above the shopping area in the center of Hiroshima. The attack came as a complete surprise, as everyone was used to daily reconnaissance flights.

Numbers of laborers, compulsory workers, voluntary women workers and most of the students of over the eighth grade, being mobilized for labor purposes, luckily were already engaged in work at some munitions factories, more than two miles and a half from the center of the explosion. Thus they were spared from the blast.

All the rest of the citizens remained in the city. Many children of preschool age, for instance, were either inside their houses or playing in the streets outside. First and second graders were studying either in temporary classrooms or in temples or churches [according to the practice of breaking up large assemblies that would be vulnerable to air raids], or on the way to these places. Most of the primary school children between the third and sixth grades had been sent *en bloc* to the country in April that year, though invalids and those who were unable to join the evacuation for one reason or another were studying either at the temple schools or their own schools. Many civil workers and office clerks were already working at their respective offices, while others were on the way there. Most shopkeepers had just opened their shops. In the central part of the city, a large-scale project was being carried out, with houses being demolished to form fire-prevention zones. All the seventh-grade boys and girls in municipal schools were working on this project. Many voluntary groups, including students and housewives from villages and towns in the vicinity of the city, were helping to get the work done quickly. The latter were mostly young mothers, some of them carrying their babies on their backs. Also assisting were men who were unable to serve in the army or work at the factories because of old age or physical disabilities.

In order to help the reader visualize the complete horror of the spectacle immediately after the explosion of the bomb, let us listen to what the children who were then between three and nine years of age say about what they were doing in the moments just before 8:15 on the morning of August 6. (80 quotes from the accounts of children follow.)

Dr. Osada wrote the following concerning the wreaking on Hiroshima of more casualties than necessary due to the surprise element and other factors.

The astounding number of casualties was chiefly caused by the complete surprise of the attack, the large number of buildings that collapsed and the rapid spread of fires from the embers of charcoal fires used to prepare breakfast — plus, of course, the devastation caused by secondary heat radiation near the blast center. Other reasons for the greater number of deaths than might have been expected lay in the state of malnutrition of the populace and inappropriate or insufficient medical aid. The field hospitals housed in the military and civil ammunition factories that had escaped the bombing were disbanded early in September when the Allied Forces landed on mainland Japan, whereupon most of the patients were deprived of medical treatment, again boosting the death rate.

The American strategic bombing commission stated that civilian injuries and fatalities could be reduced, by known techniques, to one-twentieth or less of the casualties that would be suffered were these techniques not employed.

In this section, also, Dr. Osada talks about the love for their fellow man among the people, teachers and students of Hiroshima under the impact of the bomb. He quotes from accounts of teachers giving up their own lives to protect the children; mothers, trapped by the beams of fallen houses, urging hesitant fathers to make their way to a safe place for the sake of the children, and then being consumed by the flames. Readers will see a number of such examples in the accounts.

Finally, Dr. Osada wants to show the single-minded efforts the children made to continue their studies amid all the difficulties, that they were un-bowed by the disaster. He also wants to draw the readers' attention to the daily difficulties faced by these children who had lost their parents.

In section six, Dr. Osada expressed his deep desire that atomic energy will be used for peace, as a new source of energy to serve people, and not for bombs. At the beginning of the section, Dr. Osada illustrates his point with an extract from the Greek myth of Prometheus.

In the myth, Prometheus was one of the gods living on earth prior to the creation of man. He molded some soil from the ground into the shape of a man, then he ascended to heaven and stole fire from the chariot of the sun. He lighted his torch and brought it to the man he had molded. This symbolizes his bestowal on man of civilization in the form of various techniques, which raised the latter above other animals. By means of fire, that is, technology and civili-zation, man-made weapons to conquer other animals and tools to till the land and discovered means of heating his home to protect him-self from the cold. It is to fire that man owes his mintage facilities and the institutions of commerce and trade.

Thus the early days of human habitation of the world formed the period called the golden age, when people lived in innocence and happiness in a land of milk and honey. Then came the age of silver. Zeus divided the year into four seasons, and for the first time man had to build houses for shelter. The age of copper followed; this was the age when the weak were prey to the strong, but evil did not always prevail. Finally, the most terrible of ages, that of iron, arrived. Evil predominated and crimes were as abundant as the flood. Obedience, truth and honor were replaced by fraud, cunning and violence. Possessiveness grew out of mistaken affection. The land previously shared by many on friendly terms had to be divided. Man was not satisfied with what he raised on the land and began to search within the earth for iron and gold, and with iron and gold he fashioned weapons to fight the first battle. The family was divided, with parents and children, brothers and sisters no longer believing in one another; the son wanted his father to die in order to inherit his riches. The earth was stained with the blood of murder. At last, the gods forsook the earth.

Surely, it is not only myself who senses in this myth a significant prophecy regarding the tragedies of this present age. In the Bible, it is said, "But if ye bite and devour one another, take heed that ye be not consumed one of another." (Galatians 5:15) Some American scientists have said that the atom bomb is a suicide bomb. Are human beings destined to destroy their own world by the fire stolen from heaven?

Following this, Dr. Osada describes the history of nuclear fission, using various quotes, notably from Lilienthal's declaration, emphasizing the existence of bright prospects for peaceful use of nuclear energy. He also, again, uses extracts from the children's accounts.

Written by Dr. Osada around 1950, this was an excellent outlook. Nowadays, however, the problem of nuclear power generation has become more complex, and leaving to one side the historical viewpoint of those days, we felt it is not necessary to take up so much space on this subject and therefore omitted the section. Needless to say, though, readers will be able to obtain an idea of what the children were thinking from the the accounts contained within. With this assumption, then, we would like to conclude with the following lines written by Dr. Osada himself.

Thus the phoenix born out of the ashes of Hiroshima appeals faintly but earnestly to the people in every corner of the world. It anticipates the peaceful use of atomic energy, the way to do great good. It would be more than fitting if the birthplace of the peaceful atomic age were based in Hiroshima. A reporter, who witnessed the inferno subsequent to the dropping of the bomb, was said to have cried, "Is this the end or the beginning of the world?" We must make this tragedy not the end but the beginning of the new world.

Today, on the seventh anniversary of the atom bombing, I dedicate this book of accounts to the 247,000 souls who expired in an instant and pray for them and for the establishment of a lasting peace.

August 6, 1951

Arata Osada

Professor Osada's Preface written in 1960, one year before his death (Unpublished)

The principal part of this volume consists of 105 accounts selected from those written by 1,175 individuals during the period between March and mid-June of 1951. These accounts are centered on affairs in Hiroshima on and around August 6, 1945, the day the atom bomb was dropped over the city. The editor specially wishes to remind the readers that, at the time these accounts were written, Japan was still occupied by the Allied Forces and the Korean War was then at its height.

In 1952, the Fraternity of the Children of the A-bomb was organized among the contributors to the *Children of the A-bomb*. At the inaugural ceremony on February 17, a memorial message was read to the departed soul of the late Hisato Itoh, who died of radiation sickness shortly after writing his account (*See* p. 161), which was also read out to the audience. In the memorial message, Shintaro Fukuhara stated: "No matter how powerful an atomic weapon may be, it is still a thing of man's own devising and, thus, something that man inflicts upon himself. The resultant radiation sickness is also, when all is said, a man-made evil . . . . It follows, then, that man can and should banish the weapon and cure the sickness at its roots . . . . Yet nothing has been done and we have remained abandoned in our agony for the past seven years . . . ."

This statement has since been upheld and the points it makes have remained the cause and aim of the Fraternity. It was reaffirmed at the First World Conference against the A- and H-bombs held at Hiroshima in August, 1955. At the Fifth World Conference, this statement of the Fraternity was adopted as the manifesto of the Conference.

In 1955, upon an invitation from the Soviet Academy of Science, the present editor visited the U.S.S.R. as a member of a delegation representing the Science Council of Japan. I had the honor of delivering the following message from the Fraternity to the general assembly of the Soviet Committee for the Defense of Peace: "The A-bomb reduced our city to ashes, annihilating two hundred and thirty thousand human beings. Even today, it is still decimating our parents and brethren through the curse of radiation sickness.

"Yet, in spite of its atrocity, the bomb was not able to quench the spirit of those who hate war. Instead, it has kindled the determination to make a stand against atomic wars.

"The people of the world should utilize the energy released by atoms not in annihilating, irremediable wars but for the building of a peaceful world and mutual trust. Peace is bound to prevail over conflict; it will expand and reach outwards, as does the chain reaction of atoms.

"We demand an unconditional and simultaneous suspension of experimentation in, and the manufacturing and use of atomic weapons. We specially wish to cooperate in mutual endeavors with the people of the Soviet Union, who are leaders in the campaign against nuclear weapons."

On the way back from the U.S.S.R., I visited the People's Republic of China and called at the Palace of Juvenescence in Shanghai. There, I delivered a similar message to the Chinese Fraternity for the Protection of Children. To this, Mrs. Sung Ch'ing-ling, president of the Fraternity, replied with a message of encouragement addressed to our Fraternity of the Children of the A-bomb.

On August 18, 1955, at the General Assembly of the United Nations, Mr. Khruschev, Premier of the Soviet Union, proposed a plan for the total disarmament of the world within four years. After that, he was reported to have conferred with President Eisenhower of the United States at Camp David; and the two leaders agreed that discussion, not force, should be the means of settling all international issues. These tidings assured the peace-loving peoples of the world that the prospects for peace, moving as they were in the direction of peaceful coexistence, were growing brighter. This was all the more reassuring in view of the fact that, just five years earlier in December, 1950, during the Korean War, Mr. Truman, then President of the United States, announced the government's intention to use the atom bomb over the Korean front, should the situation call for it. It was at that very time that the accounts of the children of Hiroshima were being written for the purposes of compilation and publication.

Fortunately, peace-loving people all over the world have always rallied in order to prevent the possible use of nuclear weapons in postwar international incidents.

Ironically, however, in Japan, Italy, West Germany, France, England and Sweden, nuclear rearmament is fast on its way to becoming a reality, in spite of the voices raised in protest against it by people such as the 'children' of the atom bomb. Humanity now stands at a major crossroads, faced with the choice of turning the world into another Hiroshima or Nagasaki, or of turning toward the path of peaceful coexistence. Today, when the entire human race has to decide for itself which road it should take, I consider that the presentation to the world of this anthology (already published in the original Japanese and in Esperanto) is the discharging of a sacred duty toward the four hundred thousand dead of Hiroshima and Nagasaki, the some three thousand authors of the accounts and, finally, all peace-loving individuals in the world.

Hiroshima
January 5, 1960   Arata Osada

contents

Dr. Arata Osada surrounded by schoolchildren of Hiroshima years after the atom bombing

Hiroshima at 8.15 a.m., August 6, 1945

Hypocenter after the atom bombing

primary school

By Mrs Toshiko Akamatsu

My army friend took up the seven skeletons one at a time . . . his five children, his
wife, his mother . . . and each time stared at the sky.
"We soldiers were the ones who were supposed to die."

Tomoyuki Satoh
4th grade boy (4 years old at the time)

I hadn't started school yet. On August 6, I was playing in front of a public bathhouse in our neighborhood. Sei-chan asked me to go to the fields and bring her some flowers so I was on my way there. Then it suddenly got very bright. I was very surprised, so I thought I would go into the house, but suddenly it seemed like dozens of needles were stuck in my eyes and I didn't know who I was or where I was going. I struggled toward the house and ran into the front door. When I opened my eyes, it was dim and gloomy. Then I saw my grandma running away as fast as she could with Keika-chan (my younger brother) on her back. I went with her. We went to the air-raid shelter. One of my big sisters was already inside so the four of us all huddled together. Then another big sister came running in and joined us. She was working at the Mitsuboshi Bakery making cakes. My mother had already got sick and died.

My father had gone to work as a volunteer and he came back looking for us. My oldest sister heard him calling and she took my father's hand and led him to our air-raid shelter. My father was burned everywhere above his waist. Both of my older sisters and the other people were scared, when they saw the burns. A stranger put some oil on my father's burns. I said thank you to him in my heart.

After that, we went to a hill in Fuchu. We put up a mosquito net in the ruins of a temple and slept inside. We lived there a long time. Then some of the other people began to return to their homes, so we did, too. When we got back, we saw all the glass broken, our cupboards all knocked over, our Buddhist altar all upset, the outer screens of the rooms destroyed, the roof tiles broken and the walls broken. We cleaned everything up and put Father to bed.

About sixty days later, Father called Grandma in the middle of the night and said he wanted to eat a sweet potato. "Very well," replied Grandma and cooked one for him.

"It's ready," she said but he didn't answer and I touched him to see what the matter was. He felt cold and I knew he had died. Goodbye, dear Mummy and Daddy!

Sachiko Habu
5th grade girl (5 years old at the time)

I was only five then, so I don't remember things very well. I heard many things from my grandpa though, so I'll write about them together with some things I remember myself. Six years have gone by and I have grown up. I am eleven and in fifth grade now.

Our house was in Togiya-cho, close to where the atom bomb fell and my mother was burned into white bones while praying before our family Buddhist altar. My mother's remains are now in Nakajima Cemetery. On the sixth of every month, I go with my grandpa to pray to my mother. But no matter how hard I try, I can no longer remember my mother very clearly. All I can see is the wooden post that marks her grave silently standing there. When I see that wooden post, I always cry. Perhaps my mother can see me, and she will be pleased to see how big I have grown. Grandpa told me that she was happy. Whenever I go, I take some pretty flowers and some sticks of incense. Then I say goodbye to my mother and return home with Grandpa.

August 6 this year is the seventh anniversary of the death of my mother. Grandpa keeps on saying that we'll all have a good Buddhist memorial service for her. It's already six years since Mother died. When I think that I have not been able to speak to her for all that time it's unbearable, really unbearable. When I see the mothers of my school friends, I suddenly feel lonely and feel like crying. But I have a very kind grandpa, a grandma, uncles and aunts, so I think I'm happy. Then every day when I go to school my teacher is kind and teaches me new things, and I play with good friends. I feel happiest going to school.

My grandfather was burned at the time of the bombing and this seems to have brought back all his old sicknesses so he has a hard time. He is sixty-seven this year. I want Grandpa and Grandma to live for a long time, and I pray for that every day.

Sanae Kano
5th grade girl (4 years old at the time)

When I was about five years old, it was the middle of the war. Whenever I tried to go to the store to buy fireworks, the air-raid siren always went off. So I always hid in a closet in our house. That's what always seemed to happen. My father was an air-raid warden, so no matter how busy he was, he always went out in his black uniform. When he went to his warden's post, I felt very lonely. But I thought it was better than if he went away to the war. On August 6, we were just going to have breakfast and even had our chopsticks to our mouths when the siren sounded. Then the dreadful atom bomb fell. We saw a sudden flash of light. There was a big bang and I almost fainted. The sound of the bomb was big and frightening. That time, Father hadn't gone to the warden's post. When the bomb fell, cushions and things came tumbling down from upstairs. I picked them up and tried to carry them outside, but I couldn't get out of the house. When Father finally got out, glass was falling everywhere and some stuck right into his back. He pulled out the glass himself and took us all out, too. My grandmother ran into a post and died. She was such a kind, good grandmother. My mother tried to help the neighbor's children and she must have touched some poison then because she died quite a while later. When I tried to cross the railroad track, it was so hot that I jumped back. At the river, I saw people who were burned black and were crying for water. It was so terrible I couldn't stand to watch. Some people were in the river drinking the water. The fire wardens were shouting at them telling them that it was dangerous to drink water. But many people went into the river anyway and drank the water and died. Little children were crying that they were hungry because the bomb fell before they could eat breakfast. I was hungry, too, but I was already a pretty big girl so I didn't cry. A little while later, we were each given two rice balls. Then I fell fast asleep on the river bank.

The next day, I went to where our house used to be. Only two motorcycles were left standing. They looked so lonely by themselves. No matter how hard Father tried to start one of them, it wouldn't go. So he tried the other one and it started up at once so we all got on and set off for Rakurakuen in the suburbs where we had rented a house. The motorcycle stopped many times on the way but at last we reached Rakurakuen.

Though I said my mother died quite a while later, it was really about the beginning of September when she died. After we came to our house in the suburbs, Mother worked so hard that in the end she couldn't get out of bed any more. She was in pain every day so we sent for a doctor. The doctor told us that she would soon have a baby. A baby boy came about the end of August but he died together with my mother after only his head was born. I was very sad.

My younger sister's thumb was almost ready to drop off but fortunately it got better. But in winter it's still very painful. My younger brother had a boil on his head. If you pressed it even slightly, pus oozed out. I felt like crying every-time I thought of my poor little brother and sister. I was the only one that didn't get hurt.

I was very sad without Mother. But I soon made some friends. It was decided that my little sister would go to live with my uncle about four miles away. It broke my heart to be separated from her. Quite a while later, it was decided that I would go to my uncle's, too, together with my father.

Hiroaki Ichikawa
5th grade boy (5 years old at the time)

It is already six years since the atom bomb was dropped on Hiroshima. At that time, I was only five years old, and now I am already in fifth grade. "You will never forget those terrible things as long as you live, will you?" My mother has said these words again and again. The anniversary of the dropping of the atom bomb on the sixth of August will soon be here again. It makes me sad just to think what things would be like now if my father and mother had died then and I feel sorry for my many friends who did lose their parents.

That morning just as I was going outdoors, I was trapped under the house as it fell on top of me. I wriggled with all my might. Even now, I cannot forget how frightened I felt when I crawled out crying, "Mother! Mother!" and how happy I was when I heard my Mother's reply, "Mother's coming, so don't cry." At first, it was so dark that I could hardly see people's faces. Then it grew terribly hot and everything brightened all at once. When I asked why it got so dark like that, Mother told me that it was because all the houses in Hiroshima had collapsed at once. My whole family was inside the house so nobody was burned. I alone was pinned under the house and hurt my finger. When Mother saw my finger, she said, "I'm glad it wasn't your face, but it hurts, doesn't it?"

We lived in a shack for a while and then went to live where my father was born in Shiga Prefecture. Every year on the sixth of August, we remember what happened on that day in 1945.

When the crape myrtles in our country garden were in bloom, my mother would say, "Don't they remind you of the red ones that used to grow by our hut in town?" And she would continue, "When the atom bomb fell, there were people who said that nothing would grow for about twenty years, but that wasn't true, was it? On the vacant lot by our shack, pumpkins and flowers and other things used to grow."

On the day after the bomb, we started toward the country and when we came to Hijiyama Bridge, we saw naked people with their burned skin hanging from them like rags. We saw others covered with blood, being carried to safer places in trucks. In the tobacco factory about a mile and a half from the bomb center were many people crying from the pain of their burns. Both Mother and Father often tell us that it was like hell.

After five years, our whole family was able to return to Hiroshima. After so many years, Hiroshima had changed completely. I was surprised to see what a beautiful town it had become. I pray that Hiroshima, where I was born, will become a splendid City of Peace. I also pray that peace will last forever.

Ikuko Wakasa
5th grade girl (5 years old at the time)

I completely hate thinking about the day the atom bomb was dropped, and remembering things about the war. Even when I read a book, I skip anything about war. At the movies, I shudder during the newsreels when there are scenes of the Korean War. It is part of my homework to write about the bomb and I am writing what I can, though I don't want to and it makes me tremble.

On the morning of the sixth of August, my brother's friends were waiting for him. They were supposed to go to their temporary classroom together. They were in second grade. I was five years old and my little sister was two. We were playing house in the garden. Father usually got to work by eight, but that day he said, "Today, I'm going in at half past eight." He was sitting at his desk, facing a window looking north, and was practicing calligraphy. My mother was by a south-facing window clearing the breakfast table. From the kitchen came the sound of the cups and bowls clinking as she put them down.

Suddenly, the humming sound of an airplane echoed high above in the sky. Taking it for a Japanese plane, I cried out loudly, "An airplane!" The moment I looked up into the sky, a white light flashed and the green trees in the garden looked brown like dead trees. I rushed into the house, shouting, "Daddy!" At the same moment, there was a terrific boom and the bookcases and the chest of drawers in the room fell down. Broken pieces of windowpane went flying over my head. I ran back to the garden. Mother called, "Come here, Ikuko!" Automatically, I ran toward my mother's voice and jumped into the air-raid shelter. Pretty soon, my ears started to bleed and wouldn't stop. There was a lot of blood, and even when I pressed cotton on them, the blood still kept oozing between my fingers. Daddy and Mummy were worried about my bleeding and put a bandage over my ears. Daddy's little finger was cut so badly it seemed it might fall off. He had another big cut below his eye. Mummy was practically covered with blood from the waist down. I guess she was injured by pieces of glass from the north window. A large piece of glass still remained stuck in her back. The cut was six inches long and two inches deep and was swollen like a black man's lips. It was bleeding terribly. Daddy took the piece of glass out of the cut, while Mummy cried in pain. He put a whole bottle of iodine on the cut. My brother had a big bump on his head that he got from hitting it against the desk when he crawled under it. My sister wasn't hurt, even though she was wearing only a pair of underpants, because she had crept under the veranda facing the garden.

After they bandaged me, my ears began to throb so I lay down. When I woke up, I was lying in a funny shack. I tried to lift my head but couldn't, because the blood had soaked through the bandages and my head was stuck to the sheet. Daddy carried me on his back to an Army hospital in the neighborhood, because he was afraid I might get worse. The hospital was crowded with people. Some were almost naked and others were groaning with pain. I was so frightened that I asked Daddy to take me back home. At last, Daddy said, "There are so many people here that we'll have to wait forever before your turn comes. And most of them are worse off than you." Then he took me home on his back.

From the fields, I could see that not only the part of town where we lived but the whole city of Hiroshima was burning. There were clouds of black smoke and big explosions. The north wind blew the fire closer and closer to where I was standing. I was trembling but didn't know what to do. About noon, the wind changed to the south and the fire didn't come any closer to our house.

My mother's brother was seventeen and was in high school. But before he finished, he decided to join the Army. He was big and strong and became a soldier in the Second Army stationed at Noboricho Primary School. On the night of the sixth, he didn't come home so my father, mother and I went looking for him till late at night. It was scary outside. The city was burning and there was a nasty smell. Blue balls of fire were floating in the air here and there. We were scared and lonely. It seemed as if no one else was alive in the world. Since then, I hate going out of doors.

Another soldier in the same unit as my uncle told us that my uncle had gone to bed after finishing guard duty. His bed was in the building next door to the granary. My father and mother went to Noboricho Primary School right away. I heard that they found a lot of human bones among the ashes beside the granary. They didn't know which bones were my uncle's so they just picked up a lot of them and brought them home and put them in an urn. My uncle's brass school badge and his aluminum lunch box were also found among the ashes. We tell ourselves that my uncle was smashed flat and killed instantly. We can't stand to think that he was trapped under a timber and burned alive.

There was a man lying in front of my grandfather's house next door. He was burned so badly you couldn't tell whether he was young or old. We carried the poor man to our veranda and laid him on a blanket and put a pillow under his head. In just a little while, he got about three times as big as he was. He got yellow and bloated. There were flies all over him. He made weak groans and smelled bad. He kept crying for water. Even though my father, mother and grandfather were also hurt, they were busy fixing the house and picking up broken glass, and also they had to store valuable things in the shed in the field because it was wartime. So they couldn't take care of the sick man and I often gave him water. But when I passed him, I ran with my eyes closed and held my breath. Later, some soldiers came to take him to a hospital together with the blanket and the pillow we gave him.

Our house was tilted three feet and the floor was broken. The bookcases and the chest of drawers had fallen onto each other. Part of the ceiling and the roof had fallen in. We could see the blue sky from inside the house. We didn't think we would be able to live in it any longer.

There had been ten eggs in a basket on the desk in the north room. The north room was divided from the south room by a paper screen and the eggs were smashed all over the south side of the screen!

Mother asked, "How come the broken eggs are on the south side of the screen? Did the blast send them flying first to the south and then back to the north again?"

Father said he had found a lot of broken tiles lying in a spiral. The foundation stones seemed to have moved. Maybe, the house itself was lifted into the air by the blast.

About this time, Mother got worse. The doctor said, "The poison gas you breathed while you were walking through the hot ashes looking for your brother made you sick."

Only six months ago, a ten-year-old girl lost all her hair from radiation sickness. The Red Cross Hospital doctors did their best to help her but she vomited blood and died in twenty days. I was shocked to hear such a sad story of death even after six years and it reminded me of that day again. The girl who died was no different than any of us. I think: What would I do if she were in my family! I am afraid of even hearing about the terrible pain caused by the atom bomb sickness. I want to forget everything about it.

An aunt of mine was crippled. She always reminds me of August 6 and I feel sad. Once in the streetcar, I saw a man whose ears had been burned into hard lumps about an inch across. My friend Sarada's father also lost his ears.

The atom bomb is terrible, but the radio says that an even worse bomb than the one used in Hiroshima has been made and it may be used in Korea.

What a horrible thing!

I am sure that everyone who was in Hiroshima on August 6 hates war. The primary school hasn't been repaired even yet. My family is poor now because the houses we were renting out were damaged or burned down.

The seventh anniversary of my uncle's death is on August 6. As the day gets closer, we all remember more and more unhappy things and it makes me sad.

Kikuko Yamashiro
5th grade girl (5 years old at the time)

In the morning, my big brother and I were playing upstairs. There was a blinding flash and our house fell down. Everything was a mess. My big sister got out first and helped everyone out. First, she got my big brother free and then me and one by one everyone in the family got out. We ran away as fast as we could. Many other people were also running away. Some of them were injured. There were so many people rushing along that we had to wade through the sea. I tried to climb up a stonewall to get out of the water but fell back again. Luckily, someone soon helped me out.

Then I saw a lot of soldiers sitting on a stone eating their lunch. As we passed them, they gave us something to eat. I was very glad and sat down on the ground and ate the food right away. I was thirsty but there was no water to drink.

We went on and it began to rain. We were pulling Mother with us in a cart. That night, we slept in a tin-roofed shack.

The next morning, my brothers woke me up and said, "Mother is dead."

"No," I cried and ran to her. I called to her but there was no answer. I kept calling but still she said nothing. All I could do was cry on her breast. Then we held a funeral service for her. I didn't want to part with her, but there was nothing I could do. After the funeral, we were sent to a hospital and stayed there for I don't know how long. One morning when I woke up, I learned one of my brothers had died. One after another, all my family died except for two brothers and myself.

Then I was sent somewhere else. The others were also sent somewhere but I don't know where. Then I went to Kure. Just before New Year's Day, I came back to Hiroshima. My brother Shigeyuki took me to Miyajima. It was my first visit to Miyajima by streetcar. The next day, I came back to Hiroshima to live at Shintenchi. I lived there until I became old enough to go to school. I entered Noboricho Primary School and I'm now in the fifth grade. Recently, my brother Shigeyuki has not come to see me. I hope he is working hard and that someday he will buy me lots of things I want.

Tokiko Wada
5th grade girl (5 years old at the time)

I was only five years old. One day, we were just going to have breakfast. The houses near the station were on fire, and thick smoke was coming toward us. It had a nasty smell. Grandpa was very excited and said that the fire was spreading toward us.

I ran away with my grandpa and grandma. On our way, we saw an injured soldier lying on the roadside. He was moaning and had a red face like a devil. We were so hungry that we picked up the food someone had dropped on the bridge and ate it. As we went further, we met a doctor who was treating people so my grandpa had his cuts treated with some white medicine. The sound of an airplane made me shudder again.

At last, we reached the house of someone we knew at Yaguchi. My mother had also come there. We had been worrying about her, thinking that she had been trapped under the house when it fell down. Fortunately, she happened to be out of the house to get some water when the bomb fell so she wasn't hurt. Our house was too small for the whole family and my mother had been living in a neighbor's house helping with the housekeeping. The people at Yaguchi were very kind and we had a bath there. But we didn't want to trouble them too much, so we walked further on. We stopped at another house owned by my grandpa's old friend. We stayed there for a few days before we went back to Hiroshima by train. There were a lot of sick people on the train and I felt very sorry for them.

When we got to Hiroshima, we had much trouble finding our house. Where our house had been, there were only broken tiles and other broken pieces scattered all over. It took us several days to build a shack. We grew vegetables in a garden that one of our relatives let us use.

Our restaurant was a member of the Restaurant Union so we had to help with the union work and they built a house for us to live in. But it was too small and we moved again to a bigger house which a neighbor let us use.

My grandpa and grandma tried to think of some way to earn money and decided to start a noodle shop. But Grandpa had breathed poisonous gas when the atom bomb fell and he got sick and went to the hospital. He died one night a little later and we had a funeral for him. With Grandpa dead, it is difficult for Grandma and Mother to run the noodle shop but they are still in business even though they are always worried by high prices and high taxes.

What about everyone studying how Japan can become a country where everyone can live without difficulty? People still drink potassium cyanide and kill themselves because life is so hard. The main reason, I think, is the high taxes. My mother says she has to pay a lot of money for my school lunch, PTA dues and lots of other things, too. She has to pay taxes on top of all that, too.

Yaeko Sasaki
5th grade girl (5 years old at the time)

On August 5, 1945, the day before the atom bomb was dropped, my brother suddenly got sick and had to go to the hospital. My mother loaded some blankets and things onto my father's bicycle and took them to the Funairi Hospital. My brother got sick so suddenly that Mother had no time to get any food ready.

As she left the house, Mother said, "Be sure to bring us lunch tomorrow and then something every day." I never imagined that these were the last words I would ever hear her say.

On the morning of the sixth, after breakfast, Father was getting ready the food he was going to take to the hospital. I asked him to take me with him but he said, "I'm busy today. Please be a good girl and stay at home. If there is an air-raid warning on the radio, put on your air-raid hood and hide in the shelter. Your hood is on the shelf. When the all-clear is sounded, you may go out and play."

I wanted to go out and play so I was waiting for the all-clear on the radio. I only listened to half of it and ran outside.

I was playing hide-and-seek at my friend's house when I thought a big ball of fire had fallen over us. When I crawled out from under the desk where I had hidden, every house around was on fire. Before long, big drops of rain came down in torrents. I was frightened. When I got home, I couldn't find Father or Mother. I sat alone by the roadside crying. I saw a man with burned skin hanging from his hands and feet. He was crying, "Water! Water!"

A little later, a woman who used to come to my house to clean our cesspool came and took me to the countryside near by.

I kept crying all night thinking of my mother. At breakfast, I asked the woman if my mother had come back. She said, "Maybe she has. Let's go and see."

I jumped into my shoes and the woman took my hand and led me to my house. The house had fallen down on one side. I ran into the house and shouted, "Father! Mother! Where are you?" There was no answer, I shouted again and again. Just then I saw a man who looked like my father walking with a baby in his arms.

"Daddy! It's me," I shouted at the top of my voice.

The woman was standing beside me. She looked at the man and said, "That's not your father. It's a stranger."

I was so disappointed. The same thing happened again and again, but I never found my mother or father.

Several days passed in the same way. Every evening in bed, I would think of my father when he left for the hospital. If he hadn't told me to stay at home when I asked him to let me go with him, all four of us would have died together.

I still have two sisters. One sister, Toshiko, was badly burned at the company where she worked and had to go to the hospital. I took care of her there. It was no fun washing bandages covered with pus but I was ready to do anything for my sister. Because I took care of my sick sister, I started first grade one year late. All my sister's burns had healed by that time, but one of her legs became stiff so she couldn't bend it. Even so, she wanted me to be able to go to school so she worked until late at night running the sewing machine with her one good leg.

Later, I went to attend school in Yamagata County where

my other sister, Sadako, lived. When I was in second grade,
I came back to Hiroshima and entered an orphanage called
"Hikari-no-Sono."

I was baptized when I was six years old but I didn't know
much about Christianity. When I met my second mother
(the one who runs the orphanage), she smiled at me just like
my real mother used to. Then I began to learn more about
Christ. I am so happy every day that I seldom long for my dead
mother. I am happy every day together with my second mother
and the sisters. I have made up my mind that when I grow up
I am going to be honest and kind.

Noriko Takemura
5th grade girl (4 years old at the time)

My sister and I had been evacuated to Miyoshi. On the
morning of August 6, all the windows in our house
began to rattle. My brother was somewhere else with a group of
evacuated children, but my father and mother were in Hiroshima. Finally, the rattling stopped.

I was worried that my mummy and daddy might be dead.
A few days later, they came to see us. Mummy had lost all her
hair and she had cuts on her cheeks. Daddy had a bad cut on
his head.

After that, Daddy went back and forth to his job in Hiroshima by train and this made his cut worse. Mother and I went
looking for a house to rent in Hiroshima and at last found one
in Ushita-machi. Daddy spent most of his time resting, but one
day, before he was well again, he said he was going out.
Mummy told my sister to go with him.

But Daddy said he could go alone and when my sister followed him anyway he got angry so she came back.

Daddy didn't come back by noon. Evening came, but no Father. My sister began to cry. The next day went by, but still no Father. We children and Mummy were all crying, still expecting him to come home at any moment. But now many days have passed and I think he is dead.

I hate war. Mummy told me there were a lot of people with burns on their faces, and with their mouths twisted. And children crying for water. I couldn't listen to much of this because I felt so sorry for them.

Next, we moved from Ushita-machi to Minami-machi, and then to Moto-machi, where we live now.

I've heard that many people died here and there, groaning and twisting in pain. Some had burns and others had injured or lost their legs. How terrible for them! If I had been in Hiroshima, I might have died. I hope there are no more wars. We want to live peaceful and happy lives helping one another. War causes misery. Now we can hope for peace all over the world. People should give up war because it causes much suffering. I've had enough war. I hope we can live happily without any wars.

There are many people who lost their money and their homes too, and became beggars. We should help those people. I want the beggars and everyone to live in peace and happiness, to hold hands and live happily together. And I want to help all those poor children who lost both of their parents and live happily together with them.

Toshiko Nagano
5th grade girl (5 years old at the time)

I was five years old. We had left Hiroshima and were living way back in the hills so we heard almost nothing about what had happened.

I remember that my sister seemed very worried about something and was busy sending telegrams and registered letters. My mother was already dead but I didn't know it until later.

A week passed and we still did not hear from Father, Mother or my brother who was a middle school student. Day after day, I worried about them, hoping they were all right but feeling they were not. My sister must have worried even more.

On August 18, the first letter from my father came, saying that Mother had died, crushed as the house fell. He also wrote, "I am still alive and will not let you become unhappy. Osamu (my brother) was away working with the mobilized youth so he wasn't hurt. Don't worry about me. I may not be able to come to see you very soon, though, because I have to help clean things up in the area."

When my big sister read the letter to my brother, my other sister and I, we all clung to her and cried.

Toward evening on the twenty-eighth, just as the sun was going behind the big hill in front of our house, my father and my brother came to see us. They had walked over four miles carrying their things on their backs.

Father took me on his lap at once and said that I had grown bigger. He often used to take me on his lap since I was the youngest. On that day, we brought out all the pears and biscuits that my sister had taken so much trouble to store away. It was the happiest time we had had in a long time.

But the next day Father had to stay in bed with a fever and

couldn't go ahead with making preparations for our mother's funeral. We didn't think he would die. But looking back now, I think Father knew that he had something bad. His temperature was between 102 and 106 degrees and the fever lasted for four days. Still his spirit was unchanged and he said that he would be all right even if the high temperature lasted for thirty days.

On the fifth day, his temperature went down. We were all so glad. Then, about eleven o'clock in the morning, Father said it was hard for him to breathe and asked my sister to rub his chest to help him. I also wanted to help in some way so I put a cold, damp towel on his chest. (In those days, there was no ice anywhere.) But no matter what we did, he got worse and worse.

Suddenly, he said softly, "It was really hell." Because of the pain, he could not lie quietly, so he would sit up for a while and then would lie down on his side. It was terrible to see him in such agony. His voice gradually became more and more feeble. But he was still conscious. He tried very hard to talk by writing words on the mat with his finger. But even my big sister could not make them out. Like this, he struggled in agony for about an hour before he finally died.

But at the last he quietly put his pillow under his head, clasped his hands on his chest, closed his eyes, and died as if he had fallen fast asleep. We cried as our big sister held us in her arms.

Six years have passed since then. We lost our big, hotel-like house and I am being brought up by my big sister. I am now attending a primary school in Hiroshima.

Satomi Kanekuni
5th grade girl (5 years old at the time)

My grandma and I came back to Japan from Dairen after the war. In April 1945, Father went back to Hiroshima to get my mother but he couldn't get back to Dairen because all the ships had stopped running. So he and Mother were staying in Hiroshima separated from the rest of the family.

We heard nothing from my father and mother after the atom bomb was dropped on Hiroshima on August 6 and we didn't know whether they had been killed or not. My grandma and I worried about them every day. We at last returned to Hiroshima on March 16, 1947, and were so happy to find my father and mother safe and sound.

On August 6 when the bomb fell, Father and Mother were living in Yanagi-machi. They were trapped by the house when it fell down and inhaled poisonous gas. They were sick for some time, but they were well again when we got back. In June last year, though, Father took some worm medicine he got from a doctor and after that he became weak. Then radiation sickness set in and he died. It's really too bad that he had to die after we had got through so many difficulties and we were all living happily together again. I hate the atom bomb. I really hate it. And I am not special. There are many people in Hiroshima suffering just like me. I don't want Japan ever to go to war again. I want it to be a peaceful country. We must make sure it does not happen again.

Yukio Sekimoto
5th grade boy (5 years old at the time)

I was playing outdoors when I saw a sudden flash. Fire broke out everywhere. Our house and gate burned down before I knew it. I felt very sad. Then we went under a bridge. There were many people there dying from burns. Then we went to the other side of the river and stayed there overnight.

The next morning, we were hungry. My sister went to the school near Misasa Bridge where there was an emergency relief squad and she brought back some boiled rice balls for us to eat. While we were wandering around with our sister, we met Daddy and Mummy. Mummy had burns on her hands and feet. Daddy looked as if he would die any moment. I was so unhappy I started to cry. I was very, very sad. We did our best to take care of him. He was on the verge of dying. When I brought a glass of water for him to drink, he seemed to get better.

Then we went to our relatives' and stayed there for some time. In a few days, they built a shack for us to live in.

One day, I went to the hill to play. When I came back, Daddy was dead. We put him into a coffin and carried it to a crematory. The next day, we brought back some of his bones and buried them in the cemetery.

A few days later, Mummy died, too. We put her into a coffin and carried it to the cemetery the same as Daddy. My sister and I buried the bones of my mummy beside my daddy's. We prayed kneeling in front of their grave and cried to ourselves.

I went to the hill to gather chestnuts. I boiled them and made an offering of them to my daddy and mummy. Some days later, I went to the river to dig shellfish. I came back with them and my sister boiled them. We ate them. Then we took some of them to our parents' grave. Then we went into town to buy some incense-sticks. As soon as we returned home, my sister went to the cemetery to offer them to our parents.

Kiyoko Tsuga
5th grade girl (5 years old at the time)

I was at my grandma's in Nakayama Village when the atom bomb was dropped. My parents and my sister were at Futabanosato. My father was burned very badly but even so he managed to come to Nakayama Village. My mother and my sister were crushed to death beneath the house when it fell. My brother and I had been evacuated from the city so we escaped without a single injury. I will always be thankful for our good luck.

I was eating breakfast at the time. There was a sudden flash. We were all surprised and ran out of the house. We saw a red glow above the city and there was a large cloud of white smoke that was getting bigger and bigger. We crouched among the rice-plants in the paddyfield in front of our house.

After a while, we came back to the house and went in slowly, not knowing what to expect. The house was a complete mess. About thirty minutes later, all kinds of injured and burned people started coming into my grandma's house.

I remember one of them was a girl named Yoshino. She lives in our neighborhood now. We often play together. She lost both of her parents at the time of the atom bomb and she lives with her grandma now. I feel sorry for orphans and homeless children. Then when I think of my dead mother and sister, I am sad all over again.

Now, I have a new mother and am quite happy. We are

lucky because my father runs a shop that has been a family business for many years so that it is well known. But Father's burns are making him weak and he often gets sick. Whenever anyone says 'atom bomb,' a shiver goes through me. I hope that nothing like that ever happens again.

I was only five years old when the bomb fell. I don't remember very well what my mother and sister looked like. But their pictures always remind me. We used to live in a nice house but now we live in a shack. We used to have a beautiful garden but now we only have a yard with no flowers. When I think of the difference, I feel sad. Sometimes, I tell my little brother about our dead mother and he cries.

The streets in Hiroshima have become dirty and there is nowhere for children to play.

There are some pictures in my house that were taken just after the atom bomb went off. We sometimes look at them but they always make me feel bad. One of them is a picture of our burned house and there are many dead bodies in it.

The atom bomb is really frightening. I hate it. And yet North America (*sic*) and North Korea are fighting, aren't they? I think they should stop right away. Why are they fighting? I hope Japan will never go to war again. In Japan, there are so many homeless children and poor children who have to shine shoes because they have no mothers or fathers.

The atom bomb is very, very bad.

I pray everyday for peace in the world.

Ruriko Araoka
5th grade girl (4 years old at the time)

August 6, 1945... the memories of that horrible day are still clear in my mind. At about eight o'clock that morning, I went out with my mother on an errand. My mother's sister from Kemuriishi went with us. My grandma usually told me not to follow my mother because I would cause her trouble and she wasn't so strong. On that morning, though, she told me to go with her. At the corner of Yagenbori, my aunt went a different way.

Just in front of the Moritas' house, while Mother was talking with Mrs. Yamamoto, we heard the sound of an airplane. After a short time, there was a flash like lightning followed by a tremendous boom.

I got trapped under the house. I was shouting "Mother" as loudly as I could and my mother was calling "Ruri-chan! Ruri-chan!" There was nothing wrong with my hands and feet so I crept toward her voice and when I reached her, I was so happy I couldn't help crying. Soon, Mother found an opening between the mats, and carried me out. We went back home.

Our house had completely collapsed. From outside, you could see everything that had been upstairs. I called my grandma, but there was no answer. Mother tried very hard to find her. Many people were running by trying to escape. Mother put me on her back and ran out to the main road. Just then, a neighbor came by carrying my little brother on her back. He had burns on his face and hands, and his face was very swollen. Poor little thing! He was three years old and such a sweet little boy. He died a week later. When he died, he was crying "Mummy, Mummy."

We and the woman who was carrying my little brother went to Hijiyama. There was another air-raid warning and we had to run into an air-raid shelter. The hill was almost covered with people whose clothes had been burned off. Some had burned skin hanging from them and some were all black and had already died.

My mother and I walked around for a long time looking for Grandma but we couldn't find her. At last, Mother started to cry. Grandma is still missing.

Later, we went to live in Midorii. They told me that Mother would not live long because she had radiation sickness. I cried everytime I thought of how lonely I would be without her. But then she got better. It was like a miracle. I was very happy.

Later on, Father came back safe from an island far away. I have two new brothers now and we are all happy. But whenever I remember that terrible day, I see in my mind my cute little brother who died crying, "Mummy, Mummy!" and my grandma who was so kind to us. I always pray that there will be no more *Pikadon*.

Junko Aratani
5th grade girl (4 years old at the time)

Mother was writing a letter after breakfast. There was a flash, and at the same time all the rooftiles and windowpanes broke. Though I was safe inside the house, Mother stepped outside to look for me. Just as she did a piece of flying glass cut her forehead. She walked around with her hand over the cut. Then she met a neighbor lady who bandaged it for her.

We started toward my grandmother's house where it would be safer. On our way through Onaga-cho, we saw my uncle pulling a cart with one of our relatives in it. Onaga-cho was burning so he took me through the fire to a safe place. My mother and I finally reached Grandma's house. All our relatives were there. Some of them were injured or sick. The house was so crowded that we put up a mosquito net in the field outside and slept there. The food didn't taste very good but in a few days everyone got stronger. Then Mother had another baby so she had to stay in bed for a long time. During that time, a midwife often came even though it rained a lot. My mother at last got strong enough to keep the house.

Then we returned to our house to find that all the ceilings had fallen in and all the tiles on the roof were broken. After a few days, we pretty much fixed the part of the house that wasn't damaged so much and started living there. In the evenings, lots of people went out looking for pieces of firewood. I don't know how many months passed like that.

We fixed up the house little by little so after several months it was more comfortable to live in. My brother who had been evacuated came home. Father came back from the war. We used to eat smelly kaolian and bad tasting imported rice. Both were rationed then. During the war, we usually ate porridge made from rice and vegetables or just dumplings. Gradually, we were able to get better things to eat. We used to live on white and sweet potatoes. When we could get rice, there was only enough for two or three days. Mother always told us to eat as much as we could so that we would grow big and she would go without so that we could have more.

The baby got bigger and bigger. Our rice ration got bigger too but our appetites grew even more. So Mother sighed often not knowing what to do. But we were not old enough then to understand the problem. Sometimes, we had to eat horrible smelling fish which we got on ration.

Everything is getting more expensive and we have got

little money. This makes Mother unhappy. At mealtimes, she often talks to us about when she was a little girl. I often think of the peaceful world we might have had if there had been no war and no *Pikadon*.

Our school is a make-shift building with a tin roof. In winter, it's drafty and cold.

We are grateful to Mother because she keeps us fed and clothed with so little money even though the prices are high. She has to be very careful even to save enough money to pay for my school lunches. Thanks to her, everyone in the family is well.

Keiko Ohtaka
5th grade girl (4 years old at the time)

Everyone in my family was very happy before the atom bomb was dropped but because of the bomb, we lost our house and all our belongings. We managed to rebuild the house, but my father's health has been completely ruined. He says it is hard for him to work much and he gets tired easily. We were brought up by Father alone. And now he is getting older and older.

Our real mother died long ago. Our stepmother is very kind but life is very hard even though my father and mother and big brother try hard to make us happy. Father looks tired and old so I always try to take good care of him.

Because we do not have much money, I often have to ask the teacher to wait a little before I can pay for the school meals. Every morning, I ask Father, "Can I take the money today?" Then one day, he will say, "Today, you can take it," and I feel so happy when I hear him say that. Then as soon as I reach school, I give it to the teacher. The next morning, Father, Mother and I all feel very pleased.

My stepmother is very nice. My father is old but he is happy because she is so good to him. We three children attend school. We all try to make things as easy as we can for our father, and we try not to spend much money, because it is difficult for him to send three of us to school.

We are poor but I am well and strong and I try to be a good girl and study very hard. I am trying to do what I can for my father and not spend money, but he sometimes buys some candy or caramels for me.

Kiyoharu Koike
5th grade boy (4 years old at the time)

J ust as I was eating some clams, there was a flash, followed by a great crash. All the windows broke, the cupboards in the kitchen fell down, and the whole house was badly damaged. It was a complete mess.

Thinking that it was only our house, I went outside and found that every house I could see was just as badly damaged as ours. All the people who came out looked stunned and were all dirty, and they asked each other, "What happened?" I was still hungry, so I went back and ate some more clams. I washed them under the pump myself.

Everybody said that a bomb had exploded and they ran away, leaving my grandma and me behind. Father had gone to the war and my sister was at school. I didn't know what to do.

One of our neighbors was badly burned and came to ask my grandmother if she could help him. Grandma said, "We have some oil. That should help." She brought a bottle of oil and rubbed it carefully on the burn and then put a bandage on it. The man said "Thank you" and walked away. I began to cry. So they took me to Fuchizaki. On the way, we saw a lot of burning houses, many badly burned people walking aimlessly, broken cars and many other terrible sights.

Everything at Fuchizaki was quite different. An old woman was taking a rest by the side of a paddyfield. We sat down there, too. The woman and my grandmother talked about the disaster in Hiroshima. She gave me a big ball of boiled rice. It tasted delicious. All the excitement made me tired so I took a nap.

I felt rested when I woke up, so we went on to a house in Fuchizaki. None of the houses there was damaged and everything was peaceful. The people at the house treated us to a dish of pumpkin and rice.

Some soldiers came to the house for water. Grandma asked one of them, "Is Danbara-shinmachi on fire?"

"Danbara is completely destroyed," was the answer.

Grandma told me to wait there because she would go to our house to get our ration cards and some rice and barley. So I had to wait.

A few hours later, I wanted to go to the toilet, but I was too shy to ask where it was, so I decided to go back to our own house. So, I started but I got lost because everything had changed. There were a lot of soldiers around. I started to cry and one of the soldiers asked me what was the matter. I told him what had happened. He told me, "Don't worry, Sonny. I'll find your grandma."

Night came. The soldier put his arms around me and I went to sleep. In the morning, the soldier gave me a ball of rice. It really wasn't a very good one but it tasted good because I was so hungry. Then the soldier put his rifle on his shoulder and said, "I will look for your grandma." He never came back. Another soldier came and made the same promise. But he didn't come back, either.

In the afternoon, while I was playing with another soldier, Grandma came to look for me. I was very happy to see her again. We went back to Fuchizaki and the next morning we went to my sister's house. On our way, we saw a lot of dead bodies along the road. Some of them were still standing even though they were completely scorched to death.

When we reached my sister's, Grandma called her name and she came to the door right away. She gave us some rice balls and we took them home and ate them. A little later, we learned that my mother had been burned to death at the Toraya Hotel. Everyone was sad. I cried loudly and big tears rolled down my cheeks.

One day, not long after, my father suddenly came home. We were all so happy that we had a big party. After that, life was very hard. We had almost no food and often had to eat dumplings with barnyard grass in them.

Whenever we thought of our dead mother, tears came to our eyes.

Hiroko Harada
5th grade girl (5 years old at the time)

A t the time the atom bomb fell on Hiroshima, I and my mother, little sister and brother had moved out of the city and were living at my grandma's house out in the country in Shimane Prefecture. So I didn't know much about what happened and learned about it later from Father and my big sister. My father was working for the city and my sister was attending a girls' high school. So they had to stay in Hiroshima.

Father wasn't hurt but my sister was badly injured. My sister was working as a volunteer clearing away houses near Tsurumi Bridge in order to make an air-raid defense zone. She got bad burns all over herself. Mother cried because she didn't think she would live. But she is strong now, though she has a lot of scars on her face and everywhere and she still has trouble using her left arm. She had two operations on it at the Ministry of Communication's hospital but it still is not completely well. In autumn and winter, she often suffers from cracked skin on her hands and feet because the burns she got made the skin very thin. Several times, an Occupation forces car* came to take her to a clinic for an examination. But she complained that they didn't give her any treatment and that only an examination didn't help her at all. Mother has been worrying that she will not be able to get married because of her burns. It also makes me sad when I remember how pretty she used to be. But I always tell myself that we were lucky because she is still alive and quite well while many of her friends were killed and nearly all who survived have severe injuries. I am happy to hear neighbors say that her face has got much better.

My grandfather on my mother's side lived close to the police station at Nobori-cho. His son was away to war and he lived with his daughter-in-law and her children. They lost their house and all their belongings so they moved to Iwakuni where his daughter-in-law's mother lived. Some time later, he came to our house and said that he had inhaled poison gas and now his throat hurt, and he couldn't eat anything even though he was very hungry. He lived on water alone for forty days before he died on October 30. My mother took care of him while he was sick and I learned what happened to him from her. I felt very sorry for him.

There should never be any more war or any more atom bombs dropped. I pray that there will be peace in Hiroshima as soon as possible.

* Hiroko refers to the Atomic Bomb Casualty Commission in Hiroshima. Lt. Col. C. F. Tessmer, director of the Commission, writes under the title of Atomic Bomb Casualty Commission Medical Research Program in *Hiroshima* published by Hiroshima Publishing Company, as follows:

> Does radiation produce long-range effects in human beings? Finding the answer to this question is the purpose of the medical research program of the Atomic Bomb Casualty Commission. In modern clinics and laboratories in Hiroshima, Nagasaki and Kure, specially trained American medical experts and Japanese doctors are working together to accumulate essential research data, a project which will require many years of study.
>
> The ABCC is a field study group of the National Research Council of the United States. The Welfare [and Health] Ministry of the Japanese Government, through its National Institute of Health, is cooperating in many ways including furnishing funds and personnel to this research project. Through liaison with Public Health and Welfare Section, SCAP [Supreme Commander for the Allied Powers], the ABCC has had the cooperation of the Occupation Forces in setting up the physical facilities necessary to conduct the research.
>
> The program provides for individual medical diagnostic examination of atomic bomb survivors, X-rays of lungs and bones, blood examination, urinalysis, laboratory tests for intestinal parasites, and complete physical examination. Also medical records are being accumulated on all terminations of pregnancy, normal and abnormal, occurring in Hiroshima, Nagasaki and Kure. ABCC doctors are visiting every household where there is a newborn child in order to examine the infant. These basic programs lead to special studies such as child growth and development, sterility-infertility in adults, and many others.
>
> The purpose of the Kure laboratory is to conduct identical studies in an area not affected by radiation, thereby furnishing a basis for accurate evaluation of the findings in Hiroshima and Nagasaki.
>
> Treatment of patients is not undertaken by ABCC because such matters properly are in the hands of Japanese physicians in Kure, Hiroshima and Nagasaki.

Masao Baba
5th grade boy (5 years old at the time)

T he atom bomb wrecked our big house and killed my father. My brother lost an ear and my little sister lost one of her eyes. They were hit by tiles falling from the roof as they tried to get out of our crushed house. My mother and two-year-old sister stayed inside but they also got hurt.

None of us could walk, so they took us to the country in a cart. Before the bomb fell, my father sold quilts and things and ran a big shop. Now, we are very poor and my mother is looking after us alone. My brother goes out to work early in the morning every day. Mother runs a second-hand store and takes care of us four children. My big sister does the cooking. We help Mother and Sis as much as we can.

Our old house had two floors with big rooms but the house we live in now is falling to pieces. We are now very poor. Right after the bomb, we escaped to the country, but eventually my mother managed to build a shelter at our place in the city and we moved back.

Other kids tease my little sister because she's got only one eye but she tries not to cry. Sometimes though, she cries anyway when they all start laughing at her. Then I go to tell them to stop and I want to hit them but they are too little so all I can do is tell them off. A little while later, they're all playing again and my sister looks so happy. That makes me feel good.

If our father were alive, he would take her to the hospital and her eye would get better but we don't have enough money to do that. It doesn't make any difference where I am, at school or in the country, I always worry about her and it's hard to study because I worry whether she is being teased or whether she is crying by herself. Grown-ups laugh at her too, but I always think: You just wait, you just wait!

Toshio Nakamori
6th grade boy (6 years old at the time)

When I go downtown, I often see little children walking along the street holding their father's or mother's hand. They look so happy and this always reminds me of my own parents. My father and mother were very kind and loved me very much. I feel they will come back at any time. Sometimes, I whisper "Mummy" or "Daddy." But they don't answer. I feel sad and envy my friends who have parents.

I try to accept it and I try not to miss my parents who have gone to heaven. Everybody loses their parents when they grow up. I lost mine earlier than other people. That's all. This is the way I always try to think.

I live with my grandma now. This is because of the war. Hiroshima was destroyed because of the war! I hate war. I hate fighting!

Junya Kojima
6th grade boy (5 years old at the time)

Six years have passed since the atom bomb explosion. I am now eleven years old. I am well and strong. I enjoy working and playing.

I lost my mother when I was still a baby. But my grandma and father took good care of me until I became bigger.

When I was five years old, there was the atom bomb explosion. My father was at his office then. I guess he breathed in poison gas. When he came to the country, he had a lot of colored spots all over and he soon died. I felt so sorry for him. I just can't explain how I felt. I lost both my parents. Why did

I have to be so unlucky?

Now, I am big, and I feel very grateful to my parents. The atom bomb was six years ago, and before that I was happy. My bad luck started after the bomb. But I know that I'm a lot luckier than some kids in Hiroshima. At least, I've got a place to live.

I am now in sixth grade. I'm glad I didn't end up missing after the bombing like a lot of other people.

My grandma died in 1948. I'm grateful to her, too, because she brought me up alone for four years after my father and mother died.

It's really lonely and sad to live alone without either a father or a mother or any brothers or sisters. When my father died, the tears rolled down my cheeks and I couldn't stop them. I always feel that my father and mother are watching everything I do, and I always feel grateful to them.

I was born in February and my mother died in November of the same year. So I don't remember my mother. I wish I could see my father and mother again! But I know it is impossible.

Keiko Sasaki
6th grade girl (6 years old at the time)

When I was seven years old, my father died in Osaka. Then on August 15, my mother died because of the atom bomb explosion. After that, there were only three of us: my grandma, my sister and I, and we've been having a hard time. My sister was only seventeen and just out of school, so she had a lot of trouble doing her work. This was because of the bomb, too. It was really sad without Father and Mother.

At the time of the bombing, I was living in the country with my grandmother. She heard from a man who escaped from Hiroshima that the city was completely destroyed by the bomb. When she heard that, she went to Hiroshima right away. When she came back after a week, I asked, "Where's Mother?"

"I brought her on my back," was the answer.

I was very happy and shouted, "Mummy!" But when I looked closely, I saw she was only carrying a rucksack. I was disappointed. My sister and our neighbors began to cry. I couldn't understand why. Then my grandma put the rucksack down and took some bones out of it and showed them to everybody. There were my mother's gold tooth and a piece of her elbow bone. I still didn't understand. A year passed, and then another year, but my mother didn't come home. Three years later, I was a second grader. Then I understood that my mother had died. Since then, I miss her very much and I visit her grave every day.

In those days, my sister was working for the tax office and she made enough money for us to live. But we were all lonely without our dead mother. All the other kids have fathers or mothers. I wonder why I had to lose both and I start crying. I have a kind grandma and big sister, though. Later, I learned that I had a big brother, too. Some relatives took care of him from the time he was a baby and that's why I didn't know about him. I don't think I've ever been happier in all my life than when I learned I had a brother. He lives in Kake and comes to see us on Saturdays and Sundays. He is very good to me. If my mother were alive, he could live with us. This makes me miss Mother all the more. When I think that if it had not been for the atom bomb, we could all live together, I hate the American Army. But then I think, 'Oh, well, it's over now,' and this makes me feel brighter.

I'm lonelier now because my sister got married and went to Tokyo. It's too bad she couldn't go any further in school, but without any mother.... It must have been a big job for my grandma to bring up both my sister and me.

When I look at the moon on August 15, I remember so many things and tears come to my eyes. I will take good care of my grandma so she can live for a long time. I often think that if Mother were with us, my grandma might not have to work so hard. I have decided that whatever happens I will try to be strong enough to tackle any troubles in the future.

Isao Kawasaki
6th grade boy (5 years old at the time)

There were six in our family and we lived in Hiroshima. As the war got worse, four of us moved to the country leaving my father and big brother in Hiroshima. One day, my brother turned up suddenly. He told us about what was happening in Hiroshima.

That was August 5. Mother told him that he should take the evening train back to Hiroshima but grandmother wanted him to stay longer. But then Mother said he'd better go back because Father would be waiting for him. So my brother caught the evening train.

The next morning while we were playing after breakfast, there was a big noise like an earthquake. I thought something had fallen down. Really, a big bomb had been dropped on Hiroshima. My father died on Miyuki Bridge and my brother was killed when the air-raid shelter at his school caved in. When I learned that they had been killed, I kept asking: Why Father? Why my brother? Why did they have to leave me? And I was angry.

I asked my mother, "Are you sure Daddy is dead?"

"Yes, he's dead and so, Isao, you will have to study very hard," she answered.

Then my uncle went to Hiroshima to see what had happened. When he came back, he told us that he found some tea-cups in our air-raid shelter. He brought back the ashes of my father and brother. After the funeral, I was sent to live with my uncle in Okayama. Before I left, I put my hands together and looked up to heaven and asked, 'Why did you have to die and leave me, Daddy?'

Some time later, Mother came to Okayama and said, "Isao, your aunt in Hiroshima is going to look after you now."

I live with my aunt now but I can't forget my father and brother. Hiroshima was burned to the ground. I still remember that horrible booming sound.

I always say to myself, "Daddy, why did you have to die? Why did you have to die?" My uncle and aunt in Hiroshima are now my father and mother. But how I miss my real father! Why can't he be alive? Why?

It will hurt my father in heaven if I do anything bad. But if I am a good boy, he will be pleased. So I always try to be a good boy.

Yoshimi Mukuda
6th grade girl (1st grade at the time)

The atom bomb fell on Hiroshima on August 6, 1945. This was just after I was moved to Hinoura Village in Asa County where it would be safer for us, but there were still about twenty kids left back in the orphanage in Hiroshima with Father and Mother Kitamura. I was very worried about the other children. And then I would think about Father and

Mother Kitamura and I would get so worried I wouldn't know what to do. Even though I don't have a real mother, Mother Kitamura took care of me from the time I was one year old so she is just like a real mother to me.

I came back to Hiroshima with another girl on August 10. There were no streetcars or buses from Yokogawa so we had to walk from there. I was only a first grader then. On the way back from Yokogawa, everything was burned to the ground in every direction you looked. It was frightening and made me worry about what had happened to the orphanage. I wanted to cry. There was a streetcar that was burned until you could see right through it and you could see the passengers burned black inside. When I saw this, I started to shake and couldn't stop.

And then we came to where the orphanage used to be. Not one of our beautiful buildings was left. The hall, the girls' wing and the boys' wing—there was nothing left of any of them but ashes. We had so many wonderful times in that big hall. We had birthday parties there and sometimes Father and Mother would get us together there and talk to us or have dinner together with us and we were so happy, just like a big family.

As I was standing there feeling sad and in a daze, Father and Mother came up to me and patted me on the head and welcomed me back. The tears started coming to my eyes and I couldn't stop them.

None of the children was hurt but Miss Kitamura, our Mother and Father's real daughter, was missing. It makes me sad when I think about her even today.

After that, I started going to Onaga Primary School again. It used to be a very nice school but it was burned down by the atom bomb. After that, they put up some temporary buildings. Then we had a lot of trouble getting food. Father said he didn't care whether he ate anything himself but he wanted food for the children and he went here and there and into the countryside looking for food. And he had much trouble getting donations. I was too little and don't remember much about these things, though.

I got bigger and went to the second, third, fourth and fifth grades and at the same time Hiroshima became a more and more peaceful city. A lot of temporary houses were built, too.

On August 6, we have Peace Day in honor of Miss Kitamura and the other people of Hiroshima killed by the atom bomb. We go to the Peace Tower early in the morning to pray.

A lot of little children joined us in the orphanage after the atom bomb. We try to take good care of them. We are all very happy now. I hope peace lasts for ever and ever.

Minoru Hirota
6th grade boy (5 years old at the time)

I went to live in the country before the atom bomb was dropped. That's why I wasn't hurt.

I was playing in the yard at my grandfather's house when there was a flash in the sky. Then the neighbor's house started to shake and the windows broke. I was so scared that I ran home. After I got home, I hid behind a cabinet. When I peeped out, I saw smoke coming up from the big hill in front of our house. I hid again because I was so scared. It even scares me to think about it and I'll never forget how afraid I was.

Two or three days later, my father came home pulling a cart with my mother in it. My father was at a temple in Koi so he wasn't hurt but my mother was at our house in Hiroshima cleaning up.

My mother was still quite well when she came to Grandpa's house. But then her cuts got worse and we thought it might be because Grandpa's house was so small so we moved her to the house next door. My mother groaned in pain every day. Then the man next door said he couldn't sleep with my mother making so much noise so we brought her back again. About three days later, I was playing by the river and the lady from next door came running and said, "Minoru, your mother is dying. Come home right away."

I ran home. My mother was about to die. She died about five minutes later. I tried hard not to cry.

That is what my father told me.

There used to be three women in our family. My big sister died of radiation sickness the year before last. Another sister was helping out in the house when the bomb fell and she got trapped under the roof when it fell. My mother tried to help her out but she didn't have enough strength because she got hurt too. While she was waiting for help, the fire reached the place where my sister was lying. She was burned alive. Then my mother died so now there are no women left in our family.

My brother was in Kohryo Middle School then. On that day, they were called out for labor service. We never saw him again. There used to be nine people in our family, but now there are only five.

The atom bomb is a dreadful thing. I hope this kind of bomb will never again be dropped on Hiroshima Prefecture—not only Hiroshima Prefecture but anywhere in Japan. War is a dreadful thing. I hate war most of all. War is a dreadful thing. I hope the war in Korea will end soon.

I still think about my mother. If my mother had been with my father at the temple, she would still be alive. If my sister and brother had been with me in the country, they would be living, too. But the atom bomb has already exploded and there is nothing we can do about it now.

Yukiharu Suzuki
6th grade boy (5 years old at the time)

I was five years old and I was eating some canned tangerines for breakfast one morning. There was a flash and a noise like thunder. Mr. Saito jumped up and ran outside. Then he helped my grandmother and me to get out. Mr. Saito, my grandmother and I went toward the City Office where we thought it would be safer but by the time we came to the bridge my grandmother began to ask Mr. Saito to take me on alone. She wanted to go where my mother was but she got stopped by the fire. While we were at the City Office, the fire died down so we went to Mr. Saito's house. There were a lot of other people who came there, too. Ten days later, my father and mother came to Mr. Saito's house to get me.

About a month later, I got a lot of sores all over me and all my hair fell out. No one thought I would live but they all took good care of me and I gradually got better. My brother came back twenty days later. We all went to see our house in Ohte-machi but there was nothing left but burned ground. I went to my relatives in Eba-cho and they were very good to me. They even put salts in the bath and let me get in first.

During the summer vacation when I was still in the first grade of primary school, I got radiation sickness again. I got well by the end of the summer vacation and moved here when I was in the second grade. Everyone tells me they are surprised I got well because they were sure I was going to die.

Toshie Tanabe
6th grade girl (1st grade at the time)

I will never forget August 6, 1945. I was in first grade then. Many of the children had been evacuated and those who remained went to school at a church across from where Senda High School is now. I was on my way to school with my brother and a classmate named Kiyoshi. There was a sudden flash.

When I came to, the place was covered with smoke and I was all alone in the grounds of the Technical College. I was scared and started walking around shouting for my brother and Kiyoshi. Then I saw a man running about as if he were looking for something. Then I saw that the college building had collapsed into a pile. I got very afraid and began crying for my mother.

The man came back and said, "Don't worry. Your father and mother will come for you pretty soon." He looked at me more closely. "This is bad. This is bad. I hope your mother and father can find you."

I can remember that he put me on his back and began walking about, but what happened then I don't know.

Suddenly, I heard a woman's voice saying, "Oh, you poor little thing."

I looked around but the man was gone. Then I looked at myself. My arms and back were burned. Almost nothing was left of the cloth bag I was carrying on my shoulder but the books inside were all right. My clothes were all torn and I was almost naked. Many people were crying for help and everyone was burned.

There was a lady that was burned very badly and she seemed to be in much pain. She asked me to lend her my school bag so she could use it for a pillow.

"No! No!" I sobbed. I didn't want to give her my books.

I was still crying when my mother found me. She was crying and told me that she had looked all around the church because she was afraid I might be caught underneath something. She had also walked back and forth many times in front of the Technical College. This made me cry all the more.

When we got home, the house was flattened and there was no one around. My mother had a cut on her forehead and it was still covered with blood. She went to look for my father and my brother. She found them before very long.

My father had been on the way to the doctor but got caught under a house that was knocked down. Somebody helped him get out.

My brother, the one I was walking to school with, jumped into a big gutter in front of the school to get out of the heat of the flash. Later, he crept under a concrete bridge and stayed there for a while.

I had two other brothers. One was a middle school student and he was down near the City Office at the time helping to clear the buildings. We couldn't find any trace of him and so just the four of us set off across Miyuki Bridge toward my aunt's house in Tanna.

There were many burned and injured people lying by the sides of the streets. I looked back and the city was a sea of red flames. Someone was shouting that people should get across the bridge and out of danger as quickly as possible.

Just as we were walking past the place where the Prefectural Hospital is now, my uncle from Tanna met us with his car. We got in and he took us to Tanna.

I couldn't get up for about three months.

My oldest brother was burned on the face, arms and legs and had to stay in bed for two months. Another brother, the one just above me, was in bed for three months like me.

There were two or three times when I almost died but Mother took good care of me and I got well in three months. My mother was hurt badly, too, but she stayed up many nights taking care of us three children.

When there were air-raid alarms, we ran into the hills. Later, though, we couldn't do this because we were too weak to move.

The war ended on August 15. The brother we left behind was never found. He was such a good brother. But he is gone now, killed by the atom bomb. It makes me so sad when I think that I will never see his smiling face again.

I don't want any more war. I absolutely hate war.

Sachiko Fujimoto
6th grade girl (5 years old at the time)

Whenever I remember August 6, 1945, I think of a poor middle school student.

I was sick that day and was resting in our six mat room. My mother and a neighbor lady were talking.

There was a flash.

What happened next I don't know. When I came to, I was under the wall and couldn't get loose. The kitchen cupboard was turned over, the floor of the four and a half mat room had fallen through, and everything in the house was in a mess. The neighbor lady and a boy pulled me out.

Firemen were shouting that everyone should go to a safe place at once. So my mother, grandmother and I ran away to the hills. My mother carried me on her back and pulled grand-mother by the hand on the way to the hills. I noticed that my mother had a bad cut about four inches long on her leg, but we finally got to a safe place. All around us, there were many other people like ourselves.

About sundown, we started down the hill toward home and met a middle school boy about twelve who was badly burned all over. He put his burned, swollen hands together and said to my mother, "Please help me. Won't you, please?"

"Poor child. Come with us," my mother said and took him with us.

Our house was so wrecked that we couldn't get in. So we put the boy to bed in a small shed in the yard. Even his chest was badly burned and he groaned in pain. He said that it felt as though he were being poked in the chest with a red-hot rod.

I was worried about what would happen to the boy. As my mother took care of him she tried to make him feel better by saying, "Your mother will come for you any moment. Cheer up."

A couple of days later, my mother learned that a doctor was coming to see a neighbor to treat his burns. She put the boy on a cart and took him to see the doctor. I went, too. My mother asked how bad the boy was and I noticed the hopeless look on the doctor's face. We felt very sad as we brought the boy home on the cart.

A day later, the boy's mother came and she was so happy to find him that she cried. She took him home right away but I heard later that he died.

Kimiko Takai
6th grade girl (5 years old at the time)

I shiver whenever I think of August 6, 1945, the day when Hiroshima was destroyed in just a few minutes.

I and a friend were playing at a neighbor's house when I heard the roar of an airplane.

"It's an airplane," I said. Right then, there was a flash. I was so afraid that I hung on to the next-door lady, but she was more scared than I was. She shook me loose and threw her arms around her husband. Then she took a cloth band out of a drawer and tied it around her waist. After that, she and her husband ran out of the house.

My playmate Tatsuko and I didn't know what to do. Suddenly, it got dark and something began to drop from the ceiling. We were so frightened that we just hung on to each other with our eyes wide open. It got lighter and lighter and after a while I heard Tatsuko's mother calling for her. She sounded very worried.

She took Tatsuko with her and I was left alone. I started to cry. A neighbor with dirt all over her face came out of the wreckage and said, "Don't cry. Your mother is nearby."

She ran off, too, and I was alone again. A little later, I heard my sister's voice through my sobs. I listened carefully. I could hear her calling, "Kimiko! Kimiko!" with all her might. I was so glad that my eyes got full of tears. My mother came, too.

"Oh, Kimiko, I'm so glad to find you. And now your sister. Where could she be? I hope she hasn't been burned. Maybe, she's already dead," my mother said.

But we couldn't waste time. We were scared and wanted to get to a safe place.

As we walked along, we saw soldiers with bloated stomachs floating down the river. They probably had to dive into the river to get away from the flames. A little farther on, we saw many dead people piled up at the side of the road. As we walked on, my father saw a woman whose leg was caught under a large timber. She couldn't get free so he shouted for help but no one came. Everyone was too busy trying to get away to pay any attention to anyone else. Finally, my father shouted angrily, "Aren't any of you Japanese?" Then he got the woman loose by sawing off her leg with a rusty, old saw.

Further on, we saw a man who must have been burned to death while he was walking.

Mother said that she couldn't go any further and told us to go on without her. She sat down to rest but we couldn't go on by ourselves, leaving her behind. Then she scooped up a handful of muddy water from the roadside and drank it. This must have made her feel better because she got up and joined us again.

As we got to the countryside, farmers stared at us in amazement and asked us what had happened. When we passed farm houses, people would come out and give us rice balls to eat, or ask us whether we would like to wash our faces.

We stayed with our relatives for about a month.

After we arrived, Mother complained that her back hurt. I looked at her back and found a piece of glass about ¾ inches wide and 1½ inches long stuck in it. It had gone in quite deep because she had been carrying my brother on her back. We went to see a doctor and learned that we had been rather lucky. Many people had died and hundreds had been injured.

From the next day, Father went out looking for my sister. The bomb had exploded over Aioi Bridge, near the Hiroshima post office where my sister worked. She must have died without time to call for her mother or even to say, "Oh!" My uncle and aunt had gone to a place near the post office to collect some manure that day and both were killed. Their ashes were brought back to us, though. Not even my sister's ashes have come back to us.

All but one of the workers at the post office was killed. He picked up the remains of the other workers and then took a little of the ashes to each of the dead persons' families. We put the ashes before God and prayed that my sister would rest in peace.

Asako Katayama
6th grade girl (6 years old at the time)

August 6, 1945, is a sad day that I will never forget. It was on this day that that horrible atom bomb was dropped on Hiroshima.

I was six years old, then. I often missed kindergarten because there was no one to take me.

My sister Aiko said that she had a headache and Mother told her to stay home. She went to school anyway because she didn't want to get behind.

I stayed home.

There was an air-raid warning on the radio and I put on my trousers and air-raid hood right away. Before long, I was glad to hear the all-clear siren and took off my trousers and hood. Mother went out to collect money for the rationed supplies and I played with Masao in the grounds of the shrine in front of our house. Suddenly, Masao shouted, "A B-29."

I thought he was joking and laughed, but Masao was serious. Just as we were getting near the air-raid shelter, there was a terrific boom. I was so frightened that I fell into the shelter.

After a while, it got calm outside and I crawled out of the shelter to go home. All the roads were closed by broken houses and many of the houses were on fire. I felt unhappy and didn't know what to do without my mother, but everybody was running toward Mitaki so I joined them. Someone told me it would be safe in the bamboo grove and I went there. There were many people with blistered skin and others who were bleeding. They were lying all over and seemed to be in a lot of pain.

Every time I remembered that I was alone and without my mother or my sister, I started to cry.

Just as I looked up, I saw a girl that looked like my sister.

She was limping along with her back toward me. I shouted to her at the top of my voice.

It was my sister. Her right side was burned and her skin was peeling. Some soldiers came and brought us rice balls, but I didn't feel like eating. One soldier took off his helmet and put some rice balls in it. "Eat them later," he said.

I sometimes remember that moment and what a kind young man the soldier was.

When I found my sister, I was so glad I cried. I felt much stronger because I wasn't alone anymore.

A terrible night went by and morning came. My sister was looking down the hill and suddenly said that our mother was coming. Our mother came toward us slowly with a suitcase in her hand. My sister and I ran toward her, calling her name again and again. She seemed to hear us, because she suddenly seemed to get back her energy and came running toward us. She hugged us both and said how relieved she was that we were safe. There were tears in her eyes.

Then she asked, "Where's Aiko?"

"I don't know. I thought you would know," I said.

Her face suddenly clouded and she began to sob, "The two of you are safe, but what has happened to Aiko?"

As we walked into the countryside, I began to feel the pain of burns I didn't know I had until then because I was so worried about other things. I kept walking, encouraging my sister along, but by the time we reached a country school, she couldn't walk anymore.

After that, my sister nearly died several times but she finally got better and was able to get out of bed in March, 1946.

My mother found my sister Aiko at a school on August 9. When she had left for school on the day the bomb fell, Aiko was wearing a pretty dress but when Mother found her she was lying there wearing only a pair of underpants. She was burned all over. She died about three in the morning on the tenth. She could not even see her mother's face because there were American bombers flying overhead and everything was dark.

Today, whenever anyone says the words "atom bomb" at our house, everyone becomes silent and sad.

Chikae Matsumoto
6th grade girl (1st grade at the time)

I was only in first grade then. My father was an air defense warden so as soon as the air-raid warning sounded about eight in the morning on August 6, he put on his uniform and left the house.

At the door, I said, "Hurry back, Father."

"Yes, my dear," he answered.

I had just reached the temple nearby where I was going to study when I heard an airplane. Suddenly, there was a flash and then a noise like thunder. The building fell on me and I was trapped under a large beam. It became dark. I shouted at the top of my voice. Once, I thought I could hear my mother calling me, but her voice was small and then I couldn't hear it anymore.

Some people who lived in the neighborhood finally helped me out. My face, arms and legs were bleeding. A neighbor was carrying me on her back when my mother came running back from the air defense station. My mother thanked the lady and took me. Then she washed my face with water. My mother went back into the house to get some important things and then she put me on her back, and my brother—he was a seventh grader—put my three-year-old sister on his back and we all went to the East Parade Ground. You could see fires here and there already. Everytime we heard an airplane, we lay down in one of the gutters. The fires were spreading rapidly and the sky soon became dark with smoke.

At last, we didn't hear any more airplanes. That was late in the afternoon. We heard that they were giving first aid at the shrine so my mother carried me there. She was barefoot and her face was covered with dust. She had blood all over her but she was still wearing her air defense uniform. When we got to the first aid station, there were many people with worse burns than mine. Some had burns all over. We waited a long time but couldn't get any help. Then we heard that the doctors were to leave by six so we begged them for help and they finally treated us. We and our neighbors slept at the parade ground that night. The whole city was burning and some sparks even fell on us. Morning finally came and we tried to go home, but we couldn't because it was too hot.

That evening, we went home but all we found were some tiles among the ashes.

My mother spent the next few days looking for my father. Then, on the morning of the ninth, some soldiers who were cleaning up dragged my father's terribly transformed body out of the ruins. The air defense station was near the Yasudas in Kyobashi-cho and my father was found under a large chimney that was taken down a year before. His head was burned so bad you could see the skull. We couldn't even recognize him and thought there might be some mistake, but when we saw his collar badge we knew it was our father. He looked so pitiful that we all threw our arms around him and cried. Mother went with Father's body to the crematory at Matsukawa-cho and there she saw bodies piled up in mounds. The soldiers cremated my father separately. The next morning, my mother put me on her back and my brother put my sister on his back and we all caught the Geibi Line train to take Father's ashes to where my mother grew up. The train was very crowded with injured people. When we got to Koutachi Station, we saw many people waiting for their friends and relatives but no one came to meet us. Both my grandparents had died a long time before and my mother's two brothers had been killed in action in the south. We went to my father's hometown and took his ashes to the temple where we had a funeral. On Buddhist All Souls' Day, my father's ghost came to the house, looking like a pale wisp of fire, and then all of a sudden it disappeared into the nearby woods. On August 15 when we got to Koutachi Station, there was an important broadcast by the Emperor and people were crying because Japan had lost the war. My mother and we children were very disappointed.

We had nothing left when we got back to Hiroshima and just had to get by from one day to the next. I couldn't go to school because I wasn't well yet. The sore place on my rear got worse in November and I had an operation. They took out a piece of glass about a half-inch long. On December 23, my mother had a baby boy, so my thirteen-year-old brother had to take me to school on the first day and I became a first grader again. There was nothing to eat in the house and my mother couldn't go out to work because of the baby. I still remember the hard time we had getting along.

In November the next year, Mother started work as a day laborer doing road work for the city. She had to take the baby with her and only got a little money. My brother had to quit school and work as a store clerk at Kyobashi-cho. Now, my mother is working as a bill collector for a newspaper and last year in January the company gave her a letter of commendation for her work. Our baby boy born the same year my father died is now six years old and is going to be a first grader next year. I am in sixth grade. I don't have enough time to study because I have to help my mother when I get back from school.

I always envy my friends who have fathers. But
till I'm grown up so I can build a nice house and
mother happy.

Machiko Fujita
6th grade girl (5 years old at the time)

F irst, there was a flash and then a big boom. I was very surprised and looked out the window.

We had moved out of the city and way out to Yasu in Furuichi.

White smoke rolled up toward the sky like a big storm cloud.
Then I heard the neighbors saying that Hiroshima was hit by a
bomb. A chill ran through me because my dear father was in
Hiroshima and so was my middle school sister who had left that
morning for voluntary labor service. I was so worried I couldn't
be still and I ran to my mother. I could tell from the uneasy
look on her face that she was worried, too.

From the next day, my mother went out to Hiroshima to
look for my father and sister. My seven-year-old sister, two-
year-old brother and I would always be looking down the road
in front of our house hoping that our father might return.
Every time a man who looked like my father came by, we
would run out and circle around him and stare into his face,
hoping he might be our father. But Father never came back.
There is no way to say how sad I felt.

My mother would come home sad and lonely after dark.

Once when she came back, she said, "It was so nice of you
all to wait so patiently for me." But her face was filled with
sadness and I knew she hadn't found our father.

Two days later, she got her lunch ready before dawn as

usual and was about to leave for Hiroshima, when my brother who was going to Hiroshima High School came back from Kudamatsu where he had to work. He went out with her to Hiroshima.

Three people with burns came to the Toshis' house next door and five people came to stay with us. Their faces were burned so badly that they looked like monsters and I shudder even now when I think about them. I cared for them the best I could. Every time I saw one of them, I would be filled with sadness because I knew that my father and sister might be somewhere in the same condition.

My mother and brother returned late and tired day after day. Their faces depressed me. From my mother, I learned that of the 600 city middle school girls that were there for labor service clearing the buildings, 593 were killed and only seven managed to survive, but within a week these seven died, too. The teachers in charge were also killed instantly together with their students. Many students tried to escape by diving into the river but their burns were too serious and they died. The faces of these dead students floating down the river were burned brown and their uniforms were in shreds. They couldn't be told one from another. My sister was probably one of them.

A teacher and four students were found dead in a large water tank in front of the Seigan Temple. The teacher had thrown himself over the students trying to protect them. The more I heard, the sadder I felt.

My mother grew so tired that she could no longer talk. All she could do was cry. We started to think that maybe our father was really dead and every time we did, it made us cry.

Days passed into months and our sadness returned again, and again. The time came for me to start school. Every day, my mother had to take me to Senda Primary School in Hiroshima from our house way out in Furuichi.

When I first came to Hiroshima, I was astonished. It was so changed that I could not tell where our former house was. Not many houses had been rebuilt yet but in our neighborhood two houses had gone up. They both belonged to people who had lived there before everything burned down. I would eat my lunch with one or the other of the families on my way home from school.

We started building a new house where our old one used to be in April. My brother and I moved in from the country before it was finished. We used *tatami* mats in place of the doors and slept together on only three mats in a six mat room. My brother cooked rice over a fireplace he made by stacking up a few bricks.

I had to play by myself. Sometimes I picked bowls and things out of the ashes to play house with. My brother's friends would often visit us and so it was quite cheerful.

In May, my mother and the others moved to Hiroshima, too, so my brother and I didn't have to live by ourselves any more. I was so glad I felt like I could fly. They put in a stove, too. After that, we all lived together happily.

My big sister started going to the Attached Primary School from the first of May and I changed to the same school from September.

Over the six years since then, Hiroshima has changed completely. There is a new hundred-yard-wide street and there are almost as many houses now as there used to be. The city is busy again.

Still, there is never a day I do not think how wonderful it would be if my father and sister were still living.

Yoshiaki Wada
6th grade boy (6 years old at the time)

I was at Kako-machi when the atom bomb was dropped. It was midsummer then. Some time after I got up, there was a flash and then a terrific boom. The house swayed and made noises as if it were going to collapse. My father said, "This may be an incendiary bomb raid."

It was the biggest bomb explosion I ever felt. First, I lay on my stomach for a while, but then I got scared and ran outside. Everyone in the neighborhood had run away and all the houses had fallen down except ours. I was glad that our house was OK. But just after my father, mother and sister got out of the house, it fell down, too.

There were many dead people lying on the bridge. Some were burned black, some had blistered skin that was peeling off, and some had pieces of glass stuck in them all over. Some asked for a glass of water. Their faces and mouths were bloody and they told us to go toward Yoshijima Airfield. We ran as fast as we could and finally reached the airfield. We were so tired and at the same time so relieved that we just sat down and didn't move.

My mother was burned the worst. She couldn't get up and ate almost nothing. She had a piece of glass stuck deep in her breast. But more than that, she was not very strong from the beginning and then she breathed the poison gas from the atom bomb. That's why she was so bad.

Two or three days later, we left the airfield for the country. By this time, the local railway lines were running and we took a train to a place called Kuba Village in Hiroshima Prefecture. My grandmother and little sister were living there. I guess they knew we were coming because they were at the bus terminal waiting for us. As soon as they saw us, they ran toward us in tears.

Two or three days later, we moved again. This time, we went to a place called Toyosaka Village, also in Hiroshima Prefecture. There, my mother went to see a doctor every day. It took her more than two years and two operations to recover.

My father's clothes were torn, but he only got a few scratches. Some time later, he began to work at the Ujina Railway Bureau in Hiroshima and so he moved to the city alone. He bought a camera and sent us many photographs showing the damage done by the atom bomb. They looked like pictures of hell.

My mind is so filled with memories of the atom bomb that I don't know where to begin. The war between Japan and the United States is over and it is peaceful in Japan again. Still, they have started to fight in Korea.

Yasuo Fujita
6th grade boy (5 years old at the time)

There were several hot days in a row. As usual, after breakfast, my brother left for labor service, my sister went to the Prefectural Office, and another sister of mine went to school.

Just when I was leaving the house early that morning to go catch dragonflies with the boy next door, the lady there stopped me and gave me two special rice cakes, a red one and a white one.

I went inside and showed them to my mother. While we were eating them, the boy came with his rice cake and we ate them together.

I don't know what happened then.

I finally came to several minutes later. I was caught under the wrecked house but I was saved by a table that was next to our cart. The next-door boy who was sitting in front of me when we were eating the cakes was now behind me, trapped under the house. My father helped me stand up but I was hurt pretty bad and could hardly walk. When I got out, there was a burned woman who was crying and a dead man in the middle of the street. I felt sick. The neighbor boy's mother helped me get away. We followed my father and mother. I could walk but not fast. We finally got to where there were some doctors.

There were a lot of burned people there and many of them were almost dead. The doctors were very busy treating them. My turn came at last.

I got in a car but I don't remember where we went.

That night, I stayed at a relative of our neighbor's. The next day, I had my bad cut stitched. I was only six years old and it hurt so much that I couldn't sit still. They put in only two stitches. When we got back, my father was at the house.

A little later, I went to where my father was staying. That was where my mother was born and she was there, too. My father took me to the hospital every day in a cart.

Once there was a bad flood but my father put together a raft and took me to the hospital even then. About a month later, a piece of glass about a half-inch square came out of my arm.

The saddest thing for me was that I lost my brother, sister and grandmother.

My grandmother was folding up some quilts and things and when the house fell she was caught under many beams. She screamed for help but the beams were too heavy for my father to lift alone.

They brought our sister to us about three days after the bombing but she had lost so much blood that she died two days later.

My brother was missing for about four months. Then one day, we heard they had found him but when we went to take a look all we saw was some buttons lying here and there.

I was knocked out and don't know what happened but I heard later that there was a flash and a moment later a boom. My family suffered a lot but I know other families suffered even more. That is why I hope that Japan and the whole world can live in peace.

Taeko Matsumoto
6th grade girl (5 years old at the time)

August 6, 1945. For me, that is a horrible and sorrowful day I will never forget. I was five and too young to go to school. My brother was in second grade at Danbara Primary School. "If he were alive today," my grandmother often says, "he would be in the second year of middle school."

My brother left for school without his writing brushes and was just coming back to get them when the atom bomb hit. He got back to the house but he was all burned. Our house was knocked down by the blast. My little sister Ah-chan was under the porch but she was able to get out safely because she was so little. I was playing next door and my grandmother was washing clothes in the bathroom. When the house fell down, everyone got scared and started calling each other. At last, we all got together. Grandmother was happy to see us all alive and safe. The next-door lady said another bomb might be dropped so we all ran to our uncle's in Aosaki. On the way, my brother said his head was hot and poured water over it many times. After taking many rests on the way, we finally got to our uncle's house in Aosaki about three in the afternoon. Our uncle had been very worried about us and he was so happy to see us all alive that he cried. My brother got worse and worse and kept asking for water.

But someone said that water was not good for someone with burns. So Grandmother told him he shouldn't drink water because it would make him worse. Then she wet the inside of his mouth with a moist cloth.

My uncle and aunt took good care of my brother but he kept getting worse day by day. A doctor at Aosaki gave him many injections but he didn't get any better. His hands and legs and the back of his head got soft and sticky. If you pushed these soft places with a finger, the pus oozed out. It was so sad. He couldn't eat anything and only asked for water. He couldn't get up. Once he said, "I want to get up just once. Please help me get up. Please!" He put his hands together as though he was praying. We tried to help him up but he couldn't even sit. At last, he gave up and just lay there.

He would often say, "You, Americans, look what you did to me. Just wait. I'll get even."

America and Japan were at war in those days so my brother hated America. But at last he said, "I want to go and see my dead father and mother," and died at three in the morning on the fourteenth of August.

Every time I remember how much my brother suffered before he died, I feel a deep pain in my breast and I can't help crying. At the same time, I say to myself that we must never have another war and I pray that all the countries of the world will become friends in a bright and peaceful world.

Daiji Nakamura
6th grade boy (5 years old at the time)

I was in the toilet at kindergarten when I heard an airplane. I was crazy about planes so I ran out of the toilet and started up the stairs. There was a flash. It scared me, so I lay down on my stomach and that's all I remember. When I woke up my mother was holding me in her arms and we were in an air-raid shelter.

Father brought some quilts on his bicycle. He also brought some money and medicine. When everything became quiet, Father said, "It's not safe here. Let's get out."

We started running to a safer place but my foot began to hurt. We looked at the bottom of my foot and I had a cut on the middle toe. My mother put a bandage on it and I got on the bicycle. But then we came to a hill and I had to walk again. We followed the other people and came to Kawauchi. We stayed overnight at someone's house, and then we asked the people there to take care of our bedding and things and went to Yoshida-machi. A few days later, we came back to Kawauchi and after a few more days we went back to Hiroshima. Everything was burned to the ground. When I got better, I started primary school and then when I was a second grader, I transferred to Noboricho Primary School in September.

Whenever I see a big plane flying in the sky, it reminds me of that day. Whenever I walk across Aioi Bridge,* I think what a powerful thing the atom bomb must be.

The newspaper says that America has made an H-bomb and when I asked my mother about it, she said the H-bomb is many times stronger than the atom bomb. I was really surprised. When I get big, I want to stop all the wars. Even now, people are fighting in Korea and lots of planes are carrying bombs there. I feel sorry for the Korean people.

* Aioi Bridge is located near the center of the explosion.

Nobuyuki Nakajima
6th grade boy (5 years old at the time)

On that day, Mother and I were feeding the chicks outdoors. We saw a plane flying overhead and then we heard the air-raid warning right after that. Something fell from the plane and I just stood there watching it. Then there was a terrible noise and I was blown into a gutter. Mother came running to me and pulled me onto the grass. I was burned all over. Mother and Father started to bundle up some clothes and other things.

My big brother and sister were at the temple school and we were very worried about them. We waited for a while but they didn't come home so we went to look for them. The temple and everything around it was burned down and there was no one there so we picked some bones out of the ashes and brought them with us. My big brother had been evacuated to the countryside and we wanted to go where he was, but my burns were so bad I couldn't go. Father packed up some things and took my little brother out to the country where my big brother was. I couldn't be moved so Mother and I stayed behind. I cried when my father and little brother left.

Mother took good care of me. The way the flies kept bothering me, it was terrible. I could hardly wait for my burns to get better because I wanted to join my father and brothers in the country. My mother looked after me every day and at last I got better. I was so happy then. Then Mother and I went to the country too. Later, we came back to Hiroshima, the city we love. I asked myself, "Why did we have to get into a war?" But then there is no use being gloomy after everything is over.

Susumu Mitsuda
6th grade boy (6 years old at the time)

Nobody in my family will ever forget August 6, the day when my sister Takeko was killed. She was in the third year of a girls' middle school but had been mobilized and was working at the telephone office. I often think of my brother who died in the war too. I was living in the country with Mother and my little sisters then, so I don't remember much about what happened that day but I still remember that there was a big boom. I was five years old then. I still remember Mother saying, "I hope the war ends soon so we can all catch that train back to Hiroshima."

Mother and we children were in the country but Father and Takeko stayed in Hiroshima. Whenever Takeko was able to get any hard-to-get things on ration, she would save them and bring them to us in the country on Sunday. She would tell us how things were in the city and then take the evening train back to town. So we always looked forward to her coming. And then she was killed in the air-raid. Later, Father told us a lot of horrible stories about that day. I often think of Takeko's sweet face and wonder where she died and how.

The war is over and Japan was defeated. My brother didn't come back from the front. If it had not been for the war, both my brother and sister would be here with us, and my brother would take me many places and play baseball with me. Why did they have to die? Whenever we have something they liked to eat, all of us think how nice it would be to have them with us. I will never forget them as long as I live, and I always look at their pictures and talk to them.

If there had never been any war, how happy my family would be! North and South Korea are now fighting each other. If they drop another atom bomb on Hiroshima, we won't try to

run away because we'd rather just all go to heaven where my
sister Takeko is waiting for us.

Katsuhide Tamamoto
6th grade boy (5 years old at the time)

I was six years old then. I was playing outdoors by the water
tank and then I went into the house. That's when that horrible atom bomb was dropped. The house fell down and I was
trapped underneath. The next thing I knew, Mother was carrying me in her arms. She brushed the ashes from my ears and
eyes. Our house had two floors. All the houses in our neighborhood were knocked over.

Father was in his office in Ujina and my two big brothers
were working at a factory at Yoshijima. My sister was working
on the seventh floor of the Fukuya Department Store. There
was no one to help us take things out of the fallen house and we
ran away with only one blanket. We ran along the street and
had to step over the dead bodies lying on the road.

I got so scared on the way that Mother had to carry me on
her back. I saw telephone poles on fire. Some people were
walking around in torn clothes and you could see the red burns
underneath. Mother and I put our hands together and prayed
toward the Fukuya Department Store because we thought my
sister might have been killed.

We went to Nakayama Pass and lay down in a bamboo grove
but we couldn't sleep because so many people were screaming
and crying. We spent the next night under a railroad bridge but
it was the same. A lot of black ashes like burned paper fell on
us from the sky. In the morning, we had nothing to eat so we
went to Nakayama Primary School where we got three rice

balls. Mother didn't eat any and wrapped them in paper and said we could eat them later when we got hungry. We were walking around looking for Father but I didn't have anything on my feet so I picked up a shoe here and a clog there and wore them. We found Dad and my big brother toward evening. When we got back to Nakayama, we saw my sister taking care of some burned people in front of the village office.

"We are going to get some medicine from the office," she said. We took turns hugging each other because we were so happy that all of us were alive. Then we went to the country. We stayed there for half a year.

When we came back to Hiroshima, the city was like a desert with a few tin-roofed shacks standing here and there. Who did all this to us? Who killed all our friends? I was too little to know. My friend, Okamoto, used to be a good boy when his father was alive. But now that his father is dead, he's turned bad. Really, it all makes me so mad I just feel like crying.

Toshiko Nobunaga
6th grade girl (1st grade at the time)

I was only a first grader when that horrible atom bomb was dropped. I mean, they called me a first grader but I really didn't learn anything at school because there were air-raids all the time. On August 5, I spent the whole night in the air-raid shelter waiting for morning to come but the enemy planes were still above us when it got light. We couldn't even boil rice so we had to eat parched rice and peas. Then we heard the all-clear. I got out of the shelter and went home. Just after I went into the house, it fell down. I was scared and started to cry. My big sister found me and asked where Mother was. We started looking for her right away. She was caught under the fallen house so my sister and I moved away the broken tiles and other things and pulled her out. We were relieved to find that she wasn't hurt. She said we'd better get away to some place safer so we started out but we had to wait for Grandma to catch up with us. On the river bank, we found Mrs. Fujimoto trapped under her wrecked house. We tried to help her out but the fire was coming toward us and she shouted, "You children are not safe here. Run down to the riverside. Hurry up!" So we ran down to the water.

The fire was coming toward us. It was high tide and the river was full of water. We were driven back to the edge of the water and at last we jumped in and hung on to a piece of wood. My feet hurt and when I looked at them I saw that my toes were burned. My arms were burned, too. My big sister was burned on the face and hands but fortunately my little sister wasn't burned at all. At last, the fire died down and the tide went out. I sat on the sand and Mother cleaned the dirt off my hands and feet. Then she said anxiously, "I wonder what has become of your big sister." My sister was at the Army Transportation Department in Ujina. I was also very worried about her. I felt cold from being in the river till evening. No matter which way we looked, we could see lots of people with burns. The water began to rise again so we moved onto the bridge. Some soldiers came by and one of them put some medicine on my hands and feet. After that, they gave me a ride to the parade ground and I got more first aid for my burns. Then my sister came to get me and told me that we were going to the Transportation Department in Ujina.

Mother carried me on her back to Ujina and put me in the hospital there. While I was still in the hospital, we learned that my brother had been found dead in Asano Park. We never did hear anything more of Grandmother. I was so sad that I cried almost all the time. Also, it hurt terribly when the doctor changed my bandages and that made me cry, too. I guess the doctor must have felt sorry for me because one day he brought me some cake. Afterwards, they told me that I almost died. The doctor gave me blood transfusions every day and at last I got better. My burns healed so that I could walk a little again. Mother carried me back to Ohcho on her back and everyone was glad to see me. But the children in my neighborhood laughed at me so I didn't want to go outside. This meant I couldn't go to school and anyway it would have been hard for Mother to carry me to school every day. So we asked the principal to let me stay away from school till the next school term and he said all right. I recuperated at home and started first grade in April the next year. I should really have been in second grade so I felt ashamed. Since then, I have been studying very hard.

On January 23 of this year, we came back to Hiroshima City. I could hardly wait to get back because this is my home. On the day we left, our friends and neighbors came to see us off at the pier. I cried when we had to say goodbye. And now that I'm here in Hiroshima, I keep thinking of the people back there. Mother got weaker and weaker after the atom bomb. She really wasn't well enough to make the trip here but she came anyway. The ship voyage was too hard for her and she suddenly got worse. She died on February 20. Since Mother died, my big sister has been missing school or coming home early to do the housework. I always come home right after school to help. There are five of us now—two boys and three girls. I feel very lonely. I can't sleep at night. I lie awake crying to myself and thinking how happy we would be if we had a father and a mother. My brother told me that the newspaper says there is another war. I feel like crying when I think that there might be more air-raids.

If there is a war, my brothers will have to go in the army and I just don't know what we three girls will do. I don't care what happens, just so long as there isn't another war. I just want to live happily with my brothers and sisters.

Shigeko Hirata
6th grade girl (5 years old at the time)

How fast time flies! Six years have passed since Hiroshima was hit by the atom bomb. Each year, more houses and new streets are being built and the city is becoming pretty again.

I was six years old when the bomb was dropped. I waved goodbye to Daddy when he went to work and was playing by the front porch. All of a sudden, there was a lot of yellow smoke and then a very big noise. I thought I could hear my mother's voice far away calling, "Grandma! Shige-chan!" I couldn't budge because I was caught under something heavy. The smoke went away slowly and the house became clearer little by little. Mother somehow got herself out of the kitchen. There were broken windowpanes, straw mats and plaster all over. The place was a complete mess. Grandma was sick in bed then and she was blown into the next room, bedding and all. A straw mat was lying on top of her. Fortunately, she wasn't hurt.

Someone shouted, "Help! Help!" from next door. Mother ran over and helped out the old neighbor who had been trapped under the fallen house. She was under a pile of broken tiles and pieces of wood and glass that mother had to remove one by one. A fire broke out in the neighborhood and we couldn't stay in the house any longer. Mother climbed up on the river bank with Grandma on her back. Many people came running from toward the center of the city. They all looked the same. Their skin was burned off and was dangling from their hands and chins. Their faces were red and so swollen that they didn't seem to have any eyes or mouths.

In the direction of the city, we could see a huge column of black smoke climbing into the sky. It was a horrible sight. I was scared and shook as I hung on to Mother. Then Daddy came running up to us with a terrible look on his face. He had a cut on his hip. The color was terrible, something between yellow and black. His hair was full of ashes. As we ran for safety, we saw people become too tired to walk another step and fall by the roadside. Even now if I close my eyes, I can see the many terrible things I saw then and it makes me shudder.

Father later died of radiation sickness. The cuts on my feet were slow to heal too and took a whole year to get better.

War is horrible and I hate it. I want to ask everyone in Japan and everyone everywhere in the world never to go to war again but to join hands and live peacefully together. Let's live happily like little birds. I don't think we should make atom bombs.

Shigehiro Naito
6th grade boy (6 years old at the time)

On the morning of August 6, I was eating breakfast with Mother and my little sister Naoko. It was summer so we were eating in the front room. My big brother had already finished eating and gone to the river bank nearby. He was good at telling airplanes apart by the sound of their engines. We heard a B-29. Suddenly, there was a flash and then a big bang. All three of us, Mother, my sister and I, were knocked out. About five minutes later I came to. Mother and I were all bloody. The kitchen was half caved in. Mother was scared and she took my hand and pulled me to the front door. The door was partly blocked but I could see the broken fence outside. We hurried outdoors. All the houses around us were badly damaged. We tried to get to the road that ran along the river bank but the walls along the road had fallen down. Mother asked someone to help us get through. Then we found my brother crying on the bank. He was scared and hurt. I ran to him. He seemed to be all right but he must have been burned. I looked toward the river. There were some dead bodies floating on the water.

"I'll bring some water so you can wash your eyes," my brother said and he got us some from the damaged kitchen. Mother and I washed our hands and faces. My brother was burned on both the right side and the left side.

Father came home from the school where he taught a little after noon. He was hurt. The school was just beyond the gas company. He said that he got caught under something but someone heard him shouting and helped him out. One of our neighbors also got burned on the back so he and my brother went to the hospital to have some oil put on their burns. That night, my brother swelled up tremendously. He looked like a bronze Buddhist idol.

Mother and Father watched over him every day but nothing they could do made him better. His fever wouldn't go down. Mother made rice gruel for him with the rice she had stored away but he didn't seem to enjoy it. Mother and Father were both hurt, too, and we couldn't get a doctor or find any medicine.

After about ten days, we all put my brother on a stretcher and carried him to Danbara Primary School which had been made into a field hospital. Every classroom was filled with badly burned people. They were all covered with white ointment and mercurochrome and were moaning and crying and grasping at the air. The soldiers were taking care of them. The air was sickening with the strong smell of disinfectants and the stink of pus. It was enough to spoil anyone's appetite for the rice balls that were handed out. My brother couldn't eat much and he got worse and worse. His burns got soft with pus and he made no improvement at all. Then he got diarrhea. Even my sister did. And there was nothing we could do. They gave him camphor and vitamin injections every day. Even though he was so sick, I still got into a fight with him.

"I'll bash you when I get well," he shouted at me, but he died that same night.

How horrible it was before he died! His whole body became festered and there were even maggots under his skin.

I felt so sorry for him especially because he died believing that he would get well. I miss him most when I meet one of his old friends.

I hate war. How hard it's been for my mother and father. I pray for peace in the name of all the people who died in the war.

middle school

By Mrs Toshiko Akamatsu

In the pond in Asano Park, carp swim among the dead bodies.

Masako Ohta
7th grade girl (1st grade at the time)

M y brother was five years old in those days and used to say that he wanted to become an admiral. But I hate war now. And it doesn't make any difference who wins; I hate it because so many people were killed and so many houses and so much money were destroyed in such a short time.

In 1945, I was living with Mother and my brother. Father was in the Navy and my big sister had moved to the country. On the morning of August 6, I was playing at school. Suddenly, we heard the sound of a plane and some of my friends went out to see it. I decided to go home right away. I wasn't carrying anything because I had no school bag. On my way home, I met a friend who was hurt and carried her on my back. When I got home, Mother told me to wait right where I was but I went on ahead with a neighbor lady.

On my way, I saw people caught under fallen houses, burned people wandering here and there and a man whose eyes were bleeding. I was glad that I wasn't hurt and could run to a safe place. The factories were already burning. Everyone was trying to escape. We ran away from the fire. Mother and my brother came after me.

We went to a house a long way out in the country. I wasn't very strong and got sick. The people at the house tried to help me. Only people who were very sick could get into the hospital, so I only went and got some medicine and came home.

A few days later, we went back to Itsukaichi. We couldn't get enough food and we were always sick. My uncle had been killed by the bomb while he was walking on Aioi Bridge. We went to his funeral.

Fortunately, Father came back right after the war ended. He went and brought my sister back from the country. She was so thin she looked like a stick of incense. Japan lost the war and so there are now a lot of unfortunate people and families like those on the radio program, "The Bells Ring on the Hill," and there are a lot of bad children around. It will take a long time and much work before we can get back the houses, money and food we lost during the war. Everyday, we suffer so much that I even hate to hear the word "war." If all the people in the world could live in peace, how bright our lives would be with beautiful flowers, trees and mountains, and with clothes and things to eat! Wood, tiles, glass and *tatami* mats all come from earth. So do the bombs used in war. We must not use the things we get from the earth to do evil. I hope atom bomb energy will be used for peaceful purposes as soon as possible. If we all obey the laws and are considerate of the opinions of other people, Japan is sure to become a highly civilized country.

Tokuo Nakashima
7th grade boy (1st grade at the time)

I was still in bed when the atom bomb was dropped on the morning of August 6. I heard a big explosion and jumped out of bed to see what was going on. Everything was pitch dark. I sat down and started to think about what might have happened. The minute I did, the roof tiles started coming down on my head. I jumped to my feet. The roof and the ceiling were both gone.

A neighbor woman came along and told me I'd be burned to death if I didn't get to a safe place right away. I went running off. Before long I started to feel that something was wrong so I stopped. Then I realized that I had left Mother behind. I went back along the same road to tell my mother. When I got back to the house, it had fallen down completely. I thought Mother must be around somewhere so I called her but there was no answer. I wondered where she might be.

"Have you seen my mother?" I asked a neighbor who came by.

"No, I haven't," she answered and my heart sank.

A man came by and said, "Come along or you will be burned to death," but I kept on looking for my mother.

No matter how hard I looked, though, I couldn't find her.

Then the man said, "I'm sure we can find her tomorrow morning. Come on. Let's go now."

I couldn't make up my mind for quite a while but he told me I'd be burned to death if I didn't hurry so I went with him.

"We'll be safe at least for now if we can get as far as Eba," he said.

We got to the hollow near the hill in Eba. There were lots of tomatoes growing there. There was no water to drink, so everyone was eating tomatoes.

I said to myself, 'I hope I can find Mother soon.'

From a mound a little beyond the hollow, I could see that the sky was black and that the houses were flattened and their tiles scattered all over. I could hear people crying for help all around. People with their faces burned so badly that no one would recognize them were crying for water. I spent the night on the hill. In the city the fire burned all through the night. The moon when it came out looked like a red lantern. The next morning, I went to where my house had been. I stood there for hours hoping that Mother might come looking for me. She never came.

At Funairihon-machi, there were many people lying on the ground. Some were dead and others were dying. I looked into their faces one after another, thinking that one of them might be my mother but she wasn't there. I walked along the road and came to Meiji Bridge. There were many dead bodies lying about but none of them was my mother.

I sat down on the river bank and cried as I waited and waited, but Mother never came. Dead bodies were floating by in the river.

Six years have passed since then. I live in Matsubara-cho now.

I am fed up with war. I want the world to be peaceful forever.

Toshihiko Kondo
7th grade boy (1st grade at the time)

O h! I shudder at the mere thought of the dreadful atom bomb that fell on August 6. How mercilessly it shattered out hopes!

August was my school vacation and on the sixth the sky was clear and blue.

Mother and my big brother had gone to the city hall as members of the labor service corps and Father had gone to the bank. I was left alone and was playing with my friends by the air-raid shelter nearby.

Suddenly, there was a flash and the next moment we were surrounded by black smoke. As I stood bewildered, trying to decide what to do, the house in front of us started to fall our way. We got out of the way in the nick of time. On my way home, I saw children crying for their mothers and people trying to press cuts they had received closed with their hands —terrible scenes that send shivers down my spine when I think about them even now. Fortunately, I escaped without a scratch.

When I got home, Father and Mother were not back yet, and I got even more scared. Our house had fallen over and everything was in a mess. The chest of drawers had tipped over and there were clothes scattered all over. The lady next door told me to get into the shelter, which I did right away because I thought Father might be there, but he wasn't. My friends were all with their mothers so, being the only one there alone, I crouched down in a corner by myself.

Just then, I heard my Father call, "Is Toshi down there?"

I rushed out of the shelter and there stood Father. I was so happy tears came to my eyes. 'What if he had not come?' I thought, 'Especially after my mother and brother hadn't come back.'

Then Father said, "Let's go look for your mother and brother."

The two of us set out toward the city hall. On the way, we saw a man with his lower half trapped under a fallen house. He kept crying, "Help! Help!" We couldn't bear to pass him by pretending not to hear his cries and gave him a hand. As soon as he was free, he ran off crying, "Shinji! Shinji!" He must have been looking for his child. Out on the main street, the streetcar lines had fallen to the ground so it was almost impossible to get through. A little way ahead, we could see flames leaping high up into the air. Some of the smashed houses must have caught fire. The road we took wasn't really a road. It was the roofs of the flattened houses.

I heard a baby crying a few houses away. The cry was trembling with fear. We wanted to save the baby but there was nothing we could do because the house next door was already on fire. We could hear the baby crying behind us as we went on toward the city hall. When we got to the city hall, there were a lot of people lying about on the ground. We searched for Mother and my brother but with no luck. Disappointed and tired out, we turned back, but as it was dangerous for us to go along the street, we walked on the roofs again, making a long detour to avoid the fire near Miyuki Bridge. Before long, we saw a boy come stumbling along. He turned out to be my brother. He seemed to have gone mad.

"Where is Mother?" I asked him.

"I don't know," he answered.

After a while, we got word that she was in Ninoshima and Father decided to go there. I was left alone with my brother who was still not in his right mind. How could I be expected to take care of him alone? I was only a first grader. That night, I lit a candle and held it near his face. His face was swollen and covered with blisters. He muttered something as though talking in his sleep and then suddenly he stood up and cried out: "Hurray! Hurray!" Maybe he was dreaming of an athletic meet. I hung on to him and shouted his name again and again but he wouldn't quiet down. At last, I called the next-door neighbor and he quieted my brother. By then, it was late so I went to bed but I was so worried about my mother and brother that I couldn't sleep for a long time. The next morning, Father was back.

"How about Mom?" I asked.

He simply said, "She was dead. They cremated her body on the island."

They said that Mother had been burned black all over and died in the course of the day. Father told me to open a box. In the box, I found her ashes. For a moment, I felt as if I had sunk down to the bottom of the sea. My brother breathed his last at about 12:30 that night.

We laid his body in a coffin along with some candies. The next morning, we took his coffin to the river bank, but I didn't want to cremate his body. Why? Because he had been such a good brother to me for nine years. And when I thought of how nice he had been to me, it made me hate those who had done this to him. Soon, the coffin was set on fire and in the smoke and flames I could see the faces of my mother and brother appear and disappear. I looked at Father. Tears were rolling down his cheeks. When we went for my brother's ashes in the evening, Father said, "Toshi, your mother and brother have left us. From now on, we have to go on alone. Do you understand?" The expression of his face when he said this is still deeply impressed in my mind.

I said to myself, 'I have no mother or brother. I have only a father. From this time on, it's just Dad and me.'

The next morning, when the eastern sky began to get light,

I went to the river bank where my brother's body had been burned the day before. It was not till then that it really came home to me that Mother and my brother had departed from earth forever.

Yuriko Kohno
7th grade girl (1st grade at the time)

It happened when I was in the first year of primary school. Just as I had entered the classroom and was sitting at my desk waiting for the teacher, the windows suddenly turned bright red and then with a terrific boom and clatter all the windowpanes broke. I sat there dumbfounded. Then I happened to look at my hand and was even more surprised to see that it was bleeding. I stood up and after a little while a soldier came and carried me home. As soon as I got back, Mother put my air-raid hood on my head.

It got dark but Father didn't come home.

That morning, my father had said, "I don't want to go to work today."

Then when he said he was hungry, I said to him, "Daddy, I'm full, so eat mine."

"Thanks! For that, I'll bring you something when I come home," was his answer.

"Goody!" I shouted.

But, unhappily, that was the day that the atom bomb fell. I and the other three, Mother, Motoko and Yoko, waited for him. The longer we waited, the more we worried that Father was not going to return.

Then some friends of my father came running to say, "Mrs. Kohno, we have bad news for you. Your husband is dead."

My heart seemed to stop and I couldn't say anything. Mother and we, three children, stood crying for a while at the front door. Then I realized that it was no use crying and I thought, 'He was a good father who loved you dearly but now you have lost him.'

But I was not the only one to suffer. Here, there and everywhere, the soldiers were carrying other children's mothers and dads to a kindergarten, where they treated and looked after them. I felt sorry for them and cried.

Then I went to my mother, "Mom, there are others worse off than us, aren't there?"

"Yes," was all she said in reply.

Then she said, "Yuriko, let's look for Father once more this evening."

So we took my two sisters and left them with a family that ran a glass and mirror shop.

I called, "Father! Father!" into the pitch dark night every step of the way. But there was no reply. That night, we slept in the air-raid shelter. The wind was very cold. We went searching for Father again in the morning. We went to the hospital and looked at the patient list but no one named Kohno had been admitted. Dejected, we returned home.

After that, the four of us had to work hard every day. Quite a while later, we moved to Motomachi. After I entered the second year of primary school, Mother came down with radiation sickness. In spite of how bad she felt, though, she still did all she could to take care of us. But her sickness gradually got worse and finally got so bad that I had to take over the housework, so I often had to stay away from school. I so hoped that Mother would get better and I tried to help by getting the meals ready and doing the shopping. I got so tired that I ended up sick in bed myself.

Mother worried about me and said, "Yuriko, I hope you get better right away. With you in bed, too, there's no one to take care of the house. Both Yoko and Motoko are too small to help out. There is only you. So do the best you can. I'll be getting better soon. Let's see. Here's five yen. Go and buy yourself something good to eat, dear."

I got up and went out and bought some sweet potatoes with the money. Little by little, I got used to the work and I made up my mind that I would take good care of Mother because she was all I had left. From then on, I tried harder.

When we had sports day at school, all my friends would be there together with their parents, but I had to go alone with my little sisters. When we got back to the house, Mother used to say, "Well, how did it go? Did you have fun?" and I would always nod and say "Yes."

Time passed until one day Mother said, "Yuriko, you and your sisters are going to go live at a place where they'll take good care of you."

She said this so suddenly that I asked, "Why, . . . what for? Do we have to be separated from you?"

Then Mother said, "No, it's not like that. I'm very sick so I have to go to the hospital. When I'm better, we'll be able to live together again."

Then a lady from the Child Welfare Department came to take us away. Mother was lying in bed and she cried as she said, "We'll meet again, dears." That's all. I was heartbroken because I had to leave my dear mother.

When I first came to the Hikari-no-Sono home, I thought to myself, 'Is this to be my home?' I was surprised at how quiet it was. Then I looked out the window and I thought, 'My, isn't it pretty here?' And then I looked around and, Oh! there were so many cute little children all over. That's how I started my life here. I played with my sisters and thought how lucky we were. I am so thankful to God because He made all this possible. From now, I will work hard to become a better girl. Mother is dead. Father is dead. Ah, yes, in the end Mother did die. Only three of us are left. I have made up my mind to become a good, honest, cheerful person, the kind of person that everyone will respect.

Shizuo Sumi
7th grade boy (1st grade at the time)

When the atom bomb was dropped on Hiroshima City at about 8:15 on August 6, I was playing outside with my sister. I saw a flash but I had no idea what it was. Mother ran out and picked up my sister so she didn't get burned. Mother was burned on the arms and I was burned on the face, neck and hands.

I was lying on the ground. I could see but couldn't talk. Mother was hurrying to get our things out of the house. I seethed with anger. I closed my eyes but couldn't go to sleep because my burns smarted. After a while, I could see something red through my closed eyelids and I opened my eyes. Fire was spreading from house to house. I gritted my teeth as I watched our house burn down. It was a sea of fire spreading in every direction without the slightest sign of dying down. Mother was speaking with the neighbors, and I kept on crying all the time.

Night came. Miraculously, the main shop was saved. I think this was because Mother and the others had kept throwing water on this building only. We slept there. I cried and cried and mother did all she could to make me feel better but I couldn't sleep all night. I was still crying the next morning.

Mother said the fire was still raging in the western part of the city. The day passed and night came again but I was still crying. The man lying next to me told me to shut up.

The next morning, Mother put some medicine on my burns. This hurt terribly and I cried some more. There was a doctor who passed by our house every now and then and when he did he dropped in to see me. After about twenty days, the burns on my hands were a little better but those on my face and around my neck still smarted. I hoped I would get better soon and expected the doctor to come to see me but he stopped coming, and I had only Mother to take care of me. I couldn't eat anything but soup. At night, mosquitoes and fleas bit me so hard that I sometimes cried. After a couple of months, I could open my mouth wide enough to eat boiled rice by myself.

One night, there was a terrible storm and the wind howled and made a racket as it tore the tin off the roof. My sister and I were so scared that we cried. The water rose to just beneath the floor. The wind died down by morning but we couldn't leave the house because of the water. Two or three days later, the flood receded. Mother and the others got up on the roof and put back the tin that had been blown off so that it wouldn't leak.

I got very tired of staying in the house and got Mother to put me in a cart and take me to my school. The school I had attended was gone and there were only piles of debris there. Many columns of smoke were rising from the military parade ground and the air smelled bad because they were cremating bodies. I felt sorry for those who were killed and it came to me how lucky I was to survive the blast. I went home and lay in bed with a slight headache. In the evening, my head began to ache terribly. Mother told me that the headache came from my being exposed to the sun during the daytime. I stopped going out. The headache continued for four or five days. Mother cooled my head with cold towels and this made me feel better.

About a year passed and most of the burns healed except those on my neck and cheeks. By that time, I could go out by myself. Houses were being built one after another. But the electric lights weren't back on yet so it was pitch dark at night. During the day, everyone in the house worked at cleaning up the debris. Eventually, my burns completely healed and I joined the others. The burned light and telephone poles were taken away and roads were cleared of debris.

At last, the school was reopened. Mother took me to the opening ceremony. But there were no schoolrooms and we had to study outside in vacant lots or on the side of the hill. It was very inconvenient. After I went into the second grade, they put up some temporary buildings. How happy we were! After that, I studied all the harder. Rain or shine, I always went to school. Now, there are a lot of houses all over town. Our middle school has many new buildings, too.

I will never forget that day. I want to repay Mother for everything she did for me. Six years have passed since the bomb was dropped on Hiroshima. How fast time flies! Our new constitution renounces war and I think we must keep the promise of the constitution and love peace above all.

Setsuko Yamamoto
7th grade girl (1st grade at the time)

I was in the first grade of Noboricho Primary School when the enemy air raids got bad. So Mother and I left Hiroshima City and went to stay with relatives in Miyajima.

On August 4, we went to a Buddhist memorial service held at the home of one of our relatives in Hiroshima. We had finished our breakfast and were getting ready to go back to Miyajima. Then from nowhere came that tremendous flash. Surprised, I said to my mother, "What happened?"

My mother answered slowly, "I wonder what it was?"

Then I heard a terrific crash, and it suddenly became dark —so dark that I couldn't even see my mother's face clearly, though she was right next to me.

Suddenly, I felt as if I were being pressed down by something very heavy.

"Mom, Mom!" I shouted desperately.

"Setsuko, Setsuko!" I heard my mother calling to me. Her voice seemed weak and jerky.

"Here, Mom. Here I am," I shouted back.

"Setsuko, try to move your legs," my mother's voice said.

I started kicking my legs with all my might. Then I heard some clattering sounds as if things were being taken off my chest. Finally, I managed to crawl out of the debris.

"Mom, get up! Quick!" I shouted and pulled at her hand.

She cried, "Ouch! Ouch!" but couldn't move.

I looked and saw that there was a heavy piece of wood lying across her back and right arm. She had helped me out with her left hand. I put my hands under the piece of wood and tried to lift it but it was too heavy for me. Again and again, I tried to move the piece of wood but it wouldn't budge. Cries of "Help! Help!" were coming from all directions. I shouted for help, too, as loud as I could but nobody came. The fire was right next to us. The flames blew toward me and singed my hair.

I shouted, "Mom! Quick! Get up quick!" but there was nothing either of us could do.

I heard my mother saying, "Hurry up and go! I'll come later."

I told her I wouldn't leave without her but the flames were closing in around us and my clothes caught fire and it was so hot that I couldn't stand it any longer. "Mother, Mother," I cried as I ran as fast as I could through the flames. There was fire all around and there was no way to escape so I jumped into a water tank by the side of the road. Lots of sparks were falling from the sky so I put a piece of tin over my head to keep them off. The water in the tank got hot like a bath. There were four or five other people in the tank, too, and they were all crying and shouting different names. As I sat in the water, I started to get a dreamy feeling and finally passed out.

I don't know how long it was before I came to but it seemed to be morning. Smoke was coming up from here and there and I could hear the cracking and popping of things smoldering on the ground. In the tank beside me, there was a dead woman lying back as peacefully as if she were asleep. As soon as I noticed her, I got scared and shouted to a passing man for help. He lifted me out of the tank and told me that there was a first-aid station straight ahead. I walked beside the man. Just as I started wondering what had become of my mother, I happened to take a look at my hand. The skin was burned and sore. I also felt a pain in my chest and back. At the station, they took care of me and gave me some rice balls to eat. Then I got in a truck that took me to a primary school outside the city. There were hundreds of injured people there groaning with pain. The people in charge there were all very kind, making our meals, and comforting and looking after us. But day after day scores of injured people died and there was a bad smell coming from one corner of the playground where dead bodies were cremated on piles of sticks. I was very worried about my mother and cried every day. There was a man who offered to go with me and help me search for my mother. We went back into Hiroshima City together but when we came in front of the Fukuya Department Store, he said to me, "Wait here for a while," and went away. He never came back and I trudged along by myself through the burned-down area. We had been having fair weather for several days and the sun was so strong that the ground felt very hot under my feet. I saw a lot of dead bodies by the roadside and there were also carcasses of horses and dogs. I tried not to look. The town which had once been so busy with people and traffic was now turned into a vast burned field. Only the concrete buildings remained standing here and there like so many giants. Everybody was looking for someone or other. They were dragging themselves along feebly and tears filled their eyes. I saw people digging out the burned bones of their relatives and friends and putting them into urns. What had become of my mother? Could someone have helped her escape after I left her? I ran up to every woman who passed by and looked carefully at her face partly hidden by the air-raid hood hoping she might be my mother. When I saw that she wasn't, I was sad and disappointed. Enemy planes were flying low in the sky.

I hadn't had anything to eat or drink since breakfast so I was hungry and thirsty and so exhausted that I couldn't walk any further. As I sat crying by the roadside, a passer-by placed a small bag of hard biscuits in my hand and treated me to a sip from his canteen. I still remember how happy this made me. Then a policeman came along and asked me what the matter was. After I told him my story, he took me to a police station where I stayed for the night. When I told him that my grandmother lived in Miyajima, he made out a pass and gave it to me. With the pass, I got a ride on the suburban streetcar from Koi and then took a ferryboat to Miyajima, where at long last I found my way to my grandmother's house. She was overjoyed to see me and immediately asked, "Where is Sueko (my mother's name)?" When I told her about everything that had happened to us, she broke into tears.

One day, about five days after, she said to me, "Your mother is really dead after all." A relative had found and brought back her ashes. She had burned to death, unable to get out of the wrecked house. I hugged the urn that held her ashes and I cried loudly. I couldn't keep back the tears which kept on streaming down my cheeks. The wife, son and daughter of the family we were visiting had all died in the same way.

It was decided that I would stay with my grandmother. It was about that time that my hair began to fall out and the burn on my hand got worse. At first, Grandmother was very kind as she comforted me and changed the bandage on my hand. But later she became cold toward me. Whenever I noticed this change in my grandmother, I would be filled with resentment and sadness and many memories of my kind, gentle mother and the pleasant times we had together would go racing through my head. Night after night, I cried endlessly.

I don't know how it came about. But when the bright red of the maple trees in Miyajima had faded, and the chilly autumn winds began to blow, a relative of mine in Kyoto City came to take me away with him. I spent two years in Kyoto, and when I was in fourth grade I got tuberculosis and had to stay in the Red Cross Hospital for five months. They told me that the disease was caused by the radioactivity of the atom bomb. I got well and left the hospital but I had lost so much weight that I looked like a skeleton.

One day, when the last term of the fourth year was almost over, my father surprised me by coming to see me. I left Kyoto with many memories of the city, and with Father came back to dear Hiroshima. I had been away four years and much rebuilding had been done in Hiroshima. There was a new house where our old house had been; where my mother died. In front of the house, I put my hands together and prayed, "Mother, I have come home to Hiroshima. Please watch over me so I will be happy here."

My father and new mother have taken good care of me and I have become strong and healthy. I am happy and enjoy every day. Sometimes though, I get angry when inconsiderate boys say bad things about me or tease me because my little finger is still crooked from the burn I got on my right hand.

Every day in the streetcars and on the streets, I see quite a lot of people who have large, ugly scars on their faces, necks and hands. Since I know that almost all the scars are from the bomb, I always feel like rushing up to them so that we can comfort and encourage each other. I think everyone who suffered from the bomb feels like this. All of us who suffered from the bomb know from our own experience how horrible and how miserable war is. And we all want to try to live peacefully forever with people all over the world.

Yukiko Yoshida
9th grade girl (3rd grade at the time)

I had just become a third grader of the Nobori-cho Primary School in 1945. With the war getting worse, mass evacuation of Hiroshima schools had started. I was to be sent to my uncle's in the country and attend the village school there. My mother was busy every day, getting ready the clothes and things I'd need.

When I was in the country, I worried about my mother back in Hiroshima. One day, the radio announced, "B-29s are now flying over Hiroshima." I thought of Mother and my little sisters and cried. I was so anxious about Mother that I wrote to her. To my great relief and happiness, three or four days later a letter came from her saying that they were all well at home.

Summer came. It was extremely hot on August 6. I mailed another letter to Mother on my way to school. While I was studying at school, I heard a distant rumbling. When I got home, I switched on the radio and heard the word "Hiroshima"; my heart jumped with shock. The next moment, the radio announced, "Hiroshima completely destroyed." I didn't know what to do.

On August 8, while I was helping with housework, my two little sisters, aged eight and five, came. It was a long walk for them, three hours from the city to Wada Village in Futami County where I was. I was so happy I hugged them and asked about Mother. They said our house had burned down and Mother was at a temple near the East Parade Ground. I was very happy to hear that she was alive and well. It was decided that on the following morning my uncle, sisters and I would go to see Mother and Grandmother. The next morning, we got on the first train to Hiroshima. Hiroshima Station had of course been reduced to ashes, so we got off at Yaga and set off on foot for the East Parade Ground. On the way was a small hill, and the first person we saw after we'd gone over the hill was a woman of sixty or seventy lying on the road. Coming closer, we found that she was already dead. A little further on, we saw a young man crying for water. I felt so sorry for him that I was going to give him some, but stopped when someone who was passing said, "He will die if you give him water." We walked on and finally got to the temple near the parade ground.

Mother was waiting for us, sitting on a torn straw mat. We had plenty of time before our train so my sisters and I had a look around the temple. The ground under the raised wooden floor of the building was full of dead bodies. Near where the dirty water which had been used for washing flowed out, an old man was lying dead with his mouth wide open. The temple gardens were full of the dead and injured. The injured were crying, "Give me water," "Help me," "It's agony," and so on.

In the evening, we took Mother and Grandmother and my little sisters back to the country. Even after moving there, Mother was busy every day with many things to do such as the registering at the village office, rations, and so forth. She steadily went about all this although she'd broken four ribs when the house in Nobori-cho had collapsed. Perhaps because of all that or because she'd breathed the poison which had got into her, a number of brown spots from a quarter to a half inch in diameter appeared on her body three or four days before she died, and she grew hard of hearing. My uncle and aunt thought it was very strange. After another couple of days, on September 9, she passed away. A few days later, one of my young sisters died in the same way, and later in the month another followed her to the grave, thus leaving only three of us behind—my youngest sister, my grandmother, who was badly hurt, and I.

I was sad and lonely and didn't feel like going to school for a while. At school, I'd often hear friends saying their mothers had made them new dresses or bought this or that for them. I felt sad just hearing the word 'mother.' I only had my grandmother to turn to, and she became ill every winter. It was very difficult for me because it meant I had to miss school every day to take care of her, and I'd think, 'If only Mother were here.' In the country it was hard, because Grandmother was ill a lot and we could not get enough nutritious food, so we decided to go back to Hiroshima. In Hiroshima, she wasn't ill much, but now she fell sick very easily. I think this was because the atom bomb weakened her.

I am really happy to be able to live in Hiroshima, where I was born. If only my mother and sisters were here. . . . If there had not been a war, my dear mother and sweet sisters would not have died but would still be here and we would be a happy family, enjoying life together.

Wakako Washino
8th grade girl (2nd grade at the time)

E ven the memory of the atom bomb is horrible. I was a second grader when the bomb was dropped. This is the seventh year since I was parted from my big brother at that young age. He was very fond of swimming and used to take me swimming with him, and we'd play together. In the night of August 5, his ear began to hurt because some water had got into it. It was so painful that he couldn't wait and he went to Hiroshima. He took the pocket money he had been saving up and got on the 7 a.m. train for Hiroshima on the sixth, and I never saw him again.

Mother wasn't worried because she didn't know he'd gone to Hiroshima, and thought he'd gone to school. Hardly could his train have arrived at Hiroshima when there was a dazzling flash quickly followed by an earth-shaking roar, and an ugly cloud rose up. The moment I saw the cloud, I thought of my brother on the train and ran home in a daze.

When I got to my house, I found that the paper screens had been blown outside, the light bulbs broken and the window-panes smashed. There was so much broken glass and stuff outside that you couldn't walk barefoot, and people were running around shouting. It was unbearable to look at.

This was about a month after my father had died in action. As it was very hard for us to go by ourselves to look for my brother, we went to some relatives to ask them to help us, and so two of them, a man and a lady, took us by truck to look. But, we weren't allowed into Hiroshima. Mother and I stood by the road there and looked at the face of each person coming out of the city, but they were all strangers to us, none of them even looked like my brother. All of these poor people were badly burned and injured. Even though I was very young, I lowered my head. Every day, we looked out for my brother, hardly eating, but we never saw him. We put his picture in a box and did a funeral service for him. My brother had been waiting for Dad's remains every day, saying, "Let me go and get Father's remains when they come. All right, Mother? Please?" He didn't know he was going to die. So my brother who was going to get the remains had a funeral instead, before Dad's.

When I think this is all because of the war, I hate it and hate it. As time passes year by year, I want my Daddy and big brother so much I can't stand it. I was so young when the atom bomb was dropped that I don't know what it was all about and have only told what remains strongly in my mind. From the bottom of my heart, I want the terrifying and barbaric atom bomb to be done away with from now on and to have peace.

Yasushi Haraki
8th grade boy (2nd grade at the time)

I was a second grader then. From early that morning, it was 'Air-raid,' 'Air-raid.' The all-clear was soon given, though. Then I went to school and Mother went to work with the labor service corps, so my little sister was left alone in the house.

I was studying by myself at school. It was about eight o'clock. A light suddenly flashed and right after it got dark and gloomy. At the same time, the ceiling fell down and caught me. I got out by going under the desks. When I got outside, there was a fire all around, like a sea. The school was burning hard, too. I went home but my house was burning hard, too. There was nothing else to do so I went to get away to Hijiyama Hill, but I had a pain in my foot and my stomach was hurt so I couldn't walk anymore, so I took a rest by a bridge near there. Just then my mother came along. I was ever so happy. My stomach was cut and she was also badly hurt so we went to the hospital at Ujina and were there for about two weeks. On the way from Hijiyama to Ujina, there were a lot of dead people lying all over. About two weeks later, we went to a temple in the country. We were only at the temple for a little while. Mother and I had gone into the countryside, but we didn't know where my sister had gone so we went back to Hiroshima. We searched here and there, and then a stranger brought my sister to us. We thanked him and took her, but she died about an hour later because she'd hurt her legs when the house fell on her and she'd also breathed the poison gas. We couldn't do anything so we left her body in the temple on Hijiyama Hill and went back to Ujina Hospital. Every day, we went to the temple to make an offering of water to her.

One morning, we went there as usual but her body wasn't there. They said that someone had cremated her along with some others but we could not find out who it was and couldn't get her remains. There was nothing we could do so we went to where our house had been and dug there. We found some bones but we didn't know whose. It couldn't be helped so we took those bones back to the country with us.

A little more than a month after the atom bomb, my mother's sister and all of our relatives died. Only Mother and

I were left alive. Then we came to Hiroshima again. There were shacks standing here and there. The two of us went to Ujina, and I went to the primary school there and Mother worked in a restaurant.

The war finished and lots of soldiers came back to Ujina Port and they came to the restaurant. One day, I was playing after coming home from school and there were a lot of soldiers there eating different things. I thought I had seen one of them somewhere but I couldn't remember where, so I said nothing. After a few days, a visitor came. It was the same man, but I didn't know who he was so I didn't say anything. In the end, I found out that he was my own father. Mother was very happy. My father had come back from the war, so we changed houses. Just as I thought we'd settled down in our new house, he became ill because when he was away at war he'd eaten grass and things. After only about two and a half months, he died. I was a third grader then.

After he died, Mother and I went back to the country again. It was so sad, the loss of my father and my sister. Mother started work again, and I went to the local school. At the end of the sixth grade, we came back to Hiroshima.

Six years have passed since the day the atom bomb was dropped. Now I am getting over what has happened and I want wars to stop and Japan to become a nice country.

Kiyotoshi Arishige
9th grade boy (3rd grade at the time)

I was in third grade then. My house was about one mile away from the center of the explosion, but as it had to be vacated, we were living in a small house at the back. The said it was dangerous for schools because of air raids so we were taught in a temple near there.

On the day the atom bomb fell, I didn't go to the temple because I didn't feel like it somehow. I was lying down reading a magazine in a small room with a window facing south. If I had gone to the temple that day, I might have been crushed to death under the big trees there. Later I heard that many of my friends who had gone to the temple for lessons had been killed.

I was in that small room when it happened. That is, August 6, 1945, about 8 o'clock in the morning. All of a sudden, I saw a whitish-pink flash. The first thing I thought was: 'Oh no! We've been hit. Should get out.' I rushed over to the window, meaning to get out through it. But then I didn't think I could get out from the window and I turned to the door, and just then the house gave way with a rumbling clatter, and I lost consciousness. I came round to find myself buried in the debris of the fallen house. At first, I didn't have the will left to get out; but then when I thought someone was calling me, I crawled desperately toward a gap and finally got out. It was Mother who'd been calling me.

I had thought that it was only our house that had been destroyed, but to my great astonishment, all of the houses nearby were flattened or half wrecked. The sky was gray and overcast, and pieces of cloth and paper were caught in the telephone lines, which were dangling down broken here and there. I went around to the field at the back. Five or six neighbors came running over. It was not till then that I noticed a cut on my hand. I'd probably got it from a nail or something when the house collapsed on me. I washed the wound at the pump at one side of the field, and then Mother and I went to the road, along which many people were making their way west, their hair scorched, their clothes in rags, and many of them with burns and injuries. We joined them on their escape to the west. At Kanon Bridge, we turned toward Eba Park. The road was full of people fleeing the disaster, some of whom were so exhausted by extensive injuries and burns that they could go no further and squatted down by the roadside with a vacant stare.

As we went down the bank, a black and chilly rain began to fall. I noticed bicycles, footballs and many other things scattered around the houses but nobody made a move to pick anything up. Everyone was just thinking about getting away. We came out in front of a building like a barracks, at the back of Eba Hill. We went in an air-raid shelter there and rested a while.

After a while, a soldier came in and led us to a tent pitched beside this concrete building. In the tent, there were many injured and burned people, all lying down. Toward evening, I heard my name being called by someone sounding like my sister. I rushed out of the tent and she was standing there, my eldest sister. (She was working in the National Hospital at Eba.) She took Mother and me to her hospital.

The hospital was full of the burned and injured. Among them, I found my other big sister, lying there painfully with burns all over her face. When it was getting dark, the sky began to glow redly from the direction of Yokogawa and Kamiya-cho. The houses there must have been burning. I spent that night in an air-raid shelter outside with my sister and her friends. As I lay there, it seemed as if I could hear deep, deep down in my ears the moans I had heard during the day-time. And also, the image of the hyperdermic syringe dangling from the ceiling, with its three-inch needle entering the thigh, arose in front of my eyes: sleeping was difficult. The next day, Father came to the hospital, too. He said he'd gone to Gion early that morning and this had spared him from the bomb.

That day, Father and I went to where our house had stood, but it was gone completely, and all that was left was a fig tree and the burned metal frame of a sewing machine. A telephone pole was still smoldering. The road was littered with broken tiles and bricks and only a few people could be seen here and there. We left there and went to the ruins of my uncles' house. Uncle Takagi and Uncle Yamano and the others were living in an air-raid shelter. After everyone had discussed things, it was decided that I would go to an island called Nomishima in the Seto Inland Sea with my uncle's family. Their daughter, Takae, had some burns, but was alive, but their son Taro had been killed. Takae told me later that when it happened she had been walking over Sumiyoshi Bridge near Funairi-machi, but because of the thick coat she had on, she had suffered burns only on the side of her face which had been facing north, and on her arms and hands sticking out of the short-sleeved coat.

Several days after we came to the island, someone went through the streets, shouting, "Important broadcast today on the radio from noon. Please listen to it." At noon, His Majesty the Emperor announced over the radio that Japan had been defeated in the war. The next day, my uncle and I went to Kanokawa. The house there is on a hill-side, with a very fine view of the Seto Inland Sea. Every day, I would gaze at the beautiful seascape, and involuntarily tears sprang to my eyes.

On coming back to Hiroshima some five days later, I went to visit Mother at the hospital in Eba, but she had already died. I heard that she died four days before I came to Hiroshima. Now, I feel that it may have been her death that made my eyes fill with tears when I gazed at the blue sea from Kanokawa Village. My next oldest sister was also in the hospital, but she passed away about ten days later.

Thus the atom bomb demanded a painful sacrifice of my family—the lives of my Mother and sister. And as for myself, I was forced to remain in the hospital for several months.

Takako Okimoto
8th grade girl (2nd grade at the time)

The sixth day of August, 1945! A date deeply engraved on my heart, when the cruel bomb claimed so terrible a toll of precious human lives in an instant. I go cold whenever I think of that day. I am one of those many who were deprived of their irreplaceable parents, brothers and sisters, relatives and friends. All of them died, one after another. My big brother, who had been out on labor service, is still unaccounted for. My other brother suffered serious burns all over his body and died the next day at Koi Primary School. We left his body at the school and went to the country with my parents and sisters. However, there were no good doctors there, so Mother went back to Hiroshima. The day after she went, my uncle sent us a message saying that she'd suddenly got worse, and asked us to come back to the city. The following morning, the three of us took the first train there. There was a nasty smell everywhere in the city, and the scene was most horrible. Everything in sight had been devastated as completely as could have been; we couldn't see anything of what was Hiroshima. Somehow, we got to our home only to be told that Mother had passed away just before. I cried and cried. We cremated her body on the dry riverbed. People were cremating corpses here and there. We got to my uncle's in the country with Mother's remains that evening, and there my big sister died.

Though I was too young to know what to do, I did everything I could to help my father and little sister. But despite my care, she passed away a day after the funeral services for the first sister. Father came to my big sister's funeral services, but he'd got so weak by the time my little sister died that he couldn't come. The Buddhist monk who did the service at my two sisters' funerals must have breathed the poison, because he did not come to do my father's funeral.

Father must have felt very sad and lonely to see his sons and daughters die before him, one after another, but whenever I said, "How do you feel this morning?" he would say, "I feel a little better this morning, my dear." He didn't want me to worry, but he was just getting weaker and weaker. On the morning of September 10, he departed this life, with the thought of leaving me alone weighing on his mind. Before his death, he often said, "I hope I don't die. Now that our house and possessions have been lost in the fire, I want to stay here in the country and do farming, dressed in rags but leading a quiet life with you."

Japan surrendered at last on August 15. There were lots of poor beggars in and around the station. The city had become full of thieves and robbers and things had been getting worse.

What in the world brought all this about? The war! Had it not been for the cursed war, so many people wouldn't have been made so miserable. Without war, the world can always be a peaceful and happy place to live in. In the new Constitution, it states that war is renounced. Even if there is no war between country and country, in the country of Japan, the Japanese people continue to fight each other even though they are all the same human beings. Japan will never get peace like that. I think that if we are to build a peaceful country, we should be more thoughtful toward each other.

Sumiko Watanabe
8th grade girl (2nd grade at the time)

Not a day has passed without my thinking of the atom bomb of August 6, 1945, for it deprived me of my dear father. It makes me shudder to remember the catastrophe.

I was nine years of age. My sister was twelve and my brother four years old. Mother was expecting a baby in two months. Nothing can be more sorrowful than for a child to lose her parents early in life. Mother, who had none to turn to and couldn't seem to believe Father was dead, went out with my sister to Hiroshima to search for him day after day. In the evening, she would come home exhausted and dejected, and over supper tell us what she had seen or heard in the city.

Thus the months passed. In order to get food, Mother gradually sold Father's clothes, and now hardly any are left.

Though the war was getting fierce, my family had been leading a very happy and peaceful life in Hakushima, Hiroshima City, until a month before the atom bomb was dropped. Now, I am living with Mother in Yano, a small town a little way from the city, but am I fortunate to have survived the ordeal? Far from it. I wish we all had died with Father in Hiroshima on that day. Mother says the same thing. My sisters live apart from us. As time has passed, the horrors of war have begun to worry me. And young as I am, I ask Mother many questions and reflect on such things myself. No matter how much I think of it, what a nasty and horrible atom bomb! What was the war fought for? 'Why should any mind to give their life for the cause of peace in Asia . . . ,' we sang. Many were killed, 'For peace, for peace,' they said, but where is this peace?

Oh, Father, how you must have suffered, how hard it must have been for you! Father, who disappeared at 8:15 on the morning of August 6, 1945. Look after us, Father. Good-bye.

Masatada Asaeda
9th grade boy (3rd grade at the time)

I was only a third grader then, a kid too young to understand things, but I often heard the words 'air-raid' and 'war,' and I remember them clearly. "Today we evacuate." "Tomorrow we evacuate." Everyday we wandered around new places in search of safety, but those who didn't know anyone in the country finally would come back to the city.

We had been living in Hakushima. Father was away at the war, so the five of us, me, three sisters and Mother, sweated everyday to dig a hole to make an air-raid shelter to hide in. In July, the air raids got worse, and by the middle of the month, at about eight thirty nearly every evening, the air raids started, right after the noisy announcement on the radio. We grabbed our things and jumped into the shelter. The four of us gathered around Mother, saying nothing. We'd spend the whole night like this, praying to ourselves that we'd be all right. When the all-clear came in the morning, we crawled out.

That morning, we sat around the table eating breakfast as usual, looking at each other, and hoping that the day would pass safely. Suddenly, an alert was announced by radio, but the all-clear soon followed. I went to school unconcerned. One sister went to her school and another to the factory. Only Mother and my oldest sister stayed at home.

When we were playing in the school ground, an airplane came, but we kept on playing, only saying, "Why did they give the all-clear?" All of a sudden, there was something like lightning and I covered my face with my hands. When I opened my eyes and looked around, it was dark and I couldn't see anything. While I was feeling around in the darkness, it became light. I was thinking of going home, and I found that all the houses around me had been destroyed and fires were burning here and there.

I started running home, crying and calling, "Mother! Mother!" But I couldn't tell where my house had been. I just went around this way and that, and then I heard my sister calling my name. I was shocked when I saw her, because she was stained with blood all over. I looked at myself; the skin of both my arms and feet had peeled away and was hanging off. I didn't know what all this meant, and I was frightened, so I burst into tears. Meanwhile, Mother had crawled out from the pile of tiles and dragged an overcoat and Father's cloak out of a trunk and wrapped us in them.

"We must get away from here, to Choju Park," she said in a terrified voice and began to walk. My sister and I ran for our dear life. Close behind us, the flames were rising high up in the sky. Mother was saying from behind us, "Don't be in such a hurry. Careful, you don't step on any nails." We hurried to the river bank. When we came near it, the houses on both sides of the road were burning hard. "One, two, three," we cried and dashed through the flames up to the embankment. Feeling that we were pretty safe now, I fell down on the ground with a sigh of relief. But Mother told me sternly to stand up, and we followed her aimlessly in search of safety.

We spent the night in Yasu Shrine in Gion. Because of their burns, everyone was crying for water all night. The next morning, we were taken by truck to a Buddhist temple in Kabe. That night, my sister died. How can I describe Mother's grief? How can I describe the horrible scenes I saw in the temple then? Who can imagine the miseries we went through except those who were there themselves? It is entirely beyond my power to put the terrible sight into words. Countless people suffering from burns and wounds, groaning with pain, their bodies covered with maggots, and dying in delirium, one after another. It was hell on earth. Those people must have died, not knowing about the defeat, hating war and loving peace. I still want to write about meeting my father again, and my sister, but it will get too long so I won't.

Finally, I want to ask, what is war? What is peace? Why must we make terrible atom bombs to maintain peace? Why is it that humanity and science don't advance the same?

Those are the questions that are always in my mind.

Toshihiko Tanabe
8th grade boy (2nd grade at the time)

A flash followed by a terrific sound, and the entire city of Hiroshima was annihilated. Has there been as great a disaster as this in the history of mankind? Has anything had such power? Yes, atomic energy. Atomic energy is terrible. If it is used for bad things, it will destroy the human race. If it is used for good things, the more it is used that way, the more happy people will become, and there will be peace. With that flash and bang, hundreds of thousands of lives disappeared. What a horrible scene it must have been! It was at 8:15 on the sixth of August. That was the day which impressed itself on my mind deeper than anything else in my life will.

A few days later, I came back to our house to look for my Mom and Dad. I knocked at the door and shouted, but there was no answer. I went in but it was empty. I was then only in second grade in school, and at first I couldn't understand. But as the days went by, I began to understand. Were my father and mother dead? I felt very sad just thinking that. My father was so good and strong. I thought he wouldn't be killed by a bomb like that, not Dad. And I kept telling myself that my mother was alive, too.

At midday, six days later, a soldier, dirty and bloody, leaning on a stick, hardly able to walk, lurched in the door. It was no other than my dear, unforgettable father. I was so happy! I rushed to him and hugged him. I was right, my father was strong and wonderful.

"Where is your mother?" he asked. "She hasn't come back yet," I replied. "Not yet? There may be no hope," he said. He stayed in bed after that. My happiness was short. My father had been so much affected by the poison that he passed away about noon on the sixteenth, while I just clung to him tightly and cried and cried. My mother never came back. I don't know where she died. And when I thought that it was just we and Grandmother living together, I felt sad again.

Six years have passed since then, but I have never forgotten that sixth of August. It will be the seventh anniversary of my parents' death soon. Lastly, I pray that the atom bomb is used for good and peaceful purposes, not for bad ones!

Kazuo Mori
9th grade boy (3rd grade at the time)

On July 14, 1945, I was sent together with my grandma and brother to Ohnori Village, and was attending the primary school there. With a mountain at the back and facing the sea, the village was a peaceful place, and I used to go swimming or gathering seashells with my brother and sometimes with Grandma. As he was a teacher at a girls' high school, Father had no chance to come to see us in the village, but Grandpa sometimes came.

I went to school as usual on August 6. It was during the morning assembly. Suddenly, there was a flash in the sky. I thought it was strange. As soon as I got home after school, I asked about it. People said that Hiroshima had been completely destroyed.

Two days later, a letter reached us from home through someone we knew. It said that Father was missing. I was very worried. Grandma prayed that he was alive. The next morning at school, my teacher asked me if my father was all right. I had no heart to say he was still missing, so I simply said that I didn't know.

On August 15, the unconditional surrender was announced. The villagers cried.

On the nineteenth, we decided to go back to Hiroshima. Tickets were very hard to get those days, but Grandma asked the stationmaster so hard we got them. The three of us got up early the next morning and went by the first train as far as Mukainada Station, which was before Hiroshima, and from there we walked the rest of the way, gasping for breath under our heavy loads and stopping here and there to take a rest. When we got to Toyo Industries, we met a group of men pulling a cart. At Grandma's request, they were kind enough to quickly put our things and also me on the cart. They were hurrying along to get some injured people, they said. I shall never forget how happy I felt when they put me on top. My grandmother and brother had to hurry along behind. I felt a bit sorry for them, but it felt nice riding on the cart. The cart went near the ice-skating rink in Minami-machi, which was not far from my home in Midori, so it was a big help. It wasn't far but the streets were full of hurt and burned people, with swollen, dark-red faces. It was really horrible to look at. Grandmother asked me to go and bring Mother to where we were, but I was too scared to go through those people. And I was too scared to watch over our things by myself, so we left them with some people nearby, and went to our house together.

When we went in, our house was so damaged that I couldn't say anything, I could only cry. Grandfather was lying in bed with his legs badly injured. Mother said that Father was dead, and she and Grandmother cried. I was sad too, but I was still too young to understand what his death meant for my family. Mother tried very hard to look for Father. The girls' middle school where Father had been teaching helped Mother to look for him. Finally on the twelfth, his ashes were found and brought home. Mother wept as she told us that he had died together with many of his students.

After some time, Grandfather's legs got better and the house was repaired a little, but as there was no school in the whole city, we went back to Ohnori, while just Mother remained in the city. On September 17, there was a big rainstorm. The roof leaked and the water came up to floor level. It was terrible, I heard.

Our school in Hiroshima reopened so we returned to the city in the middle of October. We had no school buildings so we had to study outdoors. The days were getting colder.

It was not before I finished primary school that I began to think about my father. I got more and more sad over his death whenever I saw my friends whose fathers were alive. My hatred against the atom bomb which not only killed Father but injured Mother and Grandmother will never end. I shall never forget this horrible event for the rest of my life. And I am only one of those countless numbers of children who are so unhappy simply because Japan started on that silly war.

With my father gone, Grandfather had to work hard to support us, in spite of his old age. But it got too much for him, and he died this year on March 11.

"Be good to each other and work together," were his last words. With this last wish of his in mind, I will work hard and make Mother and Grandma happy in the future.

Nothing is worse than war. I really hope that there will never be another stupid war. I think all the people of Hiroshima think the same thing.

Kiyoko Tanaka
9th grade girl (3rd grade at the time)

August 6, 1945, when the atom bomb fell, is the most unforgettable day in my life. Even now after so long an interval I shudder whenever I think of the day.

I had not been evacuated and was attending an annex school in the city. That morning, I went to my friend's home and was playing with her. There was a flash of light and the next moment I found myself trapped under the house I'd been playing in. I didn't know what to do, but I saw some light coming through a space in the wreckage, and I squeezed out through the gap. Now I found that not only the house I had been playing in but all the houses nearby had either fallen down or caught fire. I felt like crying at the sight, but as there was no use crying, I started back home.

Mother was frantically carrying various things out. The baby, which was one year old, had been put on our stuff, but was senseless, maybe from fright. Mother was glad to see me and said, "Let's get away. We'll be burned to death if we stay here," and she put the things on her back and held the baby in her arms, and started. I ran after her. I saw a man running blindly around with a big piece of wood in his eye. We didn't know where to go, and we joined the stream of people running away. On the way to Hijiyama Hill, some badly burned people were jumping into water tanks and ponds, and others were just sitting by the roadside, crying, "Give me water," or "Splash water on me." Still others were drinking muddy, roadside water.

Halfway up the hill, I saw a big tree burning from the middle, and from the top we saw a big sea of fire in all directions. Lying around me were lots of injured and burned people rolling around and groaning in agony. Mother and I went down the hill toward Danbara, where the houses, though all knocked down, were not burning yet. There were some houses which were still standing, but there was nothing in them. Those who had been running barefoot put on clogs they found in doorways and started running again. A bit ahead, a man with a megaphone was shouting that all the injured should go to Ninoshima Island. We decided to go there too, and got on a small boat on the river. A girl about my age was sitting in front of Mother. She was hurt, burned and covered all over with blood and kept on calling for her mother. Suddenly, she asked Mother, "Is your daughter here?" She couldn't see anymore. When Mother said, "Yes, she is," she held out something and said, "Please give this to her." It was the lunch prepared by the girl's mother that morning for her to take to school.

"Aren't you going to eat it yourself?" Mother asked.

"It's all finished for me. Please give it to your daughter," she replied, and we accepted it.

The boat floated down the stream and was soon at the mouth of the river.

"I'll tell you my name, so if you happen to see my mother, please tell her that I am here," the girl said suddenly, and hardly had she said these words before she was dead. I felt very sorry for her and cried with Mother over her death. How happy I would be if she were alive now! On the island, we were sent to a reception center, which was crowded with many people who were burned and injured. Some people were running among the patients as if they were crazy.

How happy I would be if now all those people had no burns or injuries and were alive, and if the girl in the boat wasn't burned and was alive, and I could meet that girl's mother.

Kazuko Komae
9th grade girl (3rd grade at the time)

I was a third grader then, and was evacuated to Tomomura Village some 13 miles north of Hiroshima City on April 14, 1945. It was the first time I'd been away from my parents and sister, and it made me very unhappy. I remember that I cried all the more bitterly on leaving home because, little though I was, I had come to somehow feel that the chances of winning the war were against Japan, because American planes had begun to fly over Japan, by that time. I also knew that Kure City, and Tokyo and Osaka, had been badly damaged by air raids. The rumor spread that Hiroshima was the next target, and I thought it might be so. The letters from home always told me not to worry about them and to study hard, but at night after I got into bed and I heard the sound of raindrops or the unpleasant air-raid sirens, I felt a keen sense of loneliness and my heart filled with a longing for home, and I wanted to be with my parents in the city, even if it meant dying with them.

August 6! A terrible day cursed by the devil. What I had feared happened. But was I the only one who had been comforting herself, until the bomb actually fell, with a slender hope that Hiroshima or at least my own home would be safe from any harm?

A bluish white flare many times as bright as the sun, and then a deafening explosion! In an instant, the sky was overcast with black smoke. I took shelter behind the hill at the back of the temple which served us as a school building. There, I found many people, their pale faces together, whispering, "Hiroshima has been destroyed. Hiroshima has been destroyed."

Far away in the direction of my home town, I saw a column of ominous smoke rising high up in the air. To think that that light, that sound, was the first atom bomb ever suffered by mankind! Under the smoke, what tragedy were the people of Hiroshima experiencing? That merciless bomb turned Hiroshima into a city of death and deprived me of my dear sister, at a single stroke. Days passed without a word from home, and I was very anxious about my relations in the city. Some who came from Hiroshima described the city as having been changed into a scorched field by a single bomb. Others compared it to a city of the dead with almost all of its citizens annihilated. I felt more dead than alive.

On August 14, Father came unexpectedly to see me. "Oh, Father!" I just clung to him and wept. My sister who was in the first year of high school had been missing since she left home for war work that day. For three days just after the calamity, Father and Mother searched for her desperately all over the city, where the fires were still raging. He found her canteen and uniform by a water tank, but of her, there was no sign.

It was in the middle of September that I came back to Hiroshima. The house in which we had lived for years had been razed to the ground. Thus my family came to live in a room in my uncle's house, together with all our pieces of furniture which we had moved beforehand in case of air raids. As time went by, my sense of loneliness over the loss of my only sister grew keener and keener. She was only eleven years old. If she had been but one year younger, she would have been evacuated with me.

One day, I found her diary by chance in a corner of the bookcase. It reads as follows:

[Date] Tomorrow I'll have to part from Sis. Took every care so as to make her happy and cheerful on the eve of her departure.

[Date] Kazuko left us this morning. Felt tongue-tied when I said, "Well, so long, Kazuko-chan. I have no time to see you off at the station. Good luck!"

Kept thinking of her at school. Didn't feel like playing with anybody at recess. Kazu-chan, I'll write to you very often. As I was looking at her writing practice and drawings, I found myself almost crying.

[Date] Came home from school and found a letter from Sis. She wrote many interesting things. Decided to make her some jackstones.

Thus the war separated my sister from me and finally frustrated my hope of ever seeing her again. When I look at the framed photo in front of our altar of my sister in her school uniform, memories of her crowd into my mind one after another till it seems as if I can actually see Sis, left alone in the raging fire caused by the atom bomb, being burned by the scorching blaze; and as if I could clearly hear her crying desperately at the top of her voice, "Father, Mother, Kazuko-chan."

In the shadow of war, there are always sad stories left untold. War destroys precious lives so mercilessly. Nothing is crueler and uglier than war.

Chizue Sakai
9th grade girl (3rd grade at the time)

The blazing sun of midsummer was shining in the eastern sky. All of a sudden, we saw a flash of light like lightning in the blue of the southeastern sky. Then there was a boom and the clouds turned red.

I and my class were staying at a large temple in a small town called Yae-machi in Yamagata County, where we'd been evacuated. We were scared, and ran into the temple and huddled together, shaking with fear. By the evening, lost of injured people were being carried to houses near the temple. Because it was the southeastern sky that had flashed, I was worried that Hiroshima had been bombed. There were no smiles from anyone from that day on. All we could do was to pray that our families were alive and well.

Soon, the teacher who had come with us to Yaemachi went to Hiroshima to find out exactly what had happened to each student's home, a hard job. Thanks to the trouble he took, we were able to get news about our families. As for my family, I was told that my parents and my little sister had been killed and my house burned down. Only my grandmother was saved and was staying with my relatives. When I heard that Mother and Father were dead, I didn't say anything, and I didn't cry. The tears came later, as if I'd just remembered.

Another thing that made me sad was that every day one or two of my friends I'd been living with were taken back to Hiroshima by their fathers who came for them. I was particularly upset when I had to part from my best friend, whose family had been very lucky because they were all alive. She had been very kind to me and it was a great comfort for me to be with her, but who could I turn to without her from now on? I ought to have been happy for her, but just before she went I felt so lonely that I hid myself in the corner of the temple and cried. I couldn't say goodbye to her. After that, I got more sad and lonely every day. Many of my friends were going home, but no one came for me.

October came, and something happened which made me

happy. A lady who used to live in my neighborhood came for her young sister and me. How happy I was then! But when I thought of my friends who were being left behind, I felt sad. On the bus, I gazed out the window and thought of what had happened to me. Leaving my parents, and coming along this same country road by bus, crying; not used to farming, I found it hard at first, but soon I enjoyed it; being bitten by leeches in the rice fields; looking forward to Sundays when we could write letters; how my greatest happiness was to get letters from home; how I was scared when I heard wild dogs barking at night or saw ghostly lights moving; how surprised I was that the letter I posted a few days before the atom bomb fell was returned to me; I thought of when I was first told of my parents' death; and how I was sad when I had to see my friends off; and that I had been longing to go back to Hiroshima and talk with my grandmother. Thinking of these things, the tears overflowed and ran down my cheeks. The bus went rattling along the rough road, and soon we reached Yokogawa Station.

I was so surprised when I got off the bus. It was much worse than I had expected. The ground was covered in tiles and not a house was to be seen anywhere, just a few ruined concrete buildings standing here and there, where there had been so many houses before I had been taken out of the city for safety. Before, my house had seemed to be quite a long way from the station, but now I found the distance much shorter. Where my house had stood, all that was left were some metal bits of Father's bicycle and my tricycle. For a little while, I stood there, shocked.

"It's no use standing there like that. Let's go to my house," my friend's sister urged me after a few minutes. Her house had also been burned down, and now she had only her mother and sister left. Presently, we got to her home. She and her mother suggested that I should spend the night with them, but

I wanted to see Grandma as soon as possible so the lady took me.

It was dark before we got to my relatives' place. "I'm back," I said as if I had just come back to my own home. I was welcomed by my kind grandmother and someone I didn't know. I knew that my parents were gone, but anyway I felt empty inside when I didn't see them there. The lady who'd brought me left. Grandma was very glad to see I was well.

"Father and Mother died, didn't they," I said. A shadow crossed Grandma's face, but she also seemed to be somewhat relieved.

She answered, "So you know, Chizu. I am a little relieved to hear that. I was worrying about how to tell you."

A few minutes later, I was kneeling before my parents, meaning their ashes. For a while, I just stared at the urns. Grandma told me to eat supper but I could not bring myself to sit at the table and eat.

For the following eight days, I stayed in bed. Somehow, I didn't feel like eating anything. When I had recovered a little, Grandma told me the following sad story.

On the morning of the atom bomb, the milkman did not come around early as he usually did, and Mother went to the grocery for milk for my baby sister. While she was at the store, the bomb fell and she was burned to death there. Father had been standing in front of the house with my sister in his arms and was badly burned and trapped in the wreckage of the house, but even so he crawled out desperately with the baby. Grandma was also caught under part of the house but fortunately fell into the bomb shelter, and was only hurt slightly. Hearing the baby's cries, she went out to the street and found Father there. He and the baby had been burned all over and their skin was hanging like rags from their bodies. Handing the baby to Grandma, Father began searching for Mother right away but could not find her. He could only hear people crying for help from somewhere under the flattened houses. Then they saw the fires were coming very near. All they could do was get away. On the way, they saw the woman from the grocery store where Mother was supposed to have gone, but she didn't know what had happened to her. The dead and injured were lying everywhere, the wounded groaning or calling out someone's name. The fire was already threatening to destroy the bridge they had to cross and soldiers were shouting out, "Hurry up! Hurry up!" Father and Grandmother got to the parade ground, and that was full of injured people, too. So they had to go on and after a long walk and a lot of rests, they reached a bamboo grove. This place was also crowded with people who'd been injured. One of the people there told Grandmother that her head was bleeding and was kind enough to bandage the cut. Until then, she hadn't known she was injured. Airplanes were still flying overhead. Father and Grandmother began to walk again and at last reached my relatives' house over the hill. But by then Father was exhausted and could not move any more. Even this place was not safe from enemy planes, so people took bedding to the river bank in front of their houses and huddled under it. Lots of people were dying, and their bodies were piled up in heaps here and there and were being cremated day and night.

Grandmother could not get milk for my baby sister so she gave her thin rice-gruel and sometimes milk from nursing neighbors. Right about lunchtime, six days after the bomb, she went to have a look at Father but he had already passed away. Two days after my father died, my baby sister died, too. I really feel sorry for her; she was only seven months old, and because of the continual air raids, a blackout was ordered all over the city every night and it was also dark indoors, so the baby had seldom seen any light.

– This was Grandmother's story about what they went through at that time.

That horrible event which befell Hiroshima a little past eight in the morning of August 6, 1945, when I was eight years old, will remain in my memory as long as I live.

When I hear children calling out to their parents or see happy families going out together, I am a bit envious of them, but such feelings will go soon, and I think this way: there are many many orphans like me in this world. And there are many who are worse off than I am.

I'll try to overcome the sorrow of my parents' death and live cheerfully every day and study very hard. And when I finish school, I hope I shall be able to do my share for the good of society and help bring about a peaceful world.

Shigeru Tasaka
9th grade boy (3rd grade at the time)

The people of Hiroshima had been wondering why Hiroshima had been left intact while other big cities throughout Japan had been bombed. Some thought that the city was possibly being saved for an experiment or test. Unfortunately, this was true. The fatal August 6 had been waiting for the city. The day dawned without a cloud in the sky. At 8:15, the cursed atom bomb was dropped over the center of Hiroshima City. In an instant, the whole city disappeared from the earth and 247,000 innocent people lost their lives. I was only eight then, but I still remember the day well.

I was sickly then, and that morning I was still in bed. My sister was taking the day off from work, and was in bed, too. The air-raid warning had been lifted, so I was feeling unafraid.

I was looking out of the window when suddenly there was a flare of bluish-white light. Just as I asked my sister what it was, a heavy explosion shook the house. I heard the sound of glass breaking upstairs. My home was about three miles away from the center of the explosion, and behind a hill. This protected it and the other homes from the direct blast. Mother was in the kitchen, and, wondering what the strange light was, she opened the window to look out and just then heard the sound of the explosion. Scared, Mother shoved the mosquito net up and ran in, and the three of us huddled under the bed covers. After a while, I went outside for a look. Everyone around was looking toward the hill. A huge column of white smoke climbed high up in the air. The lower part of the column was colored red probably because of the fire. No one could tell what happened.

I went upstairs. The rooms were covered with broken pieces of window glass and pieces of an inch-thick wooden frame. Usually I would have been upstairs at that time of the day, but fortunately on that particular morning I lay in bed downstairs later than usual, and this saved my life. There was a storehouse with its front facing away from the direction of the blast. The door of the storehouse was about four inches thick and had been fastened with six-inch nails, but the strength of the blast rebounding from the house pulled out the nails and blew the door off inside. The hands of the clock showed a quarter past eight. In my neighborhood, there were many houses with the ceilings blown off by the blast. This shows the tremendous power of the explosion.

About noon, the people who had been out on labor service started coming back in twos and threes. (Their job was to demolish houses to prevent fires caused by incendiary bombs from spreading.) Some of them thought the explosion was due to the arsenal blowing up, and in fact the thump of explosions could be heard. But others said that it must have been some new type of bomb. That sounded more likely since almost all the houses in the city had been destroyed, and fires were burning, and the people being carried back on carts had been burned and injured. Of course, radio, electricity and the water supply had been cut off. Those whose family members had not come back before dark were very worried and went out to search for their missing people, but they could not even approach the city boundaries, because the whole city was still on fire. On the twelfth, Father came back from Yamaguchi and described the horrible state of affairs in the city. I was shocked. You can easily imagine how dreadful the atom bomb is from the fact that I, who hadn't thought anything about airplanes before, shuddered at the remotest sound of plane engines. It was not until then that I came to realize how hateful and horrible war was. When the unconditional surrender was announced, everybody wept with mortification. I was sorry too, but somehow I felt much relieved. I even wish that during this war atom bombs had been dropped everywhere so that every country could have experienced the terror of the bombs, because if people could fully understand how barbaric, cruel, uncivilized and nasty atomic warfare is, I think they would stop the kind of ugly war that is now going on.

Now everyone in the world keeps just saying they are for peace. It would be bad if the greatest sacrifice of World War II, the 247,000 people of Hiroshima, is forgotten. It is about time we stopped fighting and tried to establish a lasting peace on earth at the earliest possible time so that their lives may not have been lost for nothing. We ought to know how terrible and disgusting the atom bomb is and understand that war wastes precious lives and materials to no purpose.

I must add here that, strange as it is, my formerly poor health has improved greatly since then, probably due to the bomb, and this is the only thing I can thank that horrible bomb for.

Yoshihiro Kimura
9th grade boy (3rd grade at the time)

E very day at that time, I had to heat the bath. After that, I used to go back to my homework. About five, I would go to the streetcar stop to meet Father and my big sister, and we'd go back home and have supper together. That was what we did every day then.

On the morning of August 6, Father was in bed because he had a slight fever. My big brother was cooking some cuttlefish to eat at work. After everyone had gone, there were four of us, me, Mother and Father and my sister. Then my sister and I got ready for school. My sister went to the main school and I to the branch school. It was a temple, really. Me and my friends were talking about the war. Then we heard an air-raid warning. I ran home and was playing there for a while. I was used to all this. Then the all-clear was given and I went to school again. Our teacher had not come yet, so we were just talking. About then, we heard the sound of an airplane and we could see it, very small, in the southeastern sky. It got bigger and bigger and soon was over our heads. I was looking at it all the time, I didn't know whether it was an American plane or ours. All of a sudden, something white like a parachute fell out from the plane. Five or six seconds later, everything turned yellow. It was like I'd looked right at the sun. Then there was a big sound a second or two later and everything went dark. Stones and tiles fell on my head and I was knocked out for a bit. Then I woke up because heavy pieces of wood fell on me and hurt my back. I crawled out into the open. There I saw lots of people lying on the ground. Most of them were burned, and their faces had gone black. I felt better when I got out on the road and then suddenly felt my right arm hurting. The skin from the elbow to the fingers had peeled off. I began to walk toward where I thought my home was.

"Sumi-chan," cried a voice. I turned around and saw my sister. Her dress was torn to rags and her face completely different. The two of us went home, but our house had crumbled down and no one was there. We looked around nearby. When we got back, we found Father, who was trying to get something out from under the fallen roof. He gave up and walked up to us.

"Where is Mother?" I said.

"She is dead," he replied weakly.

When I heard that, I felt as if I had been hit on the head. I couldn't think. After a while, Father said, "What's the matter with your head?"

I felt the back of my head. It felt rough and was soaked with blood. A nail five inches long had stuck into Mother's head, and she died instantly.

It began to rain. The raindrops looked like muddy water. We took shelter under a railway bridge which was smoldering. Soon, the rain stopped. We felt cold and went near some burning houses to get warm. There were a lot of people there. There were almost no ordinary-looking people there. They had swollen faces and black lips. A man was waving the Japanese flag as if he was mad, shouting, "Banzai, banzai!" Another was swaggering around and saying, "I am a general." I felt very thirsty and went to the river to drink some water. Many blackened dead bodies were floating down the stream. I had to keep pushing them away while I drank. Along the edge of the water were lots of dead people. Some were still alive. A child was crying, "Mother, mother." Already, when I saw dead bodies, I didn't think much about it. Some people came staggering up and fell into the river and died. Sis fell down on the road maybe because she was badly hurt. Father carried her on his back and laid her on some ground cleared by the flames. Toward evening, my brother came back.

That night, we made a shed and slept in it. But cries for help and moans of pain were heard all the night through, and continually interrupted our sleep. I kept dozing and waking. The dawn came. My brother went to our relatives in the country to borrow a cart and came back about three in the afternoon. Then my sister and I were put on the cart and all of us started out. When we got to our relatives' home, Father almost just fell down, maybe because he didn't have to worry about keeping going any more. When night came, I felt lonely. 'About this time last night,' I said to my self, 'Mom was quite well, but now she's gone!' Two of my sisters were still missing. Father, one brother, one sister and I were now all there were in my family. We couldn't say anything, we just looked emptily into space. When I went to the toilet, I cried out, "Mother." But Mother was not there any more. When I realized she was really dead, the loneliness and sadness were painful. I cried my heart out. But no matter how hard I cry, she won't come back. When I thought that, the sadness came again. The thought that I could never see her gentle face seemed to suffocate me and my head swam. I cried a lot. Then Grandmother said, "Now Mother is a Buddha, so if you want to see her, ask him." Although Father saw her die with his own eyes, I could not believe she was dead.

Then we had another misfortune. About three in the morning on the fifteenth, my sister died. By the time I was awoke, she was dead. It must have been a hard death, for her eyes were open. Her eyes seemed to be staring at me. I shouted "Sister," and shook her, but she had become a Buddha, too. That day, the war came to an end.

Some people who had been missing began to come back. I felt that Mother, too, might come back. But although I waited, of course there was no hope of her return. I hoped that at least my eldest sister would come home. In the meantime, my eldest brother had been discharged from the army. Every day was full of loneliness. Gradually, I was able to face the fact that both my mother and sister were dead. I began to be able to resign myself to the fact. My oldest sister's remains were never found, but Father got some ashes from a mass-cremation. But no matter how hard I tried, I couldn't forget my mother. The gentlest, kindest person. Two sisters were also very kind. Mother used to make cakes and give them to me every day when I came back from school. Oh, kind Mother; good Mother! Where are you now? I am sure that she has gone to a better place. I often picture to myself Mother living in Heaven and beautifully dressed, like a goddess. She always used to say, "Children, be good to each other."

Later, we moved back to Hiroshima City again, and now I have a second mother. But whenever I have something that is hard to talk to other people about, I miss my real mother so badly.

I hate war now from the bottom of my heart. It is entirely due to the war that my kind mother and sisters were killed. I don't hate anybody because Mother is dead, but I hate war. I don't want hateful war to happen again. War is everyone's enemy. Mother's soul in heaven will be happy if we stop wars and peace comes to the world.

Masayuki Hashimoto
9th grade boy (3rd grade at the time)

August, 1945. I was nine then, a third grader. Father had been drafted as a coal miner in some coal mine in Kyushu, and we were leading a lonely life. One day about three months after my father went, we received from the municipal government a notice saying that our house was to be evacuated by August 7 for demolition. We at once began to look for another house. My brother said there was a nice one in Kawaramachi, but it was dark and gloomy and there was a carpenter's workyard on the opposite side, which seemed a likely target for bombs. Finally, however, we decided to move in there. When we were quickly packing, a special delivery letter came. It was from Father. It said that he would come back to Hiroshima on urgent business on the afternoon of the fifth of August. Two days later, we moved to the new house, though we hadn't been able to take all our stuff yet. Father was due that day and I was impatient to see him. Toward evening, an air-raid alert was announced and the whole city was blacked out. Someone knocked at the door, and instantly I knew that it was Father. That night, in darkness, we ate what he had brought.

The following morning, another air-raid warning was given, but it was called off soon. I wanted to play with Father in the living room upstairs, and was halfway up when there was a flash. At the same time, various things showered down on me. When I could think what was happening, I looked around. It was quite dark, and I thought I must be dreaming. I lay motionless for a while. The northern sky gradually began to get light. I tried moving my arms and legs. They were all right. My mouth felt rough. It was full of plaster. I spat to get rid of it. I heard Mother calling me from somewhere. I hurried to where her voice was coming from. The house had been completely wrecked. I was also worried about Father and my brother and sister. My brother had gone to fetch the things still left in the old house, and my sister seemed to have gone off to Nakahiro-cho on an errand at eight o'clock. I found Mother trying desperately to help Father, whose right leg had been trapped by falling timbers. I at once got a rafter and pried him out. By then, we were surrounded by flames. I was so scared I shook. Urged on by my parents, we forced our way out through a gap in the flames. Men covered in blood and women with skin flapping around them like kimonos were plunging into the river, screaming. They all died and their lifeless bodies floated downstream. We didn't have the courage to jump into the river. But as we stayed there like that, the flames got closer. If we didn't move, we'd be burned to death, so we decided to jump into the river. Fortunately, just then a boat floated down the river. We got into the boat and went out into midstream. Looking back at the bank, we saw the place where we'd been standing was a sea of fire. Soon, the waves got bigger and our boat overturned. I nearly drowned, but Mother pulled me up onto the upturned hull. In this way, we floated down as far as Sumiyoshi Bridge, where a boatman rescued us and took us to Sumiyoshi Shrine. There were lots of people there suffering from burns, all crying for water. Soldiers were carrying them on stretchers to a safe place. With the sudden relaxation of tension, Father could not walk any farther, so we had him carried by the soldiers on a stretcher to near Minami-ohashi Bridge, where the injured were being rested.

Hard biscuit was provided at midday and evening, but we had poor appetites. Next morning, smoke could still be seen to the north. The people around me did not move. In the afternoon, we were put on a landing-craft and started for Ninoshima Island. On board the ship, there were many middle school students who'd been badly burned. They'd been on a work detail. On the island, we saw many people lying here and there. They were so badly burned their faces were completely deformed. Day after day, they died. Those suffering from burns died one after another.

On the third day on the island, we were transferred to a primary school in Hatsukaichi-machi. Here again, I saw many burned people. The three of us lay down in a crowded room of the school.

A few days passed by. One day, I was playing with the window in the corner of the room when I heard someone call, "Oh, Mother!" I turned and found my mother and sister hugging each other, crying. With the tears pouring down her face, my sister told us how our brother died.

According to her, he was pulling a cart along Dobashi Street when the bomb exploded. He was burned all over and was carried to Furuichi Primary School. Meanwhile, my sister, who was in Funairi-machi at the time of the explosion, got to Kusatsu, although she'd hurt her head, and she spent the night at her friend's. The next morning, she went to the Furuichi school. As she had thought, she found my brother there. She nursed him and did everything she could, but he passed away three days later.

Ten days after the atom bomb was dropped, Father asked me for water. So I brought some water and tried to help him drink it, but he couldn't seem to get the water down his throat. He didn't try to drink any more, and then he died.

It was two days later that we left the school with Father's ashes. At that time, we still clung to the hope that my brother in the army might come home, but an official report of his death in battle deprived us of everything to live for. But now that six years have passed since then, we are living with new hope for the future.

Hiroko Nakagawa
9th grade girl (3rd grade at the time)

I t was a clear, lovely morning. I was just leaving for school, stepping out of the door to join my friends waiting for me, when there was a flash of light. Father ran to the window and Mother to the underground air-raid shelter. As my little sister and I ran after her, many roof tiles and household things fell on us, and suddenly it turned dark. We sat down on the ground and kept on calling for Mother. She came running up to us and lifted up my sister and led me to the field at the back of the house. Sister and I were scared and cried. My face was bleeding.

Father had been pinned under the falling house and Mother, together with Grandfather who had come back from wherever he'd been, tried to get him out but it was too heavy for them. They cried for help but no one came. They desperately pried up part of the fallen house, enough for Father to squeeze out. An artery in his arm had been cut and blood was spouting out. He tried to stop the bleeding by pressing a pouch of tobacco on the wound, but it din't work. Finally, he ran to a hospital. In the meantime, Mother and Grandfather were carrying things out from the house. Hearing a rustling noise, I turned around. Some twenty yards away, fire had broken out. Shouts of horror and cries for help rent the air. I was terrified and clung to Mother and asked her to run away with me, but she was still frantically getting clothes and things out and jamming them into carrier bags and the first-aid bag. She finished; Grandfather would not leave, insisting on staying longer at the house. So Mother, my sister and I ran to the school, which was crowded with injured people. A soldier came out of the building and said, "This building is no longer safe. You had better go farther away from the city." We fled toward Ohko. As we had no particular place to go, we went to the house of someone my mother knew and took a rest. Soon, Grandfather came and all of us started out. He led us to a half-wrecked house, in the garden of which Father was lying on a mattress. We felt so hungry. Just then, a soldier came and gave each of us a package of hard biscuit. We couldn't stay there long, so it was decided to ask another friend in Ohko to put us up for the night. The house was packed with injured people and we had to sleep in the garden or near the gate. Everyone in my family had been hurt, too. It was that night that I suddenly couldn't see anything, I didn't know why.

The next morning, we went to a police box and were given some boiled-rice balls by the police. I had never eaten food more gratefully before than at that time. Soon, the ugly sound of an airplane could be heard above. I could see nothing, but I trembled, afraid that it would drop another bomb. When I think of the plane that took my eyesight, I still remember that ominous sound of engines, even though I try to forget.

Later on, we decided to go to Itsukaichi. As there were no trams or buses, I, who was blind, had to plod along all the way, and I was so tired that I was nearly dropping. The air was filled with a nasty smell, maybe of dead people, and it made me shudder. I heard that the road was lined with piles of dead bodies and bones. My parents were anxious about my eyes, and we stopped at a hospital on the way to have my eyes examined, but they could not give much treatment.

We began to live at Itsukaichi. We had to collect firewood in the hills, and also had a hard time getting food. We couldn't get rice for money or for clothes; my father even gave his precious watch, but even that was not readily accepted. As I couldn't see, I had to lie alone in bed all the time.

A few days later, Mother took me to an eye-doctor in Hatsukaichi-machi. After looking at my eyes, the doctor said that one of my eyes was ruined. His words cut me to the heart and I stood motionless, shocked. I was only nine years old then, but I didn't sleep at all that night because of grief over my great loss, and cried unnoticed under the quilt. Tears came even to the eye which couldn't see any more. As for Father, having lost a lot of blood due to his serious injuries, he was weak and stayed in bed a lot. My mother and sister were hurt, too. Auntie was kind enough to take care of us all as much as possible, but the shortage of food was such that we couldn't stay long with her.

We came back to Hiroshima City. Father and Grandfather collected pieces of wood and tin sheeting, and made a hut on a burned lot. Then came the news that Japan had lost the war. After all the strain, we were dejected; our spirits sank, our strength left us. All of our neighbors were weeping, too. The horrible atom bomb had taken away my eyesight, badly injured Father and Mother, and reduced to ashes our house, property and everything!

Why did such a miserable misfortune happen to my family? Did all the people of Hiroshima have the same fate? Was it possible for Hiroshima to rise again on this devastated area? Those were my thoughts as I stood in the midst of the vast expanse of desolation. I think all the people of Hiroshima must have thought the same way.

My family and all the people of Hiroshima worked hard after this. Many of them died from the aftereffects of the bomb before they could see the city rebuilt, but the survivors rose above their grief and carried on the work. No helping hands came from elsewhere. The citizens made the effort themselves, helping and encouraging each other. It is through the combined efforts of them all that a new city has come into being so quickly. Six years have elapsed since that day. The seventh memorial anniversary for the deceased is coming soon. I think it is everybody's job to help to make Hiroshima a city of peace, and to bring about a world where such a cruel tragic war will not happen again.

Mitsunori Sasaki
9th grade boy (3rd grade at the time)

There was a great boom and the ground shook violently. Mother, who was doing needlework, and I, sitting at my desk, were startled. Mother threw her needlework to one side and jumped up, and cried in a low, tense voice, "Atom bomb." But in an instant she realized that it had been nothing serious, and sat down slowly, with a nervous, strained smile on her face.

It had been announced previously that on that day the ruins of a burned-out hospital near Hiroshima Station would be demolished with explosives.

"Mom, that was the sound of the hospital near the station being demolished," I said.

She said nothing. She seemed to be listening to something far away, and only her hands moved, almost mechanically. The silence continued for a minute or two.

"Mitsu-chan," she said suddenly, "was there anything strange about me just now?"

"What? What do you mean?" I asked, but really I knew what she meant.

"Oh, nothing, nothing serious," she murmured.

Then followed another silence, then she said, "I've become a little nervous since then. I jump too easily at such sounds . . . ."

"Since when? You mean the atom bomb?" I said.

"That's right," she said, and stopping her needlework, she stared at me. Without thinking, I looked away.

"Mom, where was Father when the atom bomb fell?" I asked.

Slowly, she began to talk.

It was a sultry morning. The sky was blue and completely clear. Father left home for school as usual. He was a teacher at a primary school. There were very few classes, as all the children had been mobilized for the building clearance program. On that day, Father, along with two or three colleagues, led some one hundred boys to a place near Hiroshima City Hall for some clearing work.

They were almost there when there was a flash in the western sky. The shock knocked him sideways onto the asphalt and he lost consciousness. When he came to, he was still rolling. How far he rolled he did not know. He staggered to his feet, and he thought his eyes had been injured. It was the dust, whirling like mist, so thick that he could not see an inch ahead.

As soon as he could think properly, the teacher in him came to the fore. His sense of duty strengthened him.

"Assemble! All students assemble!" he shouted. His voice shook the air in the darkness, and cut through to his students' ears above the moans of pain coming from everywhere. (This was told later by some of his students who survived.) Father moved around looking for his pupils, calling out. In spite of his desperate efforts, however, only about ten boys responded. Their clothes were burned to shreds, their faces burned and swollen, the skin stripped off and raw flesh showing through the deep wounds. They were all so changed that Father could hardly tell one boy from another. He was surrounded by faces, faces devoid of any expression. It was undoubtedly dangerous to remain there so he gave up looking for missing students and took those he had to his own house in Minami-machi. There was no one in the house. A woman, one of our neighbors, happened to pass, and kindly applied some oil to their burns.

They rested a while at the house then went back to the school.

The school buildings were not so heavily damaged as they had expected; only the roof-tiles had been blown off and the windowpanes shattered. Here, Father and the boys received medical treatment and lay on the floor waiting for their families to come.

It was after Father and his pupils had left for the school that Mother and I came home from a hospital, where I had had my injuries treated, then we were told about Father by the woman. We went to the school right away, and so we were reunited, but were not allowed to stay at the school for long. We were sent to a signal corps field hospital.

The mere recollection of the scenes in the hospital makes me shudder even now. Nearly all those who were in the hospital had bad burns. They were groaning, shrieking, sobbing and writhing like mad people. It was a Hell on earth. What a horrible scene it was! Not a drop of water was given the patients. They were as thirsty as if they had white-hot iron inside them, and kept screaming and crying for water. And my dear father, burned all over, was among them. The patients overflowing the great hall died one after another. A sudden cessation of groaning from the next bed meant that another soul had departed.

After three days, on August 9, Father began to ask us to take him to some quieter place. I didn't know why but he really wanted quiet. But any hospital would have been the same. Our home might be quiet, but then there would be no doctor. Also, the roof leaked on rainy days.

"I don't care whether the roof leaks or not. No, I don't mind a bit if I die. Please take me back home," he asked me, in tears. At last, Mother took him home, and back home he went almost mad for water.

"Utako, give me water."

"No, dear, it will aggravate your burns. Try to bear it," Mother said.

"Please, please give me water. I want water. I don't care about my life. Give me just a drop of water. Just a drop, please."

"No, my dear. Be a little more reasonable and get well soon for us all."

Tears came to her eyes as she said this. The torture of deadly thirst! It may be compared to swallowing white-hot iron. And how hard for Mother to refuse him!

On August 10, Father said to Mother, "Utako, I feel sleepy. Please leave me alone for a while."

Mother went to the next room. Father's face at that moment is branded in her memory: his ears burned into black lumps and his face swollen. Soon, she heard a faint gulping sound from his room. With a start, she ran to his bedside.

"My dear!"

There was no response.

When she had come to this point, she suddenly closed her mouth.

Oh, Father! Father suffering from terrible thirst! Whenever I think of him, I offer up my fervent prayers to whoever is above us, that never again shall we commit such a cruel folly.

Yuriko Yamamura
9th grade girl (3rd grade at the time)

The most unforgettable day, August 6, 1945. The horrible atom bomb day. It will remain as one of the saddest memories of my life. Those shuddering scenes I witnessed on that day, four days after my birthday! That haunting memory I shall never get rid of. Oh, war is terrible; I'll always hate it!

At that time, we lived in Dote-machi at the foot of Hijiyama Hill. The days were very hot. Mother made me a new dress the night before. On the morning of August 6, she was sewing buttons on the dress. It was about time for our school to begin and normally I was supposed to have been at school, but on that particular morning my friends had gone to school without calling for me, although they usually did. As for Father, though he was later than usual for his office, he was smoking in the hall saying, "I don't feel so good this morning." My brother used to go out, with almost nothing on, to make mischief in the neighborhood early in the morning, but that morning he stayed at home and kept his jacket on. Thinking back, it seems that we were all behaving unusually that day.

I was sitting by Mother's side, watching her sew. We were in a six-mat room on the first floor. The next room was a four-mat. Across the passage was a sitting room. There was no one upstairs. My big brother was in the Naval Cadet Corps.

The all-clear had sounded, so we had come out of the underground shelter and gone back into the house.

Just then, I saw a great flash of light beyond the wall of our garden. It was dazzling, I really saw it. I was frightened and suddenly found myself pinned under a chest of drawers in the corner of the hall. Whether I ran or was blown there I don't know. It was quite dark. I didn't feel any pain or discomfort, but I trembled with fear. I was just a third grader then. In desperation, I cried out for help at the top of my voice. Explosions, screams, crumbling houses . . . . In the darkness, I heard Mother crying, "I'm here." But I didn't know where her voice came from. I could only hear it.

"Help me, help me," my three-year-old brother was lisping. Hearing him cry, Father frantically tore up the floor-boards and finally drew him up. His face was bloody. Father held him close and crept through the debris into the street. The stairs had disappeared, there was nothing there. We got out some-how. Cries for help were heard everywhere. How can I describe those pitiful, strained cries? Mother and I walked gingerly to the shelter, but Father first tried to help some people out. Caught by the falling house, a child of the K. family, who was one of our neighbors, was crying in a hoarse voice, "Mother, help, help." Immediately, Father and Mr. Okamoto went to his rescue, but nothing could be done for him. "Just a moment. I'll bring a saw to help get you out," Father said, but only to encourage the boy, and began rescuing other people. There were so many people in distress that it was obviously more than he could do to help them all out. The flames were steadily making their way toward us and had begun to lick at the houses right by us. All of us including those just rescued ran to a shel-ter in the river bank. On the way, I remember Father saying, "It's you being always like that!" This was about Mrs. K. I didn't understand then, but found out later what the meaning was Mrs. K. was always putting on airs and disagreeing with people just to be difficult, and the union people didn't like her. The shelter was already full of people. We squeezed ourselves into it. As Father was standing at the entrance, looking up at the sky for the airplane, someone shouted, "With your white hat, you'll attract the attention of the plane. Get in." So he came inside.

Thinking about it now, I wonder if it was possible to see a white hat from the air. Probably not. It is also so silly, I think now, that we Japanese had to practice using bamboo lances and spears, and practice throwing water with small buckets. I my-self followed Father with a short lance he had made for me when he went out to practice early in the morning, and I train-ed among the grown-ups. It is not surprising that Japan lost the war.

In the shelter, Father and Mother said to my small brother, "Try to stand. Now walk. Run." He could stand, walk and run all right. The blood on his face came from a slight cut in the forehead, and we felt relieved. A wound in the face bleeds a great deal, so at first we thought it was serious. Just then, a blood-soaked man happened to be brought past on a stretcher. He was a young man we knew. He was really soaked with fresh red blood from head to toe. I was told that he had been looking out of his room facing the river when the house collapsed, and he was thrown from one end of the room right over the river bank in front of the house and onto the road below. He went through two windows and loads of bits of glass stuck into his body all over. However, we were to see far more tragic cases.

We went up Hijiyama Hill and into an air-raid shelter. On the way, Father doused some flames on roofs and bushes here and there with water from water tanks, but it was not much use. We saw many dead bodies on the roads. I felt sick and didn't want to look at them. As we went up the hill, the number of dead bodies increased and many of them were people we had known. Tears kept running down my cheeks. We got to the shelter halfway up the hill, but Father went down again and came back with a bucket full of water and a dipper. On his way back up the hill, he saw many dying people crying for water, and in spite of some officials' objections he gave them a dipperful of water each, he said. He thought that a dying man should have any water he wants, because he was going to die with or without the water. And I quite agreed with him.

If it had not been such an emergency, I would not have had the courage to enter the shelter, because it was packed with injured people and dead bodies. It was pitch-dark in the shelter and there was a sickening smell of blood and burned flesh. American airplanes were still flying overhead and we were afraid they might drop another bomb. I heard later that the planes were examining the results of the atom bomb. What did the Americans think when they saw the miserable conditions down below? I think even they, our enemies, could not stop some tears falling.

We squeezed ourselves into the inner part of the shelter, where we saw many people we knew. After we were there for a little time, a woman we knew lying next to us died. They said that she had been out on labor service, representing her group. She'd been terribly burned when the bomb came, and the upper part of her straw hat had been blown away and only the brim remained around her head. She belonged to the Sixteenth Neighbors Group, and we to the Seventeenth. So if the bomb had been dropped on the next day, some of my family would have been out and probably killed. Maybe that is what fate is.

Soon, we left the shelter and began to walk toward my aunt's home, over the hill. On our way, we saw heaps of dead bodies by the side of a suspension bridge. Some were still alive, but they were soon buried under more bodies being piled up one after another. On our way up the hill, we saw such scenes many times, and every time I hid behind Mother. When we reached the top of the hill, a truck loaded with rice-balls came, but no one ate them. We hurried down the pathless hillside. Mother seemed to have been hurt on the breast and arm for her clothes were soaked with blood and clinging to her body. Her right arm was useless, but she did not complain of pain or anything and kept along behind us. My brother was being carried in my father's arms. We walked toward Ushita, making a long detour because of fires.

On our way, Father asked a policeman in a police box, "Will we be safe in Ushita?"

"Well, I'm afraid not; I think it's been badly damaged," he answered, pointing in that direction. We looked where he was pointing and saw leaping flames and black smoke. We were at a loss where to go, but having no particular place in mind, we decided to go there anyway. We passed a bakery where Father had worked before and he got some cookies there. Then all of us went into an air-raid shelter nearby and ate them. Again, an airplane passed overhead. I shuddered. We came to the East Parade Ground, where the grass was burning. There was no use in turning back, so I wrapped myself up in a blanket (because I had nothing on) and ran barefoot through the fire, feeling the heat scorching my feet. Other people were also running through the field with various things around them while overhead pieces of wood, tin roofing and so on were flying about. We got to Ushita at long last, but as the policeman had told us, there was only a large stretch of burned and devastated plain. The ground was so hot that now, on looking back, I wonder how I walked on it. Yes, everything was really strange. We walked on in desperation and finally got to my grandmother's home. Fortunately, the fires stopped three or four hundred feet short of her house.

My family had sent on some of our things to Grandmother's home, but not so much as others. The family living just opposite to us had sent everything, except some chemises and spare clothes, to a distant place.

It was completely dark when we reached Grandmother's. The only light was from fires on top of the mountain to the east. Her house was very small, being only for herself, and there was no room for nearly ten people to sleep. So Father and Mr. Okamoto roped some boards together to make a kind of house. Just as we were going to sleep in it, a boy about seven or eight years old appeared, crying for his father and mother. We were sorry for him and took him into our hut. We gave him some rice-balls, hard biscuit and scallions. He was so hungry he ate four rice-balls. That night, he slept with us in the hut.

The next morning, the seventh of August, the boy left us.

We helped Father lay planks across the banks of the stream in front and move our house over to the other side. The local people kept on at us while we were working at this, making fun of us. I could hardly stand it and almost shouted at them. But Mother would say to me, "We've been burned out of our home. Be patient." And I kept quiet, even though I was very cross. What worried us was that we had no food or clothing or cooking things. But kind neighbors often provided us with these. Our biggest problem was the house. Before we used to live in quite a big house, but now in Ushita we had to live in a small hut which had no running water or oven. We lived in this house for five whole years and had a very hard time. I was not so strong before, but now I am very healthy because, I think, of what I went through in those days. Looking back, I wonder how we survived those hard days. On August 4, 1950, we came to live in our present house.

It is really very lucky that no one in my family was lost to the atom bomb. We have gone through many hardships, but this is nothing when we think of those who were much worse off than we are. For example, the family that used to live next door to us lost all its men and boys in the disaster. Every day, the father went out in search of his son, a schoolboy who had been out on labor service that morning. The boy must have died somewhere. Sometimes, I saw the father digging where his house had been, but he did not live long since he had breathed the poison fumes. His own father who had been working with him died too, from the same thing. Now, the family consists of a grandmother and two girls about my age. They used to be very well off, but now they are leading a miserable life.

I am absolutely against war. I hope we are never involved in such a horrible thing again.

Toyozo Kubota
9th grade boy (3rd grade at the time)

At the time, Mother and I were staying in Gohara Village, Kamo County, which is Mother's native village, while Father was staying in the city to run his store with his brother, nephew and the men working there.

On August 6, the atom bomb day, we had no school. So I climbed up a tree like I usually did to eat the fruit. About eight, I saw a column of black smoke rising high up in the western sky. I thought maybe it was a forest fire, but I felt worried about it so I went home and asked Mother, "Is it a forest fire?" She looked a little anxious but didn't answer. I went up the hill again and played until the day ended.

The next afternoon, I came home from the hill as usual and went into Mother's room, where I found her talking with a visitor. Then the visitor left and she came out of the room, looking pale. I didn't think much about it, and went back to the hill again and did not come back until dinner time. As Mother was talking with Grandma, my sister set the table and I ate dinner by myself, and went to bed.

About one in the morning, I was woken by a strange noise. Mother, Grandma and Sister were making rice-balls.

"What's the matter, Mom?" I asked.

"Oh, this boy!" she said, surprised. Then she told me that she was going to Hiroshima. I asked her to take me, too, but she would not say yes. Grandma and Sis sided with me in getting her to agree, and at last she said, "Are you sure you can walk more than 20 miles?"

"Yes, I am," I replied.

"Then I'll take you," she said.

We started out in the darkness with some other people and were in the suburbs of the city by morning. What we saw were countless dead bodies floating in the river and a bare, burned plain. I was terrified at seeing these corpses, piled up like things. We walked through this horrible scene toward Sakai-machi where we saw the same terrible sight. Houses were flattened and cars crushed; only a lonely safe was standing in the devastated area. We didn't know what to do and felt sad. My dear father was not there and our house had fallen down. Although I had many relatives, now I really had only Mother to depend on. Mother was also helpless.

Nothing could be done, and Mother and I began to walk again. We saw many bodies on a piece of ground where a hospital had been standing. Some were still alive. Their injuries were not bandaged only some salve was applied to them. As I was actually looking, some of them died, crying, "Mother! Give me water!" I thought they might have gotten well if they had water and asked Mother about it. She explained to me that someone suffering from burns should not be given water, because they die if they drink it.

I felt thirsty myself. On the way, I saw a water tap. As I went near to it, I jumped with surprise because I recognized a man standing there; it was my father. He stroked me on the head, crying. I cried too, but at the same time I couldn't stop laughing, it was so funny. His face was burned black and his black mustache was now grizzled, he looked completely different.

Then the three of us went to my uncle's home in Jigozen. He was in bed with injuries and his eldest son was dead. Later he got worse, and did not live long. Eventually, we went to the country and stayed there.

When I went back to Hiroshima several days later, because I had to do something, there were still lots of dead bodies piled up in heaps on the scorched plain. I saw a dead woman with her two children in her arms in a water tank. But I also saw a willow tree already beginning to bud by a dead body with no face. It seemed like a symbol of the city of Hiroshima making progress against indescribable difficulties and miseries. I found in the tree a symbol of the strong will of Hiroshima's people for reconstruction—a will which even the 4,000-degree heat of the atom bomb could not melt.

high school

By Mrs Toshiko Akamatsu

No, we'll die together. I'll have nothing to live for with my husband dead anyway.
Leave this child . . . ? No, rather than worry about me, Uncle, you'd better get away
quickly yourself.

Mitsugu Hanabusa
10th grade boy (4th grade at the time)

I

In the final stages of the Second World War in which the world was split into two, when Germany capitulated and the fighting strength of Japan was gradually dwindling, suddenly over Hiroshima a new weapon, the atom bomb, was exploded. Hiroshima is my hometown. What was left after that instantaneous flash of light? It left a tragic scene showing us how miserable war could be. The city was reduced to ruins and countless people lost their loved ones and their homes. Terrified people, half-dead, desperately tried to escape to safety. It was like a Hell before one's eyes. Fortunately, everyone in my family was saved, but when I heard that our neighbor's son of primary school age, a friend of mine, was killed by a flying tile which fractured his skull, my heart was torn with fear.

As my home was some way from the center, this was about the worst that happened. While our family was escaping out of the city to the suburbs, we saw that the situation near the center of the city was unbearably inhuman. On the scorched remains of the city, barren of all plant life, bodies, burned black, lay scattered here and there. There were many people walking around, trying to find their dear ones. The air was foul with the stench of cremated bodies and in the rivers floated countless lifeless bodies. A withered bunch of flowers placed on a tile near the head of an unfortunate victim emphasized the misery of the scene.

II

We were very frightened at the tragic sight, and hurried toward Kuchita Village in Asa County, where my uncle lived. Except for my big sister who had burns all over her body, all my family escaped injury. That village, too, was full of the sorrow of bereaved families, and of fear. Refugees with no relatives in the area were put up at the local school. Here again, we saw rows of dead. Our family was fortunate enough to be able to borrow a room from my uncle, where my sister was treated. Though I hadn't noticed before, I was getting weaker. I had been so tired, physically and mentally, after being evacuated with other schoolchildren, that my father had finally brought me back home two days before the bomb, so it was hardly strange that I should become ill. When I'd been going to the hospital for a while, my father also became ill. My father, sister and I were ill in bed for several months, and that was a hard time. It was my mother and eldest sister who cared for us and it was very difficult for them, because food was scarce and hard to buy and there was no proper medicine. About the time my aunt died from radiation sickness, my father and I had got much better. By this time, things in the village had settled down somewhat, and I began to attend primary school as I got better. But as I'd lost several months because of being evacuated and hadn't been able to study since the atom bomb, I had even forgotten my multiplication table and had to tearfully ask my father to help me. The general topics of interest among the students at my school were about experiences during the evacuation and about the atomic bomb. My sister's burns had got better by this time. Of the many memories of that period, the most pleasant was when our family would go to the *tempura* restaurant near the company where my father worked, while the most dreadful was when the Ohta River overflowed. The flood waters would surge about the house and rise ominously through the night. Finally, as the room we were using in my uncle's house was needed, we later moved to Kawauchi Village.

III

About the time my family moved to Kawauchi Village, they started rebuilding Hiroshima. The noise of construction echoed in the air, and traffic and transportation began to move again. One day during Japanese class at Kawauchi Primary School, I became ill again and was put to bed. The doctor said it was pleurisy. This was the beginning of a long period of hospitalization. The hospital was crowded with patients like me with illnesses and problems caused by the atom bomb. After a long, monotonous and trying stay at the hospital, my health got better again and I was able to return to school.

The city was on the way to reconstruction and stores were

opening for business. When books again became available, I got many and read a lot. Being able to devote my time to study, I did very well in my class, but I had a physical handicap which I could not correct. This was the weakness resulting from my exposure to the atom bomb. I could only remain quiet while healthy boys enjoyed themselves in various games. I could not swim in summer nor participate in the school's autumn sports day events.

I regained my health completely during my sixth year of primary school and then was able to enjoy both play and study. I studied hard and as a result I passed the entrance examination of Sanyo Junior High School. My junior high school days sped by as if in a dream and now I am in the first year of senior high school. I am preparing myself both physically and mentally for the future.

IV

I have written my memories of the atom bombing of Hiroshima, something which seemed to me like a nightmare, but another of these dreadful bombs was later dropped on Nagasaki. What is the next target? Why does the necessity arise for such dreadful bombs? No weapons like this, or armed forces, are necessary. The need is for freedom and peace in this world. War using weapons of this nature which take a terrific toll of life means only the destruction of mankind. Does not the Bible say: "But if ye bite and devour one another, take heed that ye be not consumed one of another"?

Yohji Kawada
10th grade boy (4th grade at the time)

I t is almost time for the seventh memorial ceremony for those many people of Hiroshima who were killed by the atom bomb. It makes me recall the pleasant times when there were six in my family. My oldest sister was working at the Hiroshima University of Literature and Science; the next sister was a student of the Prefectural First Girls' High School; my brother was still in middle school; and I was in the fourth year of primary school. My mother took care of the home by herself, while my father worked at the Food Corporation near Hatchobori. Our standard of living was quite good then, and we lived rather comfortably.

I had been evacuated to a temple in Fukuki Village in Asa County. On Sundays, either my father or mother, or my brother or one of my sisters would usually visit me. For me that was always the happiest day, because only on that day could I eat as much as I wanted. I was only little then and I did not think about how hard it was for my father and mother to prepare such lovely food and how much time and effort it took them to walk to this distant place in the country, sometimes pushing a cart. All I thought of was wolfing down the food, but now when I think back to those Sundays, I feel so grateful to them.

The fifth of August was a Sunday, visiting day. My father came with my mother and oldest sister. I did not dream this was to be the last goodbye to my father and sister.

On that particular morning, after my father, sisters and brother had left the house, my mother was lying down for a brief rest, because she was tired after a sleepless night of air-raid alerts, when suddenly streaks of light like burning splinters shot in through the back door and the paper screen began to burn. She put out the flames and dashed outside to find the other houses in a mess. She rushed back into the house to get the money and other valuables, and running back outside again, she found some flames sputtering near the back of the next house. She put that out and sighed with relief, but the next moment flames began to shoot out of the second floor of the fourth house along. Mother was so confused she didn't know what she was doing, and instead of taking the whole radio she only pulled out the radio tubes and brought them. After that, with the neighbor's assistance, she managed to bring out my sister's cherished sewing machine, and then just blankly watched the house burn down. Evening came but no one returned home. Nevertheless, thinking that someone would come back, she spent an anxious night at a neighbor's house which had escaped the flames. Next morning she went back and waited by the ruins of our home. She was waiting there when my brother and second oldest sister returned.

My sister had been working at a munitions factory, so she escaped without a scratch, but it seems that almost all the younger students in her school were working on the building evacuation program, and they were almost all killed. My brother had been on labor service at the East Parade Ground and had got burned. The burns on his face are not very noticeable now, but the skin on his arm is still rather rough.

Now that my sister and brother had come back, my mother cheered up a bit, and the three of them left for my aunt's home in Furue. My sister looked after my brother's burns, while my mother went to search for my father and other sister. Mother and my Furue cousin went to the university to try to find out about my sister, but nobody there knew. They said, however, that might be at Ninoshima Island, so they went there but couldn't find her. Later, she walked through the streets of Hiroshima loudly calling my sister's name, but she could not be found. She is still missing.

Three days later, they found out where my father was, and Mother went there with my sister and brother. His face was so heavily bandaged that they could hardly recognize him. When the bandages were removed they found that there was a deep gash above his nose, his ears were lacerated and his cheeks had no skin. Fearing that he might die if left there, my mother carried him on her back to our relatives' place in Saijo Village in Hiba County. Though he was treated by a doctor when he got there, his diarrhea didn't get better in spite of the various injections he got. In fact, it made things worse, as it swelled up around the injected area. About fifty pieces of glass were removed from his cuts. The doctor had still not properly diagnosed the nature of his illness when he died, on the fifteenth.

On that morning (sixth), my father had a flat tire and ended up pushing his bicycle to the Food Corporation at Hatchobori, not far from the center of the blast. While he was repairing it, he saw a sudden yellow flash of light on the windowpanes of the office and there was a terrific boom and all the windows were blown in. My father thought that a drum of fuel at a large bicycle repair shop nearby was the cause of the explosion. He slowly got up and felt his whole body stinging, and when he touched the painful areas his hands came away covered with blood. Surprised, he went outside, but the whole area was already covered with smoke. He sensed this was something out of the ordinary, and seeing that there were no fires to the north, he quickly went that way. A truck loaded with injured people, among whom were some seriously burned about the face and arms, and others stark naked, came by, and picked him up. But his parched throat became so painful that he got off near the Ohta River, drank some water and wandered around aimlessly. Where he actually walked, he could not remember, but he finally ended up in the shelter where my mother found him.

Not knowing anything about all this, about a month after the bombing I and others walked from Fukuki Village to Hiroshima. As far as I could see lay the scorched remains of Hiroshima. I stood there for a while, gaping. We didn't know which way was which because everything was so razed by fire, but our teacher took us to our old primary school. On the way, we were bothered by swarms of flies and there was a terrible stench in the air. They said that the flies came from the dead bodies. Our school had not burned down but it looked as if it was going to collapse any moment. I was worried about my home, and started to try to find it, but it was hard.

Finally, I found where our house used to be, but there was only a pile of burned tiles, and the kitchen and bath. Under where the kitchen had been was a flat box, and opening it, I found six eggs rolling about, burned black. It all made me so unhappy and disappointed; I returned to the school. There I met a man, a neighbor, who told me that everyone in my family was safe and had gone into the country. I jumped about with joy. I spent that night on a straw mat with my teacher and classmates and on the following morning returned to Fukuki Village.

I waited now, thinking how happy I was going to be with my family again, soon. A few days later my brother came up from the country to get me, and I learned for the first time that my father and oldest sister had died. Although I was too small at the time to really understand what it all meant, I could not hold back my tears. I said goodbye to my teacher and classmates after a last meal together with them.

It was already past nine and dark when we reached Saijo. When my mother heard my voice, she rushed out to see me. I had not seen my mother for about a month and a half, and my heart was full of joy and sorrow. I could no longer see the solid figure of my father or my gentle sister. Soon I got to know the people there well, but I was homesick for Hiroshima. However, people said that in Hiroshima there was a food shortage, so we could not move back there for a while.

As it was getting difficult for us to carry on there, we borrowed a storehouse in Fuchu, near Hiroshima, from a relative, and lived there. But it was very cold in winter and too hot in summer. Finally, we decided that each of us would work, and we moved to Funairi-cho, where we are now.

At present, I deliver newspapers in the morning, and though I don't get much, it is enough to pay for my school expenses, so I think I'll continue this job. When it rains, though, and I'm unlucky and get soaked to the skin, sometimes I find it all rather hard. At such times, I find myself thinking of my father and wishing that he were still alive.

*Hisato Itoh**
11th grade boy (5th grade at the time)

O n the morning of the fifth of August, a young man working at an island lighthouse near Ogata in Saeki County brought us to Hiroshima to see my brother, a Hiroshima High School student, whom I had not seen for some time. My father was so busy then at the lighthouse that he did not have time to come.

My brother spent the night with us at an inn in Teppo-cho where we usually stayed on these occasions. It was in front of where the Toyo Theater now stands. On the morning of the sixth, my mother was standing near the entrance, talking with the proprietor before paying the bill. She was to have gone back to Ogata. By her were the young lighthouse attendant and my 14-month-old brother; I was playing with a cat on a chair near the entrance. Suddenly, a weird flash of bluish-white light shone through the front door.

When I regained consciousness, it was all dark. I managed to work out that I had been blown to the far end of the hallway. I was pinned under the wreckage of the two-story building and though I struggled to crawl out, I couldn't move. The polished ornamental main pillar of which the proprietor used to speak so proudly was now lying in front of me. Just as I closed my eyes drowsily, thinking that I was going to die, I heard my mother shouting my name. I opened my eyes and saw that one side of the building had caught fire and the flames were coming nearer. I frantically screamed for my mother, because I knew now that I would be burned alive if I did not get out quickly. Mother dragged away some of the burning boards and wood and got me out. I can never forget how happy I felt at that moment. When I got out, I was so happy that I did not know what to do, like a little bird let out of a cage. But everything was so changed that I was utterly amazed. As far as I could see, almost every building was destroyed and in flames. There were people whose skin was peeling off, leaving their bodies red and raw. They were screaming pitifully, and others were already dead. The street was so covered with the dead, the seriously injured, groaning, and collapsed buildings that we couldn't get through. I didn't know what to do, and then to the west I saw the flames coming nearer. I walked over the roofs of some wrecked buildings that hadn't caught fire yet and escaped toward where there were no flames.

I found myself on the river bank opposite the former Sentei Gardens, where I noticed for the first time that I had become separated from my mother. Near the Kyobashi River people suffering from burns were jumping into the river screaming, "The heat! The heat!" They were too weak to swim and with a last, painful cry for help, they drowned. This river was no longer a river of clear, flowing water but a stream of floating corpses. Though I have tried to describe the plight of those jumping to their death and the destruction of Hiroshima, the reality was so much worse that I am unable to express it adequately here, on paper; please forgive me for this inability. After seeing this tragedy with my own eyes, I could not understand why human beings must fight among themselves and kill each other like this. After a while I calmed down, and began to feel that I should hurry home, but the flames were all around me.

Just then a soldiers' truck came along and soldiers began to load those who'd been burned. I got on too, and the truck weaved through the flames and managed to get to a place where there were no fires and the houses hadn't been flattened. This was the Kaitaichi First Aid Station. It was getting dark, then. I looked toward Hiroshima while I ate the biscuits that the soldiers gave us; the sky over Hiroshima was a bright red. I could not sleep for worrying about my little brother, thinking he might be dead, as he'd been in the center of Hiroshima; and I worried about my big brother, and where my mother was. Because I was so worried, I left for Hiroshima early next morning, but the roads were closed off so I had to go back to Kaitaichi, where I spent another night.

On the morning of the eighth, I got to Hiroshima and walked through the streets. I noticed that there were many dead lying there, but those suffering from burns had all been taken away. The soldiers were clearing away the debris of the burned-down buildings and removing the corpses, and I stopped to see what they did with the dead bodies. A large hole had been dug in which many corpses were piled. After kerosene had been poured over them, they were cremated. In the city, many people were walking around, looking for family members, children and relatives, and some were sobbing as they picked up some ashes from where the dead were burned. When I got to where the inn had been in Teppo-cho, I found nothing there except ashes and burned tiles. I felt that my brother must have died there, but I still searched around. A friend of ours living near the inn was there, clearing the wreckage of his place, so I asked, "Do you know anything about my brother?" He didn't.

I was depressed and went back to the island. The proprietor of the inn had built a shack on the same spot, to protect himself from the weather. To assist him, my mother and father, who had come, helped by looking for old timbers and sheets of tin roofing. Here, they stayed while searching for my brothers. Several days later, the war ended and they came back to the island.

Both my mother and I had been through a great deal of strain during this time, and what with the ending of the war and having a home, we got more slack, and then we also started to feel listless and began to lose our hair because we had breathed the gases when the atom bomb fell. We were told that moxa was good for this so we got this treatment. About this time, the remains of my younger brother were recovered from the ruins. My mother was so grieved over his death that her condition became critical, but with my father's constant encouragement, we both got better and are living happy at the' lighthouse residence. Whenever I think of the great many people who lost their mothers and fathers because of the atom bomb, I cannot help but feel fortunate. Six years have passed since the end of the war and Hiroshima has made a tremendous recovery through the efforts of people who live here and of those throughout Japan, and even the world.

In conclusion, I ask that the Korean War be ended as soon as possible without the use of another atom bomb so that all the people of the world will again show the smiling face of peace. Instead of using atomic energy for bombs, I wish they would utilize it for industry, for I know that progress in industry can be made with its peaceful use.

Lastly, I would like to add that my brother who was so full of life when we parted at the inn on August 6 has not yet returned home; and that the young attendant of the lighthouse suffered every disease he has experienced and met with a very terrible death at the beginning of September.

*On December 10, 1951, shortly after writing this account, the writer died from the results of his exposure to radiation.

Shintaro Fukuhara
10th grade boy (4th grade at the time)

What I can never forget is the morning of August 6, 1945. At the time, I was in the fourth grade of primary school and was beginning to take some interest in the course of the war. When I and my friends discussed the progress of the war, we would become anxious about the uncertain future. Especially about then, with many in my big family mobilized on war work programs, we were frightened for our own safety each day, rather than about the problems of the nation. My father had been called up, and my mother and oldest sister were working, leaving us, my two other sisters, older than me but still just kids, my younger brother, and me, at home.

It was fine that morning, without a cloud in the sky. My brother and I left as usual for our branch school in Fukushima, feeling a bit uneasy. The school was in what had been a nursery school, formerly managed by foreigners. There were only a few pupils around when we got there. I followed the uneven brick wall of the school and climbed on the earth which covered the air-raid shelter which had been recently built in one corner of the school grounds.

The all-clear had just sounded, and the number of pupils coming to school was gradually increasing. I saw a red dragon-fly winging along and finally alighting on the wall right in front of me. Now when I think back, I realize I could hear the characteristic sound of B-29 engines, but what with the all-clear having been given, I thought I was safe, and wasn't worried. Just as my brother reached out to catch the dragonfly, there was a flash. I felt I'd suddenly been blown into a furnace, and I was flung into the angle of the wall. When I think about it now, I don't know how I grabbed my brother's hand and ran, after being lost in a dream and wrenched in an instant from a whirl of light beams into pitch darkness. It is strange. These fragmentary scenes remain fixed in my mind like photographs.

When I opened my eyes after being flung eight yards, it was still dark as if I were facing a wall painted black, but gradually it became lighter as if a dark veil were being slowly raised. The first thing I saw was the level ground and the swirling dust. In an instant, everything had been demolished, and the streets were rubble and ruins. I had unconsciously taken my brother's hand and started running. When I saw passengers tumbling out of a streetcar, cruelly burned, I could not speak, I just ran home as fast as I could, worried about my family.

I cannot describe the countless tragic things I saw. In this tragedy, I lost my dear father and sister. I can never, ever, see them again. There were many who suffered the same grief, or more, much more. I am filled with resentment over the disaster when I hear that there were hundreds of thousands who lost every happiness they had.

What am I angry at? Why is such a bomb permitted in this world of ours where the permanent peace and happiness of society are being sought? There is no escape from the law of retribution. Those haughty in their wealth, who take pride in their power, and glory in their arms must fall before the power of the next generation. I shall maintain forever in my mind the memory of this brutality and I am determined to help pave the way to true peace. This alone is the only road which leads to the construction of a society which shall never fade.

Masayuki Rinde
10th grade boy (4th grade at the time)

The war was getting worse, so my younger brother and I were moved to Kawai Village in Takata County, while my parents and sweet little sister stayed at 1-chome, Senda-machi in Hiroshima. My brother and I got many letters from Mother. My brother was six and I was eleven at the time. When I read these letters to him, always he was sure to ask, "When are we going back to Hiroshima?"

Sometimes, he would ask the same question so many times that I would lose my temper and tell him off. Now, I feel sorry about it. My brother was so anxious to return to Hiroshima that my grandfather finally agreed to take him. It was just a week before the atom bomb was dropped on Hiroshima. How I envied my brother's chance to go back to Hiroshima and how I regretted that I was the oldest son.

On August 6, I went to school as usual. Just as the siren for the morning assembly was sounding, there was a flash and a terrific boom which shook all the windows of our school, and I saw white smoke billow up in the east. I was so frightened that I rushed into the school air-raid shelter. The noises stopped so I crawled out of the shelter and heard people say that the airfield at Kamine had been hit.

Four or five days later, early in the morning, my grandfather got a ride on a truck going to Hiroshima. My grandmother and I had finished supper and were in bed ready to sleep when there was a knock at the door. My grandmother opened the door and saw it was my grandfather. He told us that Hiroshima was completely destroyed, and that at Senda-machi he found that my father was only slightly injured on the back, my mother was badly burned all over, and both my brother and sister had died from serious burns.

The following morning, my grandmother and I went to Kabe by bus and then on foot to Yokogawa. Here, we were astounded to find Hiroshima so utterly in ruins. As we could not find our way easily, we followed the streetcar track to Senda-machi where we found our home in ashes. We learned where my mother was from someone who used to live nearby, and immediately left for the Yamanaka ground.

Mother was covered in burns and couldn't get up at all. Almost all her hair had fallen out, her chest was just raw, and in her back was a hole about two inches across, with maggots crawling in and out. The place was alive with flies, mosquitoes and fleas and the air inside smelled foul. Almost none of the other patients there could move either. My mother's condition became worse that evening; she was clearly declining. It was painful for Mother to breathe that night, and my grandmother did her best to help. The following morning, just when my grandmother and I brought her some gruel, she started to go. Just as I thought she'd suddenly stopped breathing, she gasped deeply and passed away. That was at 9 a.m. on August 19. Near the Red Cross Hospital, the stench of cremations was very strong. I was so sad that I seemed to not know myself, and no matter how I grieved no tears came. It seemed as if my brother came back to Hiroshima just to die. How I regret that I did not postpone his departure for another week. Both he and my sister were dead before I got to Hiroshima.

Life for my father and I was hard. It was so lonely without Mother, and my sister and brother. When I think of them, I can almost hear my brother calling me, and my sister's voice calling for my mother.

How lonely and hard my life is alone with my father. But how many are there more unfortunate than I? I who have experienced the horrors of the atom bomb feel that we must prevent the outbreak of another bloody war. I pray that no one will forget August 6, so we can have peace forever.

Susumu Kimura
11th grade boy (5th grade at the time)

It must have been about ten minutes before eight when the ominous sound of the siren rang through the air. I switched on the radio and heard, "Enemy aircraft are proceeding north from the Bungo Straits . . . ."

My father had already left for the office, but we, my mother, my sister (a seventh-grade student of the Hiroshima Prefectural First Girls' High School at the time) and I (a fifth-grader) had lifted up a *tatami* mat to get into the shelter. Outside, people were rushing to and fro.

My sister was scheduled to take part in the building clearance project near Dobashi on that day. The tension lasted about ten minutes and then the all-clear was sounded. It was in fact this all-clear signal which killed most of the people in Hiroshima.

My sister left the house to go to work. I can still recall how she looked then. She had on a pair of tennis shoes and was carrying her packed lunch and her air-raid hood.

After my sister had gone, we were getting ready to go to the station to buy train tickets so that my sister and I could visit the country. I was in the kitchen and my mother in the next room in front of the mirror. It was at that moment that the atom bomb which took a toll of 300,000 lives was exploded over Hiroshima.

An intense light flashed through the window and hit my eyes. It flashed from red to yellow, just like fireworks. For a moment everything went black, I could not see an inch. "Mother," I shouted, and rushed over. We spent that dreadful moment holding each other. That moment was a very long one, it seemed as if ten years went by. Maybe two or three minutes later I started to be able to see again. The house was wrecked, the walls knocked down, doors splintered. My mother silently looked around and then said, "It's dangerous here. Let's get out."

We crawled out of the house. Outside was a world I had never seen or heard of. I saw raw flesh, people who no longer looked like human beings. My mother put her hands over my eyes saying, "Don't look." But I pushed my mother's hands away and fearfully looked around. On the street were a lot of people lying dead, and others with fatal injuries. I suddenly thought of myself and discovered that I had escaped without a scratch. My mother was not injured, either. I stood blankly by the gate for a while. A lady, bleeding badly, ran by, shouting her child's name. Her voice made me think of my sister. 'My sister might be hurt, too.'

My mother was helping a neighbor and here and there cries for help could be heard. I even felt ashamed because I had escaped unhurt. Many people were rushing to escape toward Ujina. In the sky, black smoke was rising more thickly and the flames were getting nearer. Someone called my name, and I ran to the back of the house and found it was my father, who had come back from the office. He told me that he had been blown five or six yards by the blast. Three of us were safe and together, but what had happened to my sister? We left for Ujina, taking with us the left-overs from breakfast and leaving a message on the gate of our house: "Keiko, we are going to Ujina."

Night came and we decided to sleep in a field. More and more fires broke out. The night dragged on. I woke several times. Morning finally came. My father went to the city to find my sister, while my mother and I left for our relatives'. Their home was also wrecked, but after working for half a day we were able to make a place to sleep. I was so tired from what happened the previous day that I lay down and didn't wake up till evening. I looked around hoping to see my sister, but she was not there. My father had come back. He told us that he was unable to get into the Dobashi area because of the fires. Another sleepless night came. I would doze, the alert would be sounded. The flames made the sky crimson like the glow of a sunset.

On the following day, my father and mother both went out to look for my sister, but couldn't find her. I went with my father during the afternoon and found the streets were quite dangerous, what with tangled and broken streetcar wires. We went along the bank of the river and saw school boys and girls of my sister's age lying in groups, already dying in agony. They pleaded for water from anyone who walked by. My father said, "Your father or mother is sure to come looking for you soon, so take heart and don't give up."

They said nothing, but their swollen and burned faces smiled painfully at us. We could not do anything for them. They must have come here looking for somewhere cool. What they had been wearing was burned, and they had nothing on. Their skin was slimy from burns and already infested with maggots. Was my sister in the same state? We went along this road to

Dobashi. There was even a horse, burned to death, beside the road. We asked a man looking among the dead bodies, "Do you happen to know anything about the students of the Prefectural Girls' High School? "

He answered that he had seen some at Koi. We pedaled our bicycles as fast as we could, but we were so anxious to get there it seemed as slow as walking. At the top of the hill near Koi, we did see some of the girls of my sister's school, but she was not among them.

We also spent the next day searching like that. The students on the river bank who had been livelier the day before now could not speak, and were looking wistfully at us. Many that had been alive yesterday were now dead. As we started to move past them, a frail, soft voice said, "Goodbye."

It was hard for us to leave them. When we went there the following day, all those students were dead.

We couldn't find my sister, though we searched every day for five days. I thought she had returned each time I heard footsteps at the door. We had left the door open so that she could come in, but it was useless. I had to go back to where I'd been evacuated, in the country.

Days passed and on August 15 Japan surrendered. War, war. Each time I see this word, I remember my sister's words. It was a letter she had written me when I was evacuated out of the city.

"Dear Susumu,

"You must be very lonely there, all by yourself. We are lonely too, without you. But when the war ends, we'll all live together again . . . ."

I returned to Hiroshima, but I no longer saw my sister who always greeted me with "Is that you, Susumu?" when I came in the front door.

My father was at the office and my mother was by herself at

home, thinking of my sister, when I came back. She was very happy, but in her happiness I felt there was also some sadness.

The greatest sacrifice I suffered in the atom bombing was the loss of my sweet, innocent sister. I take out and read my sister's letter whenever I feel lonely.

This letter is to me the main force that keeps me on the right path.

Iwao Nakamura
11th grade boy (5th grade at the time)

Today, as I begin to write an account of my experiences after five years and several months have passed, the wretched scenes of that time float up before my eyes like phantoms. And as these phantoms appear, I can actually hear the pathetic groans, the screams.

In an instant it became dark as night, Hiroshima on that day. Flames shooting up from wrecked houses as if to illuminate this darkness. Amidst this, children aimlessly wandering about, groaning with pain, their burned faces twitching and bloated like balloons. An old man, skin flaking off like the skin of a potato, trying to get away on weak, unsteady legs, praying as he went. A man frantically calling out the names of his wife and children, both hands to his forehead from which blood trickled down. Just the memory of it makes my blood run cold. This is the real face of war. To those who knew nothing of the pitiful tragedies of Hiroshima's people, the scene would seem like a world of monsters, like Hades itself. A devil called war swept away the precious lives of several hundred thousand citizens of Hiroshima.

I, who cannot forget, was in the fifth year of primary school when it happened. To escape the frequent air raids, I and my sisters had been evacuated to the home of our relatives in the country, but on August 2 I returned to my home at Naka Kako-machi (near the former Prefectural Office) during the summer vacation, to recover from the effects of a summer illness that had left me very weak. At the time, there were five of us living in Hiroshima: my parents, two younger brothers (aged five and two) and myself. I used to drag myself along to the nearby Prefectural Hospital every morning at eight.

It was after eight on August 6 and the midsummer sun was beginning to scorch down on Hiroshima. An all-clear signal had sounded and with relief we sat down for breakfast a little later than usual. Usually by this time, my father had left the house for the office and I would be at the hospital for treatment.

I was just starting on my second bowl of rice. At that moment, a bluish-white ray of light like a magnesium flare hit me in the face, a terrific roar tore at my eardrums and it became so dark I could not see anything. I stood up, dropping my rice bowl and chopsticks. I do not know what happened next or how long I was unconscious. When I came to, I found myself trapped under what seemed like a heavy rock, but my head was free. It was still dark but I finally discovered that I was under a collapsed wall. It was all so sudden that I kept wondering if I was dreaming. I tried very hard to crawl free, but the heavy wall would not budge. A suffocating stench flooded the area and began to choke me. My breathing became short, my ears began to ring, and my heart was pounding as if it were about to burst. 'I can't last much longer,' I said to myself, and then a draft of cold air flowed past me and some light appeared. The taste of that fresh air is something I shall never forget. I breath-ed it in with all my might. This fresh air and the brighter surroundings gave me renewed vigor and I somehow managed to struggle out from under the wall. Where were my parents?

Where were my brothers? I looked around in the dim light and glimpsed the hazy figures of my parents looking for me. I hurried over to them. Their hair was disheveled and their faces pale. When they saw me, they sighed with relief, "Oh you're safe, you're safe."

Fortunately, my mother and I were unhurt, but blood was streaming from my father's forehead and staining his dirtied shirt bright red. I tore the shirt I was wearing into strips and bandaged his cuts, at the same time looking at the scene around us. Nothing was left of the Hiroshima of a few minutes ago. The houses and buildings had been destroyed and the streets transformed into a black desert, with only the flames from burning buildings giving a lurid illumination to the dark sky over Hiroshima. Flames were already shooting out of the wreckage of the house next door. We couldn't see my two brothers. My mother was in tears as she called their names. My father went frantic as he dug among the collapsed walls and scattered tiles. It must have been by the mercy of God that we were able to rescue my brothers from under the wreckage before the flames reached them. They were not hurt, either. The five of us left our burning home and hurried toward Koi. Around us was a sea of flames. The street was filled with flames and smoke from the burning wreckage of houses and burning power poles which had toppled down blocked our way time after time, almost sending us into the depths of despair. It seems that everyone in the area had already made their escape, for we saw no one but sometimes we heard moans, a sound like a wild beast. I began to shudder as I thought that everyone on earth had perished, leaving only the five of us here in an eerie world of the dead. As we passed Nakajima Primary School area and approached Sumiyoshi Bridge, I saw a damaged water tank in which a number of people had their heads down, drinking. I was so thirsty and attracted by the sight of people that I left my parents' side without thinking, and approached the tank. But when I got near and was able to see into the tank, I gave an involuntary cry and backed away. What I saw reflected in the blood-stained water were the faces of monsters. They had leaned over the side of the tank and died in that position. From the burned shreds of their sailor uniforms, I knew they were schoolgirls, but they had no hair left and their burned faces were crimson with blood; they no longer appeared human. After we came out on the main road and crossed Sumiyoshi Bridge, we finally came across some living human beings—but maybe it would be more correct to say that we met some people from Hell. They were naked and their skin, burned and bloody, was like red rust and their bodies were bloated up like balloons. Nevertheless, since we had not seen any living person on the way, we felt better seeing them and soon joined this group in our attempt to escape from Hiroshima. The houses on both sides of this street, which was several dozen yards wide, were in flames so that we could only move along a strip in the center about three or four yards wide. This narrow passage was covered with seriously burned and injured people, unable to walk, and with dead bodies, leaving hardly any space for us to get through. At places, we were forced to step over them callously, but we apologized in our hearts as we did this. Among them were old people pleading for water, tiny children seeking help, students unconsciously calling for their parents, brothers, and sisters, and there was a mother prostrate on the ground, moaning with pain but with one arm still tightly embracing her dead baby. But how could we help them when we ourselves did not know our own fate?

When we reached the Koi First Aid Station, we learned that we were among the last to escape from the Sumiyoshi Bridge area. After my father had received some medical treatment, we hurried over Koi Hill to our relatives at Tomo Village in Asa

County. When we were crossing the hill late that evening, we could see Hiroshima lying far below, now a mere smoldering desert. After offering a silent prayer for the victims, we descended the hill toward Tomo.

Yasuhiro Ishibashi
10th grade boy (4th grade at the time)

I felt something heavy pressing down on me, and I tried to open my eyes but I couldn't until I rubbed them and pushed them open. It was all dark and yellowish. On my quilt were a lot of broken pieces of wood and bits of plaster.

Was I awake? I didn't know what was happening. After a struggle I managed to get up and go into the garden. All the walls had crumbled and only a few uprights remained jutting up. Everything was covered in a thick cloud of dust.

I stood there in a daze, until a lady living nearby came up. "Excuse me, but is it morning or evening?" I asked her. Although usually quiet and gentle, she said sharply, "What are you talking about? Now's not the time for that!" She grabbed my hand and pulled me toward the embankment.

All the roofs of the houses had been blown off, and only some pillars showed where they had been. I was only a primary school student then, so I held on to her big hand tightly and clambered over the tileless roofs of the flattened houses and finally reached the embankment. Then the woman left me, saying that she had things to do.

All around was frightened commotion. Crushed in the wreckage of a house below the embankment, some children were screaming. A man who seemed to be their father was straining to lift the big roof, ignoring the blood pouring from his leg, but it was hopeless and the children only cried all the harder. The frantic father screamed for help from the people passing by but no one went to help him; they were all just lurching along like sleepwalkers. I couldn't bear it and looked away toward the river. The River Ohta, where clear water used to flow, was filled with dust and the houses blown into it, so it looked as if houses had been standing on the bed of the river. I wouldn't have thought it was a river, if I hadn't been able to see all the debris slowly moving.

I had been in a daze till then, but suddenly I became frightened. Sobbing loudly, I walked through the roads which were strewn with big beams and broken glass. Soon, I found my mother. Mother had blood on her face and she was carrying bedding on her back.

We took refuge on the bank of the river. In the oily water of the river were floating five or six houses blown there by the blast. From about that time, everything seemed to catch fire; the railing of Tsurumi Bridge and the roofs floating on the river were burning. A man who was also taking refuge there told me to put out the fire on one of the roofs, as a fire mustn't be allowed to start where we were. I was not sure if I could do it but I swam through the oily water to the floating roof and put the fire out, but whenever I extinguished one place, another part began to burn and I was unable to get the fire under control. So I gave up and returned to where the others were. Soon, the water in the river ebbed, and we moved to the uncovered bed of the river. There were some corpses lying there with swollen faces. Then a group of schoolgirls came. Their trousers were in tatters and their faces burned and blistered.

"Let us in," said one of them and they burrowed into the bedclothes. I was so hot I got out of bed and dipped my shirt in the water and put it on again, but within ten minutes I had to do it again.

Soon, it was noon. I felt very hungry because I hadn't eaten anything since the night before. Some one said that there was an emergency kitchen on the other side of Tsurumi Bridge so we hurried over there. We found a large pot in which squashes and potatoes, apparently grown in backyard gardens, were being boiled together. We waited in line to get some of this tasteless food. Since we had nothing to put it in, we picked up some blackened tiles and had the hotchpotch put on these. We had some of the food put in an empty can and brought it back for the girl students lying by the river. While we were steeling ourselves and swallowing this tasteless mess, I saw a man with some salt. I felt ashamed but held out my hand and asked him for a little salt.

The sound of fires and the screams of people got worse and worse. I was getting hazy and didn't know really what was happening. I heard someone calling a long way off, a faint moaning that seemed to roll up from the depths of the earth. I gave a start—wasn't that my father's voice? I was sure it was Father's voice. Mother and I went in search of him.

Those who were not badly injured were being ordered by the military police to carry the seriously hurt to some trucks. To avoid this my mother pretended to be injured herself, saying she was sorry for the badly hurt but this was an emergency and it couldn't be helped. We searched and searched but couldn't find him. On both sides of the bridge were a lot of injured people dressed in worse rags than beggars, and there were many dead. All these were lying there or squatting. I was too afraid to look closely, but there a corpse from whose nostrils protruded a purplish grape-like mass, someone else dressed in ragged clothes and burned all over his face, and a charred girl student lying on her back, around her middle an elastic waistband, all that remained of her trousers. Beside her, a military policeman was leaning on his sword, weeping loudly as he stroked the girl's half-burned face and said to himself, "I have a child this age, how is she now?" A man by the river whose breath came in feeble gasps suddenly stood up and cried, "Long live the Emperor!" and toppled over on his back.

It was getting toward night. I was so hungry again that I went to the Hijiyama Shrine to get some rice-balls. They tasted wonderful! I brought two of them back and gave them to Mother.

In the dark, the cries of people and the noise of trees burning could be heard closer. We decided to sleep on the bank of the river where it sticks out a bit. It was dark where we were, but we sometimes felt our faces glow warmly from the fires in the distance. To the west, we would hear the sounds of explosions followed by flames rising high into the sky. I vacantly watched a big building burning, its iron framework collapsing in the heat, the whole scene standing out against the dark background. A military policeman shouted, "Any more injured? Hurry up, this is the last ambulance."

Mrs. Furuta, a neighbor, who had been lying beside me struggled up and said, "Mrs. Ishibashi, I'm going to die. No, I won't say any more. If you see my children, please give them this. Please do what I ask." She handed something to my mother. I was astonished, because she had only a slight burn on her arm. (Later, we heard that she died soon after.) I felt very sad and drew up the quilt, covering my face.

My ears were filled with the groans of many people, the sound of burning buildings collapsing, and the faint booming sound of distant airplanes as they passed across the night sky.

Etsuko Fujioka
11th grade girl (5th grade at the time)

The detestable war in which so many were sacrificed in an instant on August 6, 1945. How much pain and misery it gave to me, to so many Hiroshima people. I think that only those who experienced it can realize just how much it was.

At 8:15 on August 6, we were talking with some visitors in the hall. My father, a naval officer, was at the Naval Academy at Etajima. We four children lived with my mother. It was also the anniversary of the death of my older sister who drowned in a river in 1939.

Everyone was relaxed because the all-clear had been sounded. At the moment of the flash, I happened to look around and saw a strange light. It was the beginning of my misery. I felt I had to escape somewhere and ran toward my room. I was almost in my room when the ceiling, the big black pillar and broken glass came falling down on my small body, pressing me under it all.

"Mummy," I cried out three times, but there was no answer. Amid the smell, the strong smell of dust and the earth of the walls, I lost consciousness.

When I came to, my mother's and brother's anxious faces were peering down at me. My body was still trapped. I wondered why I couldn't move. I found that my legs were held by the central pillar which refused to move. Finally, a man from the wood shop came and got me free. Half of my body had received injuries, and much flesh had been stripped off. Strangely enough, I did not feel any pain.

The whole city was on fire. It burned with a terrifying sound. Cries were heard from here and there.

The next day dawned. A lot of people came from Miyoshi to help us and put us in a truck. I had to lie down, being unable to sit. They took us to some place where there were countless people who'd fled the disaster. An enemy airplane was circling over us; we were afraid of it. The cut caused by the broken glass looked like a slash in a pomegranate, a gaping wound. Just the sight of it terrified me. My injuries started to hurt. Soon, I was taken by truck to a hospital at Yoshida and given some treatment. While I was there, dozens of patients breathed their last, painfully crying out someone's name.

On August 13, we went to Etajima where my father was. I was treated every day at the hospital of the Naval Academy. The pain was terrible.

On August 15, Japan surrendered. We went into the country where we were received coldly. It was hard for all of us.

I'll have the scar on my face as long as I live. Why am I so conscious of this scar? Because people began to tease and taunt me about it, saying it was a *pikadon* scar. Thinking that it could all be worse, I stayed quiet and didn't say anything about it to my father or mother.

On June 4, 1946, I came back to Hiroshima. Even there, I was teased and made fun of by neighbors and classmates, even by students in the lower grades. But I endured all this and managed to enter junior high school.

After I entered that school, I became more unhappy with the teasing which got much worse, until my nature changed. I had been shy and reserved. I became like a boy; I myself was surprised at the change. After starting senior high school, no one makes fun of me, but whenever I run into students from my junior high school days they make fun of me wherever we are, on the street or anywhere. But I just keep tight control and say to myself: I am one of the victims of the war.

But the thought of the future terrifies me. Will they still make fun of my "*pikadon* scar" even when I'm grown up? And the terrible shame and resentment I'll feel.

Why don't Japanese try to share the sadness and pain that others feel? I sincerely pray that the time soon comes when I can smile the whole day through.

I feel sorry for the teachers and friends I knew well who died, but at the same time I envy them. I feel it would have been better if I'd died back then, trapped in that house.

Eiko Matsunaga
11th grade girl (5th grade at the time)

I was eating breakfast, sitting across from Mother. I was just going to put some rice into my mouth and was holding my rice-bowl in my left hand and my chopsticks in my right when there was a bright light in front of my eyes and an indescribable orange light surged in. I put the rice into my mouth without thinking, put my rice-bowl and chopsticks down and ran four or five steps. I do not know what happened after that because I was unconscious. It must have been ten or fifteen minutes later when I recovered consciousness. I opened my eyes but I could see nothing because the place was filled with white smoke. I had fallen down, so I tried to stand up and fell again. Then my head cleared. When I looked at my feet, I found that the right one was buried up to the ankle. I was so shocked that I lost my energy. I could not even think of trying to get rid of the boards with my hands. I pushed hard with my left foot and tried to pull up my right one with all my strength. Suddenly my foot came free. Where was I? What had happened to me? The whole place was full of white smoke. What on earth had happened?

Incendiary bomb! That was what suddenly came to mind. Where I was was just between the dining room and the living room. In the living room was a bookcase about five feet wide, thirty inches deep and thirteen feet long, and I was standing beside this bookcase.

As I looked around once more, I seemed to feel the white smoke thinning gradually. Two, three, five, seven minutes passed, and the midsummer sun shone directly into my eyes. I got dizzy, and lost consciousness again. After some time had passed, I stood up muzzily, and heard my brother calling me: "Eiko-chan, Eiko-chan!"

At that moment, I felt as if I were hearing my name for the first time in my life.

"Yes," I answered.

"Don't move from there," he said.

I looked over my shoulder and saw our house was a flattened wreck, and at the back waves of swirling flames were threatening to sweep down on us at any moment. Two or three minutes later, I suddenly heard my sister's voice calling, "Someone help me, please someone come and help me!" I was alarmed and looked around, wondering where she was, but I couldn't see her anywhere. Then my brother was saying, "Wait a minute —I'll get you out!" and he bent down. His face was bright scarlet with blood which trickled down. He was blinded by the blood getting in his eyes and couldn't see to get the boards off my sister, and he kept wiping the blood away with his right hand.

My father! I couldn't just stay there. But I did not know where my father was. I was scared and just dithered around. My brother finally managed to drag my sister free. She was my own sister but the sight of her was horrifying. Her dark hair which reached her shoulders, that hair was now pure white. At the side of her mouth was a crescent-shaped gash through which her gums were pitifully exposed, and from which bright red blood flowed. Each time she took a deep breath and exhaled,

I could hear a sighing sound from this gash. When she said she wanted a drink of water, I could see glimpses of her white teeth through the cut. She'd been in a glassed-in room, and she had fifty, sixty or probably more than a hundred pieces of glass embedded all over her body, and the blood was gushing out from the cuts. I could see her ankle bone where the flesh had been stripped away. When I saw this figure my sister had been transformed into, for a fleeting moment, I just couldn't think that it was her. I was afraid even to go near her.

My father's moans became higher. "Quick, get me out!" he shouted.

My brother went toward the voice, saying, "Where are you, father?"

"You're standing on me! Oh, the pain."

My brother leaped back, surprised.

We could not see Father just by looking from above. He was completely covered by the plaster wall, and his head was jammed into the angle of the doorsill. The strength of the blast had sandwiched his head so firmly that it was difficult to move him. When my brother pulled as hard as he could, my father cried out in pain.

When all this was happening, I heard Mother calling me: "Eiko-chan! Eiko-chan! Help! Help!"

Even now, I don't know what I had been doing till that time. I rushed over towards where my mother's voice came from, but she couldn't be seen, either. Her voice seemed to quiver with pain, surprise, and terror.

"Mother, where are you?"

I got closer to her voice. Under the fallen roof, Mother was tapping on something that sounded like tin. But her voice gradually became fainter and fainter. I had no strength at all, how could I lift up the big walls, the supports, the glass? In tears now, I cried out without thinking, "Mummy, I can't get

you out. There's the big roof and the beams, and the upstairs
. . . ."

Mother's voice faded away. I didn't particularly think I
was sad or even that I wanted to get her out. I just stood there
in a daze, gazing in through the roof. I couldn't hear the tapping sound any more either.

"Eiko-chan!" called my brother.

There was a deep cut about four inches long on his abdomen, as if he had had an appendix operation. When he made
any effort, blood flowed out. With his insides exposed and
bright red blood spurting out, he didn't seem like my brother.
My sister said she felt ill and sat down heavily. Just then, my
father came crawling out from under the wreckage. As he was
talking about us getting Mother out, my brother urged us to
get moving, saying, "Quick, out, out, or we'll be all burned to
death. Hurry up!"

When I looked around, the waves of flames had become
bigger and were threatening the four of us. We tried to get out
to the left but the flames crackled higher, making a fearful
noise that sounded like gunpowder going off. Quickly we
turned to the right, but that way, too, the fire seemed about to
swallow us. But the flames looked strange, extending straight
up. Gradually the flames advanced, reducing our space. The
four of us cringed away, thinking that we were about to be
burned to death there.

[Unfinished]

Hiromi Sakaguchi
11th grade boy (5th grade at the time)

A ugust 6—the terrible day on which the atom bomb made me an orphan. That terrible flash, the earth-shaking roar, and the devilish, dark atomic cloud, all this I saw from where I was in the country, twenty-five miles from Hiroshima. But I did not know that my parents, my brother and sisters, and my best friends were already dead in that instant. My home was in Saiku-cho near the center of the explosion.

I had four brothers and sisters. Fortunately or unfortunately, in April that year I had been evacuated with others my age to a village in Yamagata County, away from my mother and my father. I never thought that that was the last time that I would see my family.

It was a month after the atom bomb, on the night of September 7, that I learned my whole family had been totally annihilated. That evening, my uncle from Kure suddenly came to the temple where we were staying. He hadn't taken off his shoes yet, and as soon as he saw me he told me my family had died. I cried, and loudly I continued to cry. My teacher cried, too. The matron also cried, holding her apron to her face. At that time, I felt neither sorrow nor loneliness, perhaps because the shock was so great. I just cried and cried. That night I slept next to my uncle. His strong figure seemed like my father's. The face of my father, of my mother, and the dear faces of my brothers and sisters—how many times I remembered them. And now those dear faces have disappeared from the world forever! Many times, I said to myself that it was not true, not true. But the actual sight of the terrible devil that I had seen that morning gave the lie to my thought.

In bed, my uncle told me about how my family had died. Two days after the atom bomb had been dropped, my uncle and some other relatives went to the burned out remains of my house. All they found there was a big water tank and an iron bathtub. They tried digging there to search for remains, but they did not find any. They threw bits and pieces of iron and broken tiles into the water tank. But then they started thinking of the water tank itself and searched it again, and suddenly they found what had been my brother. He had been in the second year at the Prefectural Technological High School. Twenty days later, three skeletons were found under the safe at the burned-out company where my father had worked (in front of the Hiroshima Post Office). Afterwards, it was found that one of these was Father's. The remains of my mother and sisters had not been found yet. This is what my uncle told me that evening.

Three years later, however, we found out everything. My mother had been clearing sites after buildings had been demolished and was still alive after the atom bomb dropped, but she was worried about my little sister (who was five at the time) who she had left at home, and went to look for her, but was never seen again. The lady next door took my sister with her, but she said that my sister died and grew cold in her arms. My oldest sister worked at the Telephone Office and had been on night duty the previous day, and the atom bomb went off while she was on her way home that morning. Her body was not found. My next sister (I think she was in the sixth grade at the time) was also caught by the atom bomb while she was on her way to school.

When I heard of my family dying these miserable unforeseen deaths one after another, I couldn't help feeling a keen hatred of war. And at the same time I felt war was the most efficient weapon for annihilating all mankind. I lost six members of my family because of the terrible power of science. But some families had much greater losses. The new weapon had destroyed not only the people of Hiroshima but also their houses, priceless cultural properties and even the great city of Hiroshima itself.

However, Hiroshima did not die. The waters of the Ohta River flowed clearly through its seven channels. The pure and limpid water was very beautiful.

I wanted to become that water, because water knows neither pain nor sorrow. The clear stream of the Ohta washed away the suffering from my heart. By letting my heart merge with the water, I have been able to feel some of the happiness I felt before. The nameless plants that sprang up among the scorched remains also had the strength of life. They grew upward against all obstacles—bricks, tiles, debris. They have fought against all hardships.

I want to live like these plants. Even now, this is my conviction. I think everyone who has had the kind of experience I have has probably survived like this.

Now, Hiroshima has the Memorial Tower, the Peace Monument and other buildings and facilities in memory of the atom bomb victims, and Hiroshima has become a city of lasting peace which will never resort to arms. This will allow my family to sleep in peace.

Yasuko Ise
10th grade girl (4th grade at the time)

The meaningless sleepless night ended. It was the sixth of August, the sky was beautifully clear and a fresh morning breeze came in through the open window.

I had returned home, after a long time, from where I had been evacuated, and after the sleepless night I was dozing, stretched out on the *tatami*. Was I asleep or awake?

There was a sudden flash, and I felt I was exposed to the strong light and heat of the sun; at the same time, hot tiles and timbers came crashing and clattering down.

I was very frightened and just as I thought of escape, I found I was caught under something and couldn't move. It was very painful; I felt hot as if I had been burned all over.

"Mommy! Mommy!" I shouted out as loudly as I could, but it was deadly silent everywhere. I was crying as I thought I was going to die.

After a time, I heard my mother's voice from somewhere above me, and also my little brother's.

Mother was calling my name, "Where are you, Yasu-chan? Where are you?" I could hear my little brother crying. At last, the things over my face were taken away and I could breathe easily and see my mother's face. The house had been smashed to pieces; the gray sky could be seen.

"Just wait there a minute. I must help your father." I could hear Mother frantically looking for him, but then he appeared at the front door, so covered with blood that he looked like a red devil. Mother and Father came and dug me out. Apparently, he had been reading the newspaper in his room, with no clothes on, so he had gotten cut all over with the glass from the door.

Although my small brother, who was only two months old, had been beside me, we couldn't see him.

Mother began to cry. At the back, someone was shouting. "The fire is getting near!"

"It may be hopeless. We have to give up," Father said and pulled my mother away. We were almost out when we heard the baby wailing.

Mother got down and dug frantically, and there he was in among tiles and boards, crying.

Mother hugged him tightly and cried. We all cried, and Father murmured "Good. Oh, how good." The flames were coming closer. We could hear them crackling at the back and the sound of people's shrieks grew louder. When we got outside, everything was wrapped in a gray mist as far as one could see.

Flames were shooting out here and there among the wrecked houses and spreading very rapidly.

Blood-spattered people were moving past along the street, their tattered clothes trailing.

The skin of the arms of some was peeling off and dangling from their finger tips. They walked on silently, holding their arms up in front of them.

A girl came up to Father, crying, and said, "Please help me, please take me somewhere." Father said, "All right now, all right now. We'll all go together, right?"

Holding out her peeling hands, she said, "I want some water, please."

"You must not drink water now," said Mother.

But she continued crying for water, so Father gave her a drink, filling his cupped hands with water from a faucet. This made her so happy.

I looked back and saw that my dear home with its many happy memories was already enveloped in flames. We had all stopped to look back, but it was very hard for us to watch this, and when Father said, "Come on. Let's go," we hurried on till we came to the river embankment. We thought it was safe there and sat down for a short rest. There were many people taking refuge there.

Though there shouldn't have been any fire there, fire started to flicker in four or five trucks in an open space in front, and they quickly went up in flames. The light poles were burning. The wooden fences were burning, too. I felt wretched and didn't know what was happening, whether I was alive or was in some other world; it was like a bad dream.

Just then, the sky suddenly changed and heavy rain began to fall. However, the fury of the fire wasn't reduced in the least, and toward the west it burned reddish-black, more and more fiercely. I didn't have the strength to watch it any more. I was almost dropping, there. My wounds started to hurt badly. I also felt hungry, and it seemed as if I was going to faint. We had taken shelter from the rain in the driver's cab of a wrecked truck. After a while, the rain stopped, and we started for Koi. As my father and the oldest of my little brothers had hurt their legs badly, it was decided that we'd get a car to take them to a hospital. As our place of refuge was Jigozen we decided to walk as far as Kusatsu. Mother carried the baby in the front of her *kimono* and took my three-year-old brother by the hand. We went along, with Mother encouraging my other little brother and I, always to the west, the west, following the train tracks. I wondered what time it was. We had eaten nothing since the morning and my little brothers were complaining of hunger. I, too, didn't feel like I could go any further.

On the road, somebody gave us some biscuits and we stuffed them into our mouths, but they didn't taste good. It was getting dark. We kept saying out loud that Kusatsu was just over there, to encourage ourselves to keep on.

At Kusatsu, we tried to get on a streetcar but couldn't because there were so many already on it. While we were waiting for an empty streetcar, we found that they had stopped. So we asked to stay the night at some temple whose name we didn't know.

About ten people were packed in the room, so we had to pass the night, crouching and sitting around. What a long night it was! As soon as the sky began to lighten, we started out for Jigozen to find my father and brother.

There were many injured people.

The hall and the classrooms of the school were so full of injured people lying around in pain that there was no room to walk.

People breathing their last as they lay there, because there was no treatment for them; people faintly calling the name of their mother or children crying with pain; people with grotesquely swollen faces from their burns. Children hoarsely crying out to their mother for water! Oh, could such dreadful misery be imagined in this world?

When I was little, my grandmother often told me there was a hell in the other world, but I wondered if this weren't the real hell. Is it false, is it real?

Why did they have to drop such an inhuman bomb and give us such cruel suffering? Throughout the world, the use of poison gas is forbidden, but wasn't this suffering worse than poison gas? That day, my father, brothers and I stood all day long among the crowds of dead and injured, without getting any treatment for our injuries. On the morning of the eighth, we finally received some simple treatment, but our wounds were very painful and we could not sleep. Father's cuts seemed to be starting to fester, so it was decided that he would have to go to Rakuraku-En to receive more thorough treatment from a doctor before returning.

From Koi Station to Yokogawa Station, injured parents and children walked on slowly under the scorching sun, trying to encourage one another in the midst of the scenes of disaster. The smell of dead bodies almost made me feel dizzy. Along the way, some places were still burning.

As I got on the train, my pain suddenly got worse. When we arrived at Kameyama Station, it was pitch dark. From there, we had to walk more than thirty minutes along a mountain path over the pass. Father's leg was so bad that Mother carried him on her back, and so we made our way along the pitch-dark path, urged on by Mother. When we finally reached the house, it was already about eleven o'clock, and they were frightened because they thought it was our spirits that had returned. They had thought we were dead.

I slept every day like the dead. Before long, my wounds became infected but it was impossible for me to get to the doctor because he lived more than two miles away.

Mother was very busy tending the injuries of five people every day. The bandages immediately got sticky again with pus. Many times, I thought I was going to rot to death. We all got very thin and had no energy left.

The only food there was wheat, and as the farmers wouldn't let us have any vegetables, Mother would pick the parsley and mugwort beside the brook and we'd eat this with pickled plums. We had the same things day after day. When I saw the tomatoes and cucumbers in the fields, I would dreamily think how much I wanted to eat them.

On August 15, Japan finally surrendered. Many of those who were killed by the atom bomb died, believing that Japan would win. I thought it such a terrible shame that the sacrifice of so many had been wasted.

We pray more strongly for peace and that the people of the world may never again have to endure the cruel sufferings which Hiroshima sustained because of the atom bomb.

Akiko Ohga
10th grade girl (4th grade at the time)

Up to six years ago, I had a happy and joyful life, with my whole family there—parents, brother, and sister. War shattered this happy family. And not only this home; it destroyed the happiness of uncountable houses, tens of thousands of homes. Around that time, my big brother was called up and had to leave our home. As for my father, a carbuncle had formed on his face and he had been going to the hospital every day for about the last five days. The memory of August 6 makes me shudder and sends a chill down my spine. My unsuspecting father and big sister set off in high spirits for Hiroshima. A few hours later, the fate of the people in Hiroshima had been completely changed. This was of course the result of the single atom bomb. My father and sister were able to get back home. But I would like to tell about the three weeks from the time my father was atom-bombed to when he died.

A little after eight o'clock on August 6, my father was waiting in the waiting room of Taruya Surgical Clinic at Dobashi in Hiroshima for his turn to be examined. Suddenly there was a flash and a great noise and the house began to break apart. It became so dark that you could not see even an inch in front of your face. He thought someone would come to rescue him, and so he was waiting quietly with his eyes closed, when he suddenly heard the people around him starting to call for help. As he peered around him, he saw it was gradually getting brighter in one direction. As he began to crawl toward this light to get out, he bumped into someone who was already dead. He climbed over the dead body and kept going toward the light. But what do you suppose the brightness was? It was a fire, furiously blazing.

Outside was a sea of flames. His way out was gone, and he

just stood rooted to the spot, in a daze. Then a calm old man of about seventy came walking up, and Father regained his spirits and began to feel much more confident. The man told him that they would be all right if they went to the river bank, so together they made their way toward the Honkawa River. But when they reached the bank, they found it a sea of fire there, too. Not only that, flames were licking at the parapet of the bridge, and when they looked at the river, they saw fire there, too. Buildings and timbers and doors had been blown into the river and these were blazing with a crackling noise. There was nothing to do but to turn back toward Motohara, where they stopped for a while. But as the flames advanced toward them, the heat drove them on. As they were wandering around, they came out on some train tracks, but even some of the ties were burning. There was no place left to avoid the flames. Together with many other people, they began to walk along the tracks toward Koi; the flames of the burning houses on both sides of the tracks looked like the tongues of devils.

Afterward, Father said to us, "With that long procession of people, the scene was more horrifying than any picture of Hell."

It was after eleven when Father finally managed to reach home after wandering all over. And what a sight he was! We clung to him, crying. He was in bed for three days, but he had work to do. His external injuries were not so serious, so he got up. Saying how hard it all was, he kept working on the problem of providing food for the victims of the atom bomb, and put up with the pain and discomfort. But the horrible atomic radiation had already eaten deep into my father's body. On August 20, he finally collapsed. He had a constant high fever with no clear cause.

We tried every treatment, exchanging our precious food

provisions for medicine and going without food but he only got worse. His temperature went up to about 107 degrees and would not come down, whatever we did. Patches appeared on his body and his white blood count steadily decreased. His gums bled and the bleeding wouldn't stop. The family provided blood for transfusions, and he got many injections to stop the bleeding, but they had no effect.

What was for us the most tragic end was approaching. It happened on the night of the twenty-seventh. Father's bleeding, which we hadn't been able to stop before, now stopped by itself. About eleven hours later, he grasped each of our hands and, anxiously calling the name of my brother who was away at the front, over and over again, my father departed on the journey from which there is no return.

[Added later]

I saw the film *The Beginning or the End?* and want to try to write what I thought while watching it.

Those scientists* who invented the uranium atom bomb— they knew what would happen if they dropped it, and how many hundreds of thousands of innocent people would be given tragic memories. They knew it well from their tests. In spite of that, they built the atom bomb and dropped it on Hiroshima.

This was to win the war. If there had been no war, there would have been no need to commit such a crime. Many fine scientists would not have been lost. And happy home life would not have been destroyed.

I really believe that no matter what happens, we must maintain peace so that such a tragedy will never be repeated.

*Among the scientists who made the atom bomb were some humanists. In June 1945, . . . a "Committee on Social and Political Implications," appointed by the Metallurgical Laboratory in Chicago, presented a report to the Secretary of War. The Chairman of this Committee of seven scientists was Professor James Franck. . . .

. . . . To reinforce the effect of the Committee's report, a petition on similar lines signed by sixty-four scientists associated with the Metallurgical Project was sent direct to President Truman.
Blackett, P. M. S., Military and Political Consequences of Atomic Energy. p.104–6.

Russia and even allied countries which bear less mistrust of our ways and intentions, as well as neutral countries, may be deeply shocked by this step. It may be very difficult to persuade the world that a nation, which was capable of secretly preparing and suddenly releasing a new weapon as indiscriminate as the rocket bomb and a thousand times more destructive, is to be trusted in its proclaimed desire of having such weapons abolished by international agreement. . . . The military advantages and the saving of American lives achieved by the sudden use of atomic bombs against Japan may be outweighed by a wave of horror and repulsion sweeping over the rest of the world. . . . From this point of view, a demonstration of the new weapon might be made, before the eyes of all the United Nations on the desert or a barren island. . . . After such a demonstration the weapon might perhaps be used against Japan if the sanction of the United Nations (and public opinion at home) was obtained after a preliminary ultimatum to Japan to surrender . . . . We believe that these considerations make the use of nuclear bombs for an early attack against Japan inadvisable. If the United States were to be the first to release this new means of indiscriminate destruction of mankind, she would sacrifice public support throughout the world, precipitate the race for armaments, and prejudice the possibility of reaching an international agreement on the future control of such weapons.
Brodie, Bulletin of Atomic scientists. May 1946.

Noriko Iwata
11th grade girl (5th grade at the time)

My mother, sister, brother and I had moved to my aunt's home in Miiri Village in a remote part of Kabe, leaving my grandparents at our house in Hiroshima. On the day the atom bomb was dropped, my mother had gone to a parental meeting and my little sister had left on the evening of the fifth to visit our grandparents in Hiroshima. It was summer vacation and I was loafing around the house. But then I got bored and went outside. Soon after, there was a flash followed in a moment by a loud, thunderous noise. Then, before long, a cloud that looked like cotton candy rose into the clear, blue sky beyond the mountain. While I was talking with my cousin about the cloud, my uncle and the others returned from the field. My mother came back from the school a little early. She had a strange, uneasy expression on her face but she sat down to her sewing as soon as she came in the house. It was a little after lunch when my cousin came home from the Nagatsuka Factory where he was working under the Student Mobilization Program. He had heard that the Yokogawa area was seriously damaged. When my mother heard this, she began to worry about our grandparents and my younger sister. She went as far as Kabe, but couldn't learn anything about Hiroshima.

When my mother and I went out to take in the washing that evening, we saw a little girl plodding toward us along the river bank. I thought she might be my sister and ran toward her. The little girl I met was indeed my sister but, oh, how different she looked.

"Yoriko-chan! Yoriko-chan! What a long walk you must have had," my mother cried, hugging her and pressing her cheek against Yoriko's again and again. Suddenly there were tears in my eyes that seemed about to roll down my cheeks. My sister's face was dark as if covered with soot and the inside of her mouth was bleeding. The twenty-mile walk over the sun-scorched asphalt road must have made her so tired that she became sick. On her *mompe* trousers were the stains of what she had vomited. (This was during the war and even the children wore such trousers.) My mother carried her to the well and gave her a dipperful of water to rinse out her mouth with. Then she washed the dirt off her face and hands. Thinking she was hungry, we gave her some boiled potatoes. As she sat eating them slowly and with difficulty, she began to tell us about what had happened to her.

"I was at the barber shop. There was a flash and the shop fell down. Some boards and posts fell on me and I couldn't get up. So I thought I was going to die. I wriggled hard. I tried to climb up, but I couldn't. The more I tried the deeper I seemed to go. I was so afraid that I cried for help. The barber shop girl helped me out. Then I went to our house, but it was smashed to the ground. Grandfather and Grandmother weren't there. I thought they might have gone to the barber shop to look for me. So I went back to the barber shop. They weren't there. I wondered how I could get to Kirihara. I crossed the bridge to Nakahiro. There, I heard one man ask another the way to Yokogawa. I followed this man and got to Yokogawa. Then I walked straight on and came here."

I was impressed by my sister's cleverness. Even when my sister was less than two years old, she returned home from our relatives in Funairi Kawaguchi-cho all by herself.

From the following day, many burned people were brought to our school by truck. There were no classes for two or three days. According to an uncle who called on us three or four days later, both our grandparents had escaped without a scratch and had gone to the house where my grandmother was raised. My uncle stayed overnight and on the following day our grandparents came. After they arrived they would start out every morning pulling a cart toward their house in Hiroshima and in the evening they would return with the cart filled with things they had stored in the air-raid shelter. They made a round trip every day for a whole week. As our house was too small, they rented an annex of the largest house in Shimo Kirihara and started to live there.

It was about this time that both my grandmother and my younger sister began to lose their hair. Their pillows were always covered with a lot of hair and if you even so much as touched their hair it would come out in clumps of about fifty strands.

My grandfather also suddenly began to have severe headaches and was finally confined to bed. Our village was literally stricken with fear. People who had escaped from Hiroshima without a scratch began to lose their hair, break out in colored spots and eventually die. There was nothing the doctors could do to help them.

It was on the thirtieth of August. Our school was full of patients, and we were studying on the steps of the shrine behind the school. My teacher came up to me and said quietly, "Your grandfather is in critical condition. You'd better go home at once."

I hurried to Shimo Kirihara, but when I reached my grandfather's house he had already passed away.

My grandfather loved to drink sake. Saying that he might die any time so he was going to enjoy his sake now, he started to drink. After he was quite drunk, he stood to go to the toilet but he was wobbly on his feet and fell into the garden. He struck his head on a sharp stone, opening a gash over an inch wide from which blood spurted like a fountain. By the time his funeral was held, my grandmother was sick in bed. As Grandfather's funeral was the first, he was placed in a beautiful cedar coffin. My grandmother's condition gradually became worse and the black spots that appeared on her skin were followed by purple ones. She couldn't eat anything at all so she didn't have any ordinary bowel movements. Instead, she passed black mucous fluid as if her intestines were melting away. She became nothing but skin and bone and lost all of her hair. What a horrible sight she was when she finally died on the fourth of September! By that time, everyone was sure that anyone who was exposed to the atom bomb in Hiroshima would die. Grandmother's funeral was quite different from Grandfather's. Instead of being placed in a coffin, she was put on a wide board with a nightgown thrown over her. It was a simple cremation.

My aunt carried my sick sister to the hill where my grandmother was cremated and as they stood watching, she said, "Yori-chan! You will be like that soon, too."

"Auntie! Only the old people die. I'm not going to die. My mother promised me that I am going to get well."

Everyone there was in tears to hear her talking of getting well when they all knew that she was destined to die.

On the eighth of September, my uncle told Yoriko that it wouldn't do for her to go and die before he could take her for moxibustion treatment. She must have realized that she was close to death because she only smiled sadly. My uncle's face became tense and twisted. It was like a smile but it was something else. On the following day, the ninth of September, my sister passed away at the very young age of eight.

My mother put lipstick and rouge on her face. Then, like Grandmother, she was placed on a board and taken to the hill for cremation. Just as the fire was to be lit, Mother suddenly ran toward Yoriko's lifeless body screaming in an anguished voice, "Burn me with her!"

Hisayo Yaguchi
11th grade girl (5th grade at the time)

Though I was once evacuated, I returned to the city to live at home with my mother. We had to spend more time for air-raid drills than we did studying in the classroom, but it was much better than being separated from my mother. I thought I was very lucky being able to live with my mother.

Our house was in Yokogawa but for the safety of my paralyzed grandmother and my little brother, we built a house at the foot of the mountain near Uchikoshi. My father's family and my uncle's family took turns living for a week at a time in Yokogawa and Uchikoshi.

It was my father's idea that we all get together for dinner once in a while, and we gathered on the evening of August 5. My grandmother couldn't walk and was brought by car to Yokogawa where we had dinner together. We had a very pleasant evening, but suddenly there was an air-raid warning. We hurriedly prepared to leave for Uchikoshi to take shelter. However, the air-raid alarm was soon lifted. Since we were all together, we decided to spend the night at Yokogawa.

On the following morning, there was another air-raid warning, but this was also lifted soon. Then my sister left for the West Police Station, my elder brother for labor service, and Ken-chan and I for school. It was during the morning assembly in the school ground that there was a sudden, terrific flash and we were all blown to the ground. There was a deep yellow light around us which was so strong that we couldn't open our eyes. "It's hot!" I cried and tightly covered my face with both hands. Just as I had turned away from the heat, somebody suddenly shouted that we should lie down. I dropped to the ground immediately. A few seconds later, I could hear excited voices that seemed to come from the back gate on the north side of the school. I raised my head and saw everybody running in that direction. I jumped up and ran after them as fast as I could go.

The school building hadn't caught fire yet, but the roof tiles and windowpanes had all been destroyed by the blast. We ran over a lot of tin roofing near the back gate with a loud clatter and headed in the direction of the hills. Just outside the gate was a vegetable garden but there wasn't a sign of a vegetable anywhere. It was a mad race to escape with everyone for himself. The blast had destroyed some houses completely and left others tilting badly to one side. I felt so hot that I got some water from an emergency water tank in the neighborhood and poured it over my head. Then I began running along with the others again. Before long though, I discovered that I was all by myself. It wasn't until I ran into a cart in a lane leading to the Mitaki River that I regained my senses. This was the first time I noticed how I looked. I was bare from the waist up and all that was left of the trousers I had been wearing were the elastic bands around my waist and ankles. I was stripped to my underpants by the bomb. I suddenly grew weak. To my left, I could see flames shooting up from behind the house nearest to me. I got away as fast as I could and jumped into the Mitaki River. The Mitaki is not a real river but more of a creek. I washed my head in the water, but as I lay in the creek I began to feel as if I were going to faint. I let go of the red-and-white flag that I had been unconsciously clutching in my hand.

"Hey! Don't let it go!" I suddenly heard a voice shouting at me. It was my cousin, Ken-chan.

This was like a ray of hope for me, but it seemed to disappear in a moment as I lost my very last ounce of strength.

Finally though, Ken-chan pulled me to my feet and I was able to get out of the creek and start walking toward our house in Uchikoshi. However, I soon could walk no longer, since the burns all over my body sapped me of what strength I had. My arms and legs were stiff. The burned areas were blistered. My right thigh was also blistered with the skin peeling downward exposing raw flesh. On my feet, I could clearly see the marks left by the thongs of my wooden clogs. Ken-chan took my hand and pulled me onward.

At the foot of the hill, we met some nurses from the Mitaki Hospital who led us to a nearby air-raid shelter. Our house was close by and I wanted to ask them to let us go out, but both of us were so weak that we didn't even try to ask them. We went into the shelter and rested on a rock. Soon the shelter was full of burned people. My burns gradually became painful and I began to cry when I could no longer stand the pain. Ken-chan also began to cry. Not only the two of us but the others in the shelter were crying, too. These cries . . . . They were not just ordinary cries but screeches of agony that sent shivers down my spine and made my hair stand on end. Still the nurses didn't offer us any treatment but only brought more injured people into the shelter.

I looked at the man next to me. He was a wounded soldier dressed in a white hospital robe. He sank lower and lower even as I watched him. A nurse rushed outside and returned with several boards which she placed on the ground and covered with a dirty blanket. The soldier lay down on the blanket. The nurse asked the soldier his name and wrote it on a piece of paper. This she placed by his head and then she left. A little later, I looked around but couldn't see anyone who seemed to be alive. So many people had died even in this small shelter. I became frightened. People were dying one after another before my very eyes.

I took Ken-chan's hand and started to leave the shelter but it was raining hard outside. Both of us were crying from pain; both blowing our breath against the other's burns to soothe the pain. We didn't know what would happen to us and our sobs were also our prayers.

About an hour must have passed. The rain had stopped. As no nurse came for us, Ken-chan and I left the shelter. Our legs had become so stiff while we were sitting in the shelter that we could no longer bend them.

There was a procession of burned victims coming from Uchikoshi. Their hair was hanging over their faces and their bodies were red with burns. Almost all of them were naked. These people moved slowly onward, with one and then another dropping by the roadside. On the riverside and in the fields, men and cattle lay dead and dying side by side. There was a pregnant woman with burns over her entire back lying near the bridge, stark naked. It was truly a pitiful scene, but each had his hands full trying to save himself. Everyone was fleeing to save his own life.

Flames were rising from Yokogawa. Both Ken-chan and I were crippled by the contractions caused by the burns, but we finally managed to reach our house at Uchikoshi. The roof on the eastern side of the house was completely blown off; the doors and windows were gone; the kitchen utensils were scattered about; and everything else in the house except the uprights and floor was destroyed. The large tree on the hill behind the house had fallen onto the road and everything was in such a mess that there was almost no place to walk. Everyone had returned except my aunt and older sister, but they all had severe burns and cuts and could hardly move about. My big brother, the one who had been doing voluntary labor, said that an incendiary bomb had exploded right in front of him. His face was a burned mass. I looked at him once but I couldn't bear to look at him a second time. My little brother was lying next to him on the veranda. His face was also burned. He kept on shouting, "Mummy! Daddy!" My father and mother were at his side holding his hands but he still kept moving them as if he were groping for someone's hand. Father had been pinned under the wrecked house and received a severe blow on his left arm which was now in a sling. Mother had burns all over and crouched beside my brother because she couldn't sit all the way down. As I wiped the sand off my feet, I called my brother's name, but he just kept calling for Mother and Father. Nobody could do anything for him. My brother's soul was slowly leaving us to go to another world. We were all in tears and helpless as we watched him leave us forever.

My brother had been playing in the street with the other children of the neighborhood at the time. When Father had finally got out from under the wrecked house, my brother ran up to him shouting, "Father! Father!" They were able to get away to Uchikoshi before the area began to burn. According to Father, my brother took Father's hand and looking into his eyes, he asked, "Why did this happen?" My brother used to put on his air-raid hood during the air-raid drills and shout, "We'll get them!" but he didn't really understand what air-raids were about at all.

It made me cry to hear him call first for Father and then for Mother, and I called out his name many times. But I, too, was burned all over and I lay weakly on my side crying together with Mother as we watched him die. After that, I got a fever and I can't remember much of what happened. I do distinctly remember though that his dead body was placed in a cabinet without any doors. Also burned sharply into my memory is a picture of the sea of fire that hung over the city of Hiroshima that night.

On the evening of the ninth, our entire family was evacuated to Yamazaki Hospital in Kirikushi, Etajima Island, the home of an acquaintance of ours. Here we received the best of treatment, but our burns would not heal. The war continued and whenever an air-raid signal sounded, many of the patients moved into the air-raid shelter along with the doctors, who took their instruments with them. Those of us with severe burns couldn't be moved though, so they boarded up our room and this made it so much hotter that it was almost unbearable. I faintly remember our doctor telling us that the Emperor made a radio broadcast on August 15 but I had no idea what the broadcast was all about.

Our burns were getting no better and it was about this time that our doctor told us that he had come to realize that he just didn't know how to treat them.

I didn't actually hear the doctor say this but my father told me about it later. Father and the whole family were depressed by this news. Father suffered a relapse and became as bad as ever, throwing a cloud of gloom over everyone. I didn't know anything about this though because I was delirious with a high fever. On the twenty-first, my sister Sadako passed away and on the twenty-seventh my mother died. My big brother had died on the tenth but I didn't know about it at the time and have only a faint memory of Mother telling me about it later.

"Hisayo, when you get well, you must be good to your aunt. You must repay her kindness. Yes, your mother is going to die . . . ."

I cried out frantically, "Mother! You mustn't die! You mustn't die alone. If you're going to die, I am going to die with you!"

"Hisayo! Hisayo!"

"Mother! Mother!"

If I could have gotten up, I would have clung to my mother and wept. Yes, I would have been able to watch her pass away from this earth. But at that time both of us were so badly burned that we couldn't move even a finger. We were delirious with fever and only half conscious. And that is how I was when my dear mother passed away. Death comes but once in a lifetime, the full-stop at the end of life. Though Mother and I were lying side by side in the same ward, I couldn't even see her and, being almost unconscious, I lost my precious, precious mother, the only one I'll ever have, without so much as a chance to look after her as a good daughter should.

With our family suddenly so much smaller, we moved to a new house that had been built some time before. Our doctor had built it as a summer cottage for my grandmother when Ken-chan and I were evacuated.

They carried us on stretchers. This was the first time in many days for me to see the clear blue sky and beautiful green trees.

I don't remember the exact date but it was certainly after the fifteenth. The weather changed suddenly, bringing heavy rains. On one rainy night, there was a landslide and almost all the houses in Kirikushi were demolished. Fortunately, the house into which we had recently moved was located on high ground and escaped the slide. Still, when the floodwater almost reached the floor, we were at a loss what to do. The hospital wards where we had been were buried in the slide together with many of the patients and their relatives who were looking after them. All of the medical equipment and supplies at the hospital were lost too so that the doctors couldn't treat the patients who had survived.

The following morning everyone in the village turned out to dig out the bodies of the victims. The smoke from cremated bodies rose from all parts of the island and the houses that were there only yesterday were now completely gone. After being hit by the atom bomb in Hiroshima, we had escaped death by coming to the Yamazaki Hospital. And now here again, we had survived another narrow scrape with death. But we could no longer obtain the medical care we had been getting so we had to seek the help of another doctor that my father knew. It was on the twenty-first of September that we took a boat and returned to Furue in Hiroshima. We again had to be carried on stretchers and even after we arrived we lay on these stretchers for another two months. Our burns were so bad that we couldn't be moved off them. After returning to Furue, we suffered pain that was pure pain and nothing else. I cannot remember how many times I cried for my arms and legs to be ripped off.

It was truly so painful that I lost all desire to live any longer. By the end of November, our burns were quite a bit better and with the help of a visiting relative I was able to get off my stretcher for the first time.

They had said that no one would be able to live in Hiroshima for seventy-five years, but once we were back we missed our old home and started preparations for building a new house on the same site. After much planning and help from our friends, the house was completed on the ninth of February and we got ready to move in. In the meantime, on the tenth of January, Ken-chan's father, who had done so much to help us, finally passed away.

Ken-chan and I rode on a cart to our newly built home in Yokogawa, passing for the first time through the burned city of Hiroshima. The city was completely changed. Only a few houses had been built here and there and only one or two of our former neighbors were still around. It was now a place of strangers and strange houses.

The green was gone from the bank near the Military Hospital across the river, with the spread of the cold winter. From our kitchen, we could even see the train passing over Misasa Bridge located several hundred yards from the house.

How Hiroshima had changed! The only things that could be seen were burned buildings, the remains of burned trees, and burned and rusted machinery. I heard that until recently the farmers had been picking up the dead bodies in the burned area and putting them in their carts to be used as fertilizer.

The more we heard and saw, the more astounded we were. No sign of the past remained. I know that it is a natural phenomenon for things to change with the passing of time. However, these changes which seemed to transcend the element of time simply left me with a feeling of bewilderment and disbelief.

There are seven urns standing in the alcove, the ashes of

my grandmother, mother, older brother, older sister, younger brother, uncle and sister Sadako. When Father and I used to kneel before the Buddhist altar, my mind would become completely blank with the enormity of it all. Tears would come to my eyes when I thought of the hard life ahead and of my fate. I would begin to hate myself and be overcome by an urge to commit suicide. I could think only of man's meanness, his weakness and the hardships of life, and I could find no pleasure in living at all. I feared that I would become a warped and twisted person. But still, there was no desire in me to lead a good and bright life. I felt as if I were destined to ruin.

Five years have elapsed since then and as things around me have become more settled, so has my mind.

When we fall, we struggle to our feet. Yes, and though we may fall once more, we again try to stand up. Life is a thorny mountain path. We must get up when we stumble. If we keep trying, eventually a beautiful and clear fountain will appear before us. We must walk forward until we are able to scoop this clear fountain water with our own hands. Such is life.

Yasuko Moritaki
10th grade girl (4th grade at the time)

When I think of what most of the people of Hiroshima suffered because of the atom bomb, my family's case is hardly worth mentioning.

We were lucky because, with the exception of Father, who remained in the city to supervise students working at a factory, we had all left the city by April, 1945. The four of us took a lot of baggage, and went to live at my folks' hometown some fifty miles from Hiroshima. My brother was in ninth grade then, and he and his class had already been evacuated to a place even farther away from the city than the place where we moved.

We lived in the village with Mother and went to school there, so since April we did not know the fear of the bombings that constantly menaced the city. We just left the city life we were used to and lived in a hut in the country. I cannot begin to tell you of all that we went through there, the unsufferable way that the people in the village treated us, the lack of food
. . . .

But all of our hardships were nothing compared with what the people of Hiroshima were faced with—forced evacuation from their homes, more and more intense air-raid drills, sometimes risking their lives to go and buy food. They were exhausted and their lives joyless.

Nature was always there to give us comfort in our sufferings. Even now, the memories I have of hardships are also accompanied by more memories than I could write down, of the beautiful and happy times we had living so close to nature.

On August 6, 1945, news reached the village that an atom bomb had been dropped over Hiroshima.

We were not able to imagine what it was like in the city from the reports we heard after that. We were most worried for Father's safety. He and the students were in what was likely to be the most dangerous part of the city, the district where the arms factories were.*

On August 23, we children went swimming in the Saijo River. When we got back up to the road from the river after our swim, we saw Father coming toward us, walking with a cane, and with bandages wrapped around his head covering one eye.

None of us remember much about what happened when we met him, or how we got him home. But even now, the sight of Father coming up the road toward us, his head wrapped in bandages, using his one good eye, and walking with a cane, is engraved on our memories. Recently I remember the scene more vividly, with the passage of time.

Father's eye could not be saved. There had been a flash of light from the bomb, and the center of his eye was pierced by a piece of broken windowpane.

At first, we thought that he might lose the other eye, too, but it was saved by medical treatment and the long rest he got in the quiet country hospital.

Father lost his eye because of the atom bomb.

My parents' four eyes were reduced to three. Still, there is an infinite difference between losing one eye and losing both.

Father told us what he had seen on the day the atom bomb was dropped as he rode on a truck from the factory to the Red Cross Hospital in the center of the city. All the houses had been destroyed and there were clouds of smoke and terrible flames everywhere. Injured people were fleeing in droves. He was not able to get to the Red Cross Hospital because the roads got too crowded for the truck to go on.

The people who found themselves surrounded by fire each thought that a bomb had been dropped on his particular neighborhood, and so everyone was running around, trying in vain to get out of danger.

In their panic, the people all ran to the rivers and the bridges. Several bridges collapsed under the weight of the people that had rushed on to them. From the river banks, people jumped into the rivers one after the other, and were drowned. It was hell on earth. And while this was going on, countless people were being roasted to death in the air-raid shelters.

In this way, a tremendous force released in an utterly evil act wiped out the lives of 247,000 innocent people.

Not long after, Japan surrendered and the war came to an end. Democracy came pouring into Japan, along with the Occupation Forces of various countries. The Japanese people accepted this democracy. They not only accepted it but completely new institutions were immediately set up to replace the old. All the world rejoiced. In Japan, too, how many people there were who rejoiced! That we had finally won true freedom! But wait, people of the world!

Do you think that we Japanese are completely happy? Do you think we have true happiness? How many innocent people were sacrificed before we won this democracy?

Was there no other way for us to win democracy than through the horror of Hiroshima? Each of the uncountable victims of the bomb carried with him the light of his own personality. Each of them was going through life step by step. At the very least, each of them had the intrinsic value as a human being.

The price we paid in order to achieve a democracy, the most important purpose of which is to insure the precious dignity of the individual, was that 247,000 individuals were reduced in seconds to the greatest indignity, that of being slaughtered. This great contradiction always gnaws at my heart.

As for the Pacific War, which came to such a miserable end, Japan's crime was very great. She was moved by a barbaric and bandit-like greed. However, the other nations are also equally at fault. Both sides used their weapons irresponsibly against the other.

The call for 'No more Hiroshimas' has been raised all over the world, and it is the heartfelt wish of all people. It is human nature to love peace.

But look at the present state of the world. We are in the shadow of an anxiety that might even be called despair. The United States has got control of the United Nations, which should be neutral, and is making it increase its military strength in the name of preventing the expansion of communist countries. The U.N. is also recruiting soldiers. Is it right that we should try to prevent a communist invasion, one that we cannot be sure will even occur, with weapons?

World War I was supposed to be a war to end all wars, but all it did was bring about World War II.

The vast amount of money which is being spent on the production of arms should be used for the recovery of the nations of the world and the advancement of civilization. If weapons are used again, more innocent people's lives will be lost and cultures destroyed.

More and more testing and production of atom bombs is going on in countries where people are crying, 'No more Hiroshimas.'

I saw a newsreel that compared Soviet and U.S. weapons. It was totally barbaric and inane. The more inhumane the weapons people use, the more degraded people become, till they are even worse than barbarians. No matter how much it seems we may be invaded, we should remember, 'Whosoever shall smite thee on thy right cheek, turn to him the other also.' We must not resist attacks with weapons. We must not make weapons for defense.

It is my strongest desire that all countries renounce war unconditionally. The fact that certain countries do not disarm is not an excuse for other countries not to disarm. I believe that the world will never have lasting peace while countries have weapons of war. Even if war settles matters temporarily, in the end it only sets the stage for the next war. World War I was proclaimed to be a war to end all wars, and that was written into the declarations of war of the countries involved. But all it did was become the cause of World War II. Why do the nations of the world still go on pursuing the same barbaric course of action, when there are many international organizations of people who want real peace in the world and are working for it, and when we have all suffered so much?

This is too much of a contradiction in this era of advanced civilization. How can the draft system in any way conform with respect for the rights of the individual? I believe that the blood flowing through my veins is the same as that which flows through the veins of all people on earth.

Let us join together, beyond the bonds of politics and nationality, to make a world filled with peace, with not even one weapon in it, where everyone has respect for all.

It is my hope that this, the wish of a young girl, will be of help in the "Study for World Peace."

*The large munitions factories in Hiroshima were all on the outskirts of the city, two or more miles from the hypocenter. The writer's father was injured by the blast from the explosion when at a munitions plant at Mukainada, a distance of three miles from the hypocenter.

"However, the big plants on the periphery of the city were almost completely undamaged and 94 percent of their workers unhurt. . . . It is estimated that they could have resumed substantially normal production within thirty days of the bombing, had the war continued." United States Strategic Bombing Survey. Summary Report (Pacific War), Vol. 4.

Akira Shinjoh
12th grade boy (6th grade at the time)

In those days, the B-29s flew almost anyplace they wanted over Japan, leaving cities in ashes. But the rumor* at the time had it that Hiroshima, along with Kyoto and Nara, would not be bombed, because it had no war industries and was famous for the beauty of its rivers. Alas! Only God could have known that Hiroshima was an ideal place to test a new weapon, the atom bomb!

I was a sixth grader at Nakajima Primary School then. Not all of the children who went to my school could be evacuated to the country. Of those remaining, children in grades one through four went to shrines and temples in the area for lessons. The fifth and sixth graders went through the motions of studying in the auditorium of Nakajima Primary School,** a wooden building covered with mortar.

On the morning of August 6, 1945, the air-raid siren sounded, but it stopped soon. Since we were all used to hearing sirens by then, we went off to school. I had just started talking to my friends by the windows on the south side of the auditorium when it happened. There was a flash of yellow light and I felt an indescribable sensation, as if I were falling into a bottomless pit. I can remember that much even now.

I lost consciousness. I do not know how much time passed before I found myself lying among some things. At the time, I was sure that the building had been directly hit by a bomb. I tried to bend my arms. They bent. Next, I tried to move my legs. They moved. I realized I was still alive. I had no difficulty in standing. It was pitch-dark. I wiped the dust out of my eyes and shouted the names of my teacher and friends over and over into the darkness. Somehow, I was able to get together with three of my friends who were going home in the same direction. One of them, N., was bleeding badly from the base of her ear. She suddenly cried out "Mother!" and started crying. I was a leader at school then, and was fairly strongwilled. I told her to be brave, and she and I went out of the school gate, along with H. and K.

About a hundred yards from the school gate, there was a house on fire. A woman in torn clothes, who looked like a mother, went running away to the north, with a child on her back. At the foot of Sumiyoshi Bridge, we saw a lot of people going off in all directions through the thick dust. Electric wires had snapped and were dangling down, and there were roof tiles all over the place. People were standing dazed in front of their houses. There was a man of about fifty lying by the side of the road, all covered with blood, his breath coming in feeble gasps. There was a loud cry for help from the inside of one of the collapsed houses. I saw all of this hell on earth, but I was not able to do anything to help. I thought only of my own family as I ran barefoot over the roofs which had fallen into the street and blocked the way. I parted with my friends one by one as I went, my anxiety for my family growing. I finally reached the door of my house. My mother and sister heard my voice and came out. When they saw me, they exclaimed, "Oh! Your head!"

I put my hand to my head and looked at it. It was sticky with blood. My sister washed off the blood in a hurry at the broken wash basin, but strangely enough, I had not been injured at all. I was shocked when I saw that my mother had a blood-soaked bandage over her left eye. I said, "Mother, what happened to your eye?" She answered, "I have lost my eye. But it doesn't matter, because everybody is home safe. I'm so glad." It was terrible! One of my mother's beautiful eyes, an eye that had been filled with love, was closed forever. Tears welled up in my eyes at my mother's words. My father and brother had managed to get home all right, though they were both badly injured.

I kept on vomiting something yellow and did not have any appetite. My mother worried that I would not be able to keep my strength up, and gave me some orange juice to drink, but I was not able to keep it down. We spent that night on the bank of the river in front of the house, anxiously watching the night sky over Hiroshima burning red until dawn.

Several days passed. Gone forever were most of the children that I had played with in the auditorium on the third floor of Nakajima Primary School that day. Most of the friends that I went out of the school gate with afterwards, injured, arm around shoulder, hand in hand, had died, too. I spent the empty days going to the funerals of my teachers and friends.

I started to feel the injuries I got when I was knocked out of the third floor, and I had to stay in bed. A few days after I was confined to bed, I saw a lot of hair on my pillow. I touched my head, wondering what was wrong, and bunches of hair came falling out. It made me sad to think that I might never have any hair again. My father's and brother's burns got worse, and they entered the former Department of Communications Hospital at Hakushima. The rest of us entered the hospital after they did. The whole family was there.

My stay in the hospital was long and hard. I hated the shots, so I cried and tried to pull away. Even now I cannot bear to think about the great big syringe that hung from the ceiling and that big needle. My white blood count went down to 800. I was told later that the doctor had told my parents that I would not live much longer, so they let me do whatever I wanted. But by the third or fourth count, the number had miraculously risen to 8,000! The doctor was amazed.

In the beds around mine at the hospital, there were people whose open wounds had rotted and were breeding maggots. There was a child of about six years old, who screamed every time the doctors peeled the gauze off his burns to treat them. Each day one or two of the people with me died, and new patients came in. They died, too. The bodies were cremated at night in the hospital yard. The wind carried the smell of the burning bodies into the rooms of the hospital. The area around the hospital must have been completely razed by fire because the train station sounded so close. I could clearly hear the lonely drawn out whistle of the trains. To me, it seemed to be the sound that the souls of the dying made when they left their bodies for the other world.

Whenever I recall those days of six years ago, which were filled with bloodshed and tears, I want to speak out and say, "May man never cause such a tragedy again!"

This is what we, the survivors of the atom bombing, truly want to shout from the bottom of our hearts.

"However, the advice and warning of Professor Franck's committee were not heeded, and the bombs were dropped on Hiroshima and Nagasaki without warning. A generalized threat had previously been issued to Japan, and thirty-five towns were specifically warned that they were open to attack. Hiroshima and Nagasaki, chosen among other things for their dense population, were not amongst them . . . ." Blackett, P.M.S., Military and Political Consequences of Atomic Energy, p. 106.
    **Approximately 1,100 yards from the hypocenter.

Mineo Yamamoto
12th grade boy (6th grade at the time)

That morning a little after eight o'clock, when I was in the school playground, I saw something like a bright swirling flash of reflected light in the eastern sky. The next instant, the ground shook as if we were having an earthquake; there was a strong blast of wind, and dust rose and made the sky dark. I ran into the building at full speed, thinking it must have been a bomb. In a little while, it got light and things settled down. I looked around the neighborhood, but there were only some windows broken in a few of the houses.

I think it was about ten o'clock when I heard people saying things like, "Koi was razed." "Kamiya-cho was razed, too." Later I heard, "Hiroshima is totally lost. The whole city is on fire." It was then that I started worrying about my brother.

He was a student at the First Hiroshima Junior High School, and had gone out to work with the Labor Service Group that morning as usual. Was he alive or dead? I had no way of knowing.

Two o'clock, then three; my brother had still not come home. My mother and I were so afraid for him that we decided to go out to meet him on his way back. We thought we would take a streetcar, but no streetcars were running so we had to walk.

Soon after we had started walking, we saw groups of people in ragged clothing coming from the direction of Hiroshima. Their faces were so scorched that we couldn't tell if they were men or women. They were fleeing the city. One of them had a five- or six-inch piece of wood stuck in one eye, but he just hurried on away from the city, without seeming to be in pain! What could have happened in Hiroshima? Imagining all sorts of terrible things, we approached Koi. We started seeing children and adults lying on the ground like so many stones. Looking closer, we saw that they were people who had been terribly burned and had fled that far, but then could go no farther. Some had already drawn their last breath. Others were crying out in agonized voices, "Help me! Please give me some water." There were children crying for their mothers, too. Walking through such awful scenes, we finally reached Koi. We were refused permission to go on from there.

There was nothing for my mother and I to do but wait there until my brother returned. Many hours passed. We gave up hope and began to go back home by the same road, dragging our heavy feet. On the way home, we met someone we knew at Itsukaichi, who told us, "Your brother got home safely hours ago." All of our sorrow disappeared with that and we hurried home. When we got home, there was my brother without a scratch on him, not even looking particularly tired.

He told us, "I bet all of my friends were killed. The house I was in came down on top of me, but I was saved because I happened to be under a desk. By the time I had crawled out, there were fires all over and there was no way for me to get home. So I went in the opposite direction, toward Hijiyama. I found myself near Hiroshima Station and walked around there a while. Then I started feeling bad and vomited a lot of un-digested rice from breakfast. I jumped into a river near there and swam across, got away to Ushita, and back to Yokogawa. A train was just getting ready to leave there, so I got on it and came back home."

But from that day on, my brother was not his usual self. He lost his appetite, and did not want to eat anything but fruit. Of course, it was difficult to get fruit in those days. One hot day, my brother went out to the sea to fish. He stayed out all day long, and that evening he suddenly said he had a head-ache and went to bed. Being outside all day killed him. It was not until the middle of September that most people were told that people who had been exposed to the atom bomb should stay out of direct sunlight. It was not until after my brother had died that we heard that people who had been exposed to atomic blasts should not exert themselves. He got worse rapidly, and his condition became critical in a few days. About half of his hair had fallen out by then. He was still clearly conscious when the doctor told us that there was no hope of saving him.

"Mother, help me, please," he said, grasping her hand and crying. "I don't want to die. Please help me." He kept calling out in pain and asking for water. About an hour before he died, he seemed to be in great pain, lifting up his body and shaking his head. It was so bad I could hardly bear to be with him. He vomited something strange; it was as big as the guts of a big fish, and I could not tell if it was coagulated blood or part of an organ, or what. Whatever it was, it must have caused him a lot of pain before he vomited it. He died shortly after that. At the time of his death, my brother did not have a hair on his head, he was completely bald.

I still do not know what the big thing my brother vomited was, a clot of blood, or something else. Whatever it was, it must have been what killed him. Maybe it was something that was formed inside his body when he breathed in the gas from the atom bomb. He died less than an hour after he vomited up the thing, at two a.m. on August 25, 1945.

He started out on his journey of death only ten days after his friend. He was thirteen years old.

high school (senior) and college

By Mrs Toshiko Akamatsu

She died two days after she came home. An elderly cousin died on the third day.
Not being able to give them a proper cremation, the old man and the old woman dug
a hole in the field and burned their bodies. "The grief; oh, the grief."

Naoko Masuoka
Student, Hiroshima Women's Junior College

H iroshima—a city reduced to a seared patch of earth in
a single instant. On August 6, 1945, a day that I will
never forget, I lost many of my beloved friends; I lost my
teachers; and the school where I had had so many pleasant
times was transformed into a pile of ashes.

The sixth of August was hot; a beautiful, cloudless day
from morning. At the time, I was in the second year of middle
school and had to go to Zakoba-cho to help clean up after
demolition of buildings under the building clearance program.

The teachers and students assembled in the school grounds and exchanged good mornings. Who would have dreamed that this was the last morning they would do so?

We left the school at seven thirty, singing "Blossoms and buds of the young cherry tree . . ." as we moved along. It must have been just after eight when we arrived at Zakoba-cho.

In those days, we carried our first-aid kits with us wherever we went. We had just put them on the ground and were standing in the work area when someone cried out, "A B-29!"

Even as this shout rang in our ears, there was a blinding flash and I lost consciousness.

I don't know how long it was before I came to, but when I did, I was lying on the ground surrounded by total darkness. The dust was so thick that I could hardly breathe. Not knowing what to do and not knowing what had happened to me, I began to feel afraid and lonely. When I tried to rise, I thought I could feel my feet touch someone.

I heard a voice wailing, "Mother, Mother, come help me!"

I was crying, too. Maybe I was just going to die like this. Maybe I was going to be burned to ashes. There was an urgent voice within me telling me that I didn't want to die. I had no idea which way to run. Before long, things around became a little clearer. I could see my friends, and I was shocked. Some were covered with blood; others were red with burns. But for the circumstances, my eyes would have turned away from them. Oily sweat oozed from my black, burned arms. There was a strange, unpleasant smell. Tears suddenly welled up in my eyes. What had we done to deserve such terrible punishment?

I started to think about my parents and my brothers—how they were and how surprised they would be to see how miserable I looked this moment.

I tottered on after the others as they ran away. I could hear voices shouting for help coming from every direction.

I saw a man screaming for help as he lay with the lower half of his body caught beneath a toppled concrete wall. None of the people running by paid him the slightest attention.

I don't know how long I wandered about like that. The city was so completely changed that I didn't know which direction was which. I came to a bridge. (Later, I learned that it was Hijiyama Bridge.) There was a horse tied to an electric light pole, all covered with blood and kicking about wildly. The sun shone down on me as I walked barefoot across the bridge and sat down near the edge of the river. No sooner had I sat down than I saw some girls from another school, all pitifully burned from head to toe.

"Water. We want a drink of water," they cried and began drinking the dirty water of the river.

"You'll die if you drink water," someone warned them from the bridge.

One of the girls, suffering terribly, jumped into the river screaming, "The faster I die, the better."

A rescue squad that happened to drive by picked me up and took me to Ujina. I was given very good first aid treatment and was then put on a boat for Ninoshima. In the boat, there was a woman with burns all over her completely naked body who writhed in agony as though she had gone mad. Our arrival in Ninoshima was the beginning of five days that I'll not forget till the day I die.

We lay on blankets spread over straw mats. Every day, people died, one here and one there, until it was nearly impossible to distinguish the living from the dead. People who had seemed full of life when I spoke to them one day would be cold, dead bodies the next morning. 'Is life so meaningless that people should die so simply as this,' I would think and I would feel forlorn, hopeless. But before I died, I wanted to see my mother and father and my brothers again, if only once.

This desire filled me completely.

On the second day, the girl lying next to me drew closer and closer to death and at last, saying only one word, "Mother," she died. Just at that moment, a lady came in, the dead girl's mother. The mother threw herself over her daughter's body and sobbed, "I looked everywhere for you, dear. I should have come here to find you sooner, but I was just a little too late, wasn't I?"

Everybody cried, and I cried, too.

I wanted to see my mother. I wanted to go home. I didn't want to wait a second longer. But there was nothing I could do.

Just after noon on the fifth day, I suddenly heard someone calling my name and opened my eyes.

"Father!" It seemed like months since I had last seen him. Tears rolled from my eyes. Father cried silently, as men do.

"Naoko, Naoko, how glad I am to find you," he said again and again.

Even today, a horrible chill goes through me when I think of what might have happened to me if Father had not come to get me.

We went home together. Our house on the outskirts of Hiroshima had not been damaged. I learned that not only my parents and brothers but also my other relatives and even our neighbors had gone looking for me every day.

Mother hugged me to her and cried. Then for two or three months, she nursed me desperately, and saved my life.

That I am alive today, I know I owe to the efforts of many people.

I really feel it strange that I am alive. Most of my friends died. Only about five in my class survived and all of our teachers were killed.

But when I see children who have lost their parents and must struggle just to stay alive, I realize how insignificant my little bit of suffering was.

Setsuko Sakamoto
Student, Hiroshima Women's Junior College

Hijiyama Hill may be rather bare, but patches of grass have come up here and there on it, showing the power of nature. I have been rather sickly since the day the atom bomb was dropped, and whenever I look up at the cream-colored quonset buildings* on the hill, frightening images of the day of the bombing flash through my mind, and I shudder. I was the only one in my class who survived.

I remember August 6, 1945. It was the day we were sent to Zakoba-cho to clear an evacuated area. We had been having terribly hot weather and everything was roasting, but we all started to work enthusiastically, hauling roof tiles and chanting to keep in rhythm. About 8 a.m., we heard the peculiar roar of a B-29 in the distance.

Our teacher shouted, "B-29! B-29!"

We looked up and suddenly there was a terrific flash of lightning. We were blinded for the moment, and in a daze. What did I see when I regained my senses? The whole area was in darkness. There were red flames licking toward the sky, getting bigger and bigger. The faces of my friends, with whom I had been working so hard minutes before, were burned and blistering, their clothes were in shreds. They wandered around shaking like frightened chicks. Our teacher gathered us up around him like a mother hen. Some of my classmates tried to bury their heads under his arms. His hair had turned white all of a sudden, and he seemed to have gotten much bigger. I kept shouting to him, "It's me, Sakamoto!"

After the third time, he nodded in recognition. Although I had lived in Hiroshima for a long time, I did not know my way around the city. So I was determined to stay close to my teacher, no matter what. But within ten minutes, I found myself standing alone in the midst of strangers. I was standing there in a daze, when I heard my friends calling me, and I joined them. Some of them were sobbing over their burned faces, some were crying out for their parents. Burned hand in burned hand, we went looking for our teacher.

The next thing I knew, we were jumping over tombstones to escape from the fire. The pine trees around us went up in flames with a crackling noise, and it looked as if we would be trapped. We did not know where to go. We just followed the crowd moving away from the flames. There were children screaming for their mothers and mothers trying to find their children. Burned people got into water storage tanks to escape the heat. We were all the color of blood. I was with another girl. We had been going along with the crowd, but for some reason or other started going in the opposite direction. We ran along the river bank until we got to a small stone bridge. It was the Fujimi Bridge. All the stores and trees that had lined both sides of the street to the bridge until that morning had been burned to the ground. Power poles had fallen over and the electric wires were on the ground. There was a baby lying on the ground by the wires, his cute little hands clenched, his eyes closed. 'Hell on earth' is the only way to describe it. My friend was going wild from the pain of her burns and her thirst. I put her on my back after we got to the Hijiyama Bridge, and we headed for the first aid station. It was just about noon when we reached the foot of Hijiyama. There were hordes of people in the shade of the trees there. They were so badly injured I could not bear to look.

As we stood there not knowing what to do, we heard,

"Enemy plane coming! Take cover in the hills!" We desperately scrambled up a steep embankment and hid in the bamboo. I suddenly felt sick, and vomited a lot of thick yellow stuff. Then I drifted off to sleep.

A voice said, "Any sick or injured here?" and I awoke to find that we had both been carried to an air-raid shelter at the Ordnance Bureau Depot and were being taken care of. When I looked out from where I was on the hill and saw all the houses in ruins, I began to worry about our empty house. About then, we happened to meet a neighbor of my friend, who arranged to have her taken away on a stretcher. I said goodbye to her. It was getting dark when I got to my house. It had been so badly damaged no one could live in it.

Our two teachers, who in spite of their own serious injuries helped us unselfishly, died because of the atom bomb, and my forty classmates died one after the other. Who but God could have known that that morning would be our last one together. On August 29, I went to visit the family of the friend I had escaped with, and spoke in tears with the bereaved family for about two hours. I was in a pitiful state then, myself. Though I was eventually able to put on my hat and go back to school again, there were things all round to remind me of my dead teachers and friends. I felt as if my heart would break when I thought of them.

Every August 6, I go back to the evacuation station at Zakoba-cho, and I visit four or five of my former classmates' homes on Buddhist All Souls' Day. This is most painful for me. After the atom bombing, I have been sensitive to changes in temperature, and suffer when it is very hot or cold. I am often sick, and sometimes wish that I had died with everyone else. It makes my mother cry to see me this way. I get injections more to relieve my anxiety than anything else. I sometimes encourage myself with the thought that the souls of the more than forty I knew who died are protecting me. When I am feeling better, I feel ashamed that I have not got more done in the life I have been allowed to continue. Above everything else, I realize that I must be determined and work hard to be worthy of my forty classmates.

* The buildings of the Atom Bomb Casualty Commission.

Toshiko Ikeda
Student, Hiroshima Women's Junior College

It has been six years since the atom bomb exploded over Hiroshima. As time passes and the city is rebuilt, even those of us who were plunged into the depths of fear and sorrow appear to have forgotten the horrors of that day. There is an old saying in Japan that 'once you have swallowed the food, you forget how hot it was.' But no, it is not true. People are simply afraid to stir up such painful memories. If they let their minds go back to that day, they would see those terrible sights before their eyes again, as vividly as if it were only yesterday. It was much too high a price to pay to end the war. Even I would like to avert my eyes from what happened on August 6.

I was a second year student at the Prefectural First Girls' High School at the time. About a week prior to the bombing, we started commuting from our homes to the Hiroshima Printing Company, located in Minami Kanon-machi, under the Student Mobilization Program. I had breakfast alone early that morning as usual.

"How was the soup?" I heard my aunt say. I put on my big air-raid hood, put my emergency bag over my shoulder, tied a band around my head, put on my wooden clogs and hurried off to the printing company. I heard a warning siren as I went along, so I tried to keep under the eaves of the houses I had to pass. I suddenly got an ominous feeling that it might be a bad day.

Before starting work, we completed a series of hard military drills with wooden rifles in the schoolyard of the Second Grammar School, the present Kanon Lower Secondary School. Then we assembled outside, at the west end of the long school building, and practiced a new song, the "Song of the Student Corps." The lyrics of the song were posted 6½ feet up on the wall, and we read them as we sang. We heard a B-29, but it sounded as if it were at a very high altitude. We all looked toward the sound to see if we could locate it. Since our attention was diverted by the approaching bomber, our voices got lower and we got out of rhythm. Just as I looked back at the lyrics, something thick and yellow and heavy flashed before my eyes, something like a huge spark. I dazedly took two or three steps toward the school building and threw myself on the ground. There was a noise like thunder that left my ears ringing painfully. I looked up and saw five or six people run to the air-raid shelter about seven yards away. It was no time to be slow! I burrowed into an empty place in the shelter over the backs of the people who had got there first. About two minutes had gone by. We all got back together again. It had only taken us seconds to scatter. We were still alive!

Somebody said, "Maybe they aimed at us because we were wearing uniforms." It was then that I noticed that the two-story school building was leaning to one side, and girls who had been doing printing work in the building were screaming. Those who managed to get out of the building were bleeding from the face and from inside their torn clothing.

"Help! Help! Help!"

I was momentarily frozen there and my heart beat fast;

I stood undecided for an instant, but then I realized that I would have to act fast if I wanted to save my own life. I went back to the printing company, apologizing in my heart to the girls for my indifference to their pleas.

The wooden buildings were in ruins. We had to climb over collapsed walls and beams with big nails sticking out of them to get to the front of the building where we worked. It was made of ferroconcrete, and was the only building left standing. A friend of mine went in and got my emergency bag, coat, and clogs for me. I looked around at my friends after I had got my things on, and saw that many of them had been burned badly on their faces, arms and legs. The burns were dark red and swollen and were only on one side of their bodies. One friend of mine, who had been only two feet behind me when we were singing, was badly burned. My hand went automatically to my own face. I was very fortunate in that I was uninjured, except that a nail had gone about a third of an inch into the sole of my right foot.

Under the direction of our teacher, we set out for the bank of the Fukushima River in groups of twos and threes. On the way, we saw a child of about three, crying, "Mummy! Mummy!" in front of a half-wrecked house. Some people were bringing bedding out of the houses and wrapping it around them, then walking along in the same direction as us.

"Little girl, would you be kind enough to lead me by the hand?" I turned around and saw an old lady of about seventy, whose head was bandaged up. Her eyes looked straight at me out of a stark, pale face. I felt a chill go down my back, but I took her hand anyway and led her to the river bank. Almost everyone there was groaning with pain.

"Aigoh! Aigoh!" some injured Koreans were crying in high-pitched voices. There was the wretched figure of someone, probably a girl, by the side of the road. She was burned so terribly that there was no hair on her head, and her head, limbs and body were swollen up to more than twice the natural size, and her skin was brownish-red and blistered. She was still uttering a faint noise. There was filth around her.

Four or five of us walked down to the sandy bank of the river and rested. Then we walked toward the mouth of the river. All along, we could hear loud banging sounds, as if fuel drums or something were exploding. There were swarms of people on the two bridges we could see from where we were standing, all moving toward Koi. Black thunder clouds appeared in the sky, and big drops of black rain came falling down.

"It's gasoline! They'll come and light it!" a man shouted. I pressed my wet jacket to my nose, but I couldn't smell any gasoline. We noticed a group of our classmates in the shelter of some hemp palms, and went and sat with them while the weird rain fell, and helped take care of one of the girls, who had a cut about an inch long on her head.

After it stopped raining, we assumed that the danger of fire had lessened and went back to the printing company. There we forced down our lunches, only to find to our distress that we had been mistaken. The whole city was in ruins. It was one big fire. We were told that it was no longer possible for us to return to our homes in the city.

We headed for Koi, to a place where our factory had been scheduled to be moved up on the hill. I still remember that we filed across the Minami Ohashi Bridge, but after that, the area had changed so that I cannot recall which road we took. The houses there were still standing somehow, but their insides and furnishings had been completely blasted away. Bedding and stuff had been laid out on both sides of the road, and on it were the hideously burned, with their grotesquely swollen bodies and dark red skin.

Three middle school students staggered slowly down the road like sleepwalkers, encouraging each other and calling for water. They had their hands up in front of their chests, with fingertips pointing down, something like kangaroos. Loose pieces of skin dangled from all over their bodies and fluttered like bits of tissue paper. The remains of their burned gaiters dragged behind them as they went, looking like sleepwalkers, encouraging each other and asking for water. They must have been students who had been mobilized to clear a site in the city where buildings were being demolished.

We met some younger students of our school (the first year students), who had been clearing the ground in the Dobashi area, at the foot of the hill at Koi. They and their teachers were suffering from terrible burns. Those among us who were still relatively strong managed to get about a half gallon of oil and went out to put it on the burns of our schoolmates to ease their pain. We tried to distinguish which of the people lying on the ground were students at our school. We got those we thought belonged to our school to tell us their names and their teachers' name before we applied the oil. Even the very seriously injured answered in distinct voices. Some of the girl students from other schools who wanted to have some oil put on them, too, would say that they were from the Prefectural First Girls' High School, but they could not give their teachers' name. It was terribly cruel, but there was so little oil and there were so many people.

The eastern horizon was turning crimson. To us, who were anxious about our dear ones and keenly felt how precarious life was, the approach of night was most unwelcome. We all went into the temporary building on the hill, laid some boards on the dirt floor, and sat down. We had our air-raid hoods on. We rested our heads on our knees and tried to go to sleep, but our minds kept reliving the horrible scenes we had experienced.

It was a sleepless night for everyone. In spite of that, I did not in any way connect the terrible things I had seen that day with my two aunts, and Keiko and Sadako. I thought I would be able to see them when morning came.

After seven the following morning, we were each given a small amount of roasted beans to take with us and wrapped them in our handkerchiefs. We went down the hill, each for her own home. The number of refugees at the foot of the hill had increased from the day before but many of them were already dead. An injured baby was sobbing feebly beside its cold, lifeless mother. "Oh . . . Oh . . . Water . . . Water . . . ."

I and four of my friends made straight for Nekoya-cho. Our faces were tense with worry about our loved ones. We walked across the streetcar bridges over the Fukushima and Tenma Rivers. We could not keep our eyes off the bloated bodies floating down the rivers. It was so frightening we could hardly keep on walking. I do not remember just when my classmates left me. Suddenly I was all alone. Near Dobashi, there were swollen bodies with gruesome faces all around. A few people had already started going from body to body in almost hopeless attempts to find their loved ones. I tried to walk with my eyes focused on the road just in front of me. I got to a place that I thought must be Dobashi, though it did not look like it. I was sure it was Dobashi, when I saw the ferro-concrete building of the Kohdoh School (then the Military Police place) on the left. There were no houses, or even any people. All I could see were piles of roof tiles that were still smoldering.

I was so shocked by the change that tears started running down my cheeks. When I opened my eyes, I noticed that there were some soldiers with picks and shovels sitting on the ground. I could not stay there for long. I was supposed to go to Kawauchi Village for my Refugee Certificate. I should be able to find out what had become of my aunts there. I started walking toward Yokogawa. I heard moans coming from the inside of a burned-out streetcar I passed on the way, a sound which pierced my heart. There was a procession of people coming from Yokogawa, looking for those who had failed to return home. I almost felt guilty for being alive when several women, whose daughters were first-year students, stopped and asked me for information. But by the time I had reached Yokogawa, even those who had been terribly injured and all the bodies charred to a reddish black were not people, but only moving objects.

I took a train from Aki Nagatsuka Station to Kawauchi Village. I rushed to the Village Office and opened the ledger. Nothing on page one, nor page two, nor page three . . . I went through the entire ledger, but I could not find the names of my aunts, or anyone who had been living with them. I was distraught, but since I could not return to the city, I hurried on to my mother's home in Yamagata.

"You're alive! You're alive!"

Everyone was glad to see me back safe, and the atmosphere in the house became bright and merry. But gladness turned to anxiety with the news that my aunts' whereabouts were unknown. A dark cloud of grief came over the house, a grief that I have carried with me in my heart ever since. Three days after I got home, Keiko arrived at the house of her relatives in Togouchi. She was alone. She died on about the fifteenth, joining her mother and aunt.

Keiko related that after she had got out from under the wreckage of the house, she called her mother, her aunt and Sadako. Only her mother answered. "I can't get out. Go and get the Military Police to help, dear."

Keiko, who was a first-year student in middle school, ran to get help from the Military Police. But when she returned, the house was enveloped in flames. I can practically see the house burning before my eyes when I think of my aunts' death.

How I longed to see Keiko again! But I was too weak to go to her. My family and I were worried sick when we heard that people who had returned, seemingly all right after the atom bombing, would suffer from loss of hair, skin blotches, bleeding of the gums, and diarrhea, and die without losing consciousness to the very end. I took plenty of vitamin C, had moxibustion treatment, and had white blood counts taken. I was much worried. Even the small wound on my foot and places where I had been bitten by mosquitoes took a long time to heal. We left my emergency bag and air-raid hood outside for two or three months to expose them to the sun and rain, because they were supposed to be contaminated. My fear of atom bomb sickness proved to be groundless. I gradually regained my health. Of the six people who were living at my aunts' house that fateful morning, I was the only survivor.

Yukihisa Tokumitsu
12th grade boy (6th grade at the time)

My house was in Osuga-cho. It was by the river, near a place called Hakushima. I had been working at a place called Mukainada, digging holes for a factory. But I was suddenly switched to building demolition work and told to be waiting near Hijiyama Bridge that particular morning. It was a hot day, with no clouds in the sky. We were already exhausted by the heat when our teacher called us to assemble. Just as we had started moving slowly into a group, somebody shouted, "Airplane!"

Looking up, we saw a B-29 flying right over our heads, but

the air-raid siren was not sounding, so we didn't worry about it. Suddenly, everything was flooded in bright light, and I felt dizzy. I do not know what happened next. When I regained consciousness, I found that I was not where I thought I had been, in the middle of the road, but was on all fours by the side of the road, where there had been a house only minutes before. After I had calmed down some, I thought, 'That bomb must have exploded right in front of me! I've got to get home! What will I do if they drop another one?' I started running toward Hijiyama Hill. When I got to the top, I looked down on the city of Hiroshima.

I felt a little queer, as if I was in a daze. I remembered only the screams of people trapped in collapsed houses that I had heard on my way to the hill. I went down the hill and started mechanically walking after the other people in the street. All the houses were in ruins. In the middle of the street in front of Hiroshima Station, there were bloated, purple bodies. There was a lady whose head was bleeding badly. A stark naked child was crying. People pinned under wrecked houses were calling for help but no one would stop to help them. Probably, everyone was too busy trying to save his own life. I was in such a hurry to get home that I felt neither fear nor pity. Was my house all right? Was it on fire?

Suddenly realizing that I would be trapped in the fire, I went to the East Parade Ground. The people there had dazed, hopeless expressions on their faces. I was exhausted so I lay down under a tree to rest. Some soldiers came up and told me to put my name on my chest. I saw some friends of mine who had burned, swollen faces. My face must have been the same, because it was getting hard for me to keep my eyes open. I got up to look for a more comfortable place to rest. As I was wandering around, I met my mother, who looked as if she had been quite badly burned, too. We crawled into an air-raid shelter. Things got dark and I passed out. The seventh and eighth of August must have gone by but I could do nothing more than tell whether it was night or day. About noon on the ninth, we were so thirsty that we had to go out of the shelter to look for water. Before we had walked very far, someone called to us. I looked around and saw some railway workers. They put us on stretchers and took us to the Railway Hospital. I was so glad I almost cried. I was taken care of at the hospital. I looked funny with my head, arms and legs all bandaged up. We were put on a railway bus and taken to a hospital in Saka Village, Aki County, where there were doctors. There were three or four funerals at the hospital every day. Not many people got well and left but the number of patients steadily decreased. I did not even feel sorry for the people who died. I was too weak to feel anything.

However, when my mother suddenly died, I felt that this earth was hell. I cried. I was indignant. Nothing I could do would help. I felt as if grief had driven me mad that night. I saw Mother in my dreams and heard her speaking to me. I awoke to face grim reality. I will never forget what my mother said before she died, "The devils are coming! The devils are coming!"

Hiroshima was literally hell. Mother must have been thinking of it when she spoke her last words. War is horrible! Why did they drop that evil bomb? These thoughts never leave me. Everyone who was close to me died. They have gone to heaven, and are looking down on us now. My good friends, the neighbors, the people at the hospital, I'll never get them out of my head. Living in a home without a mother is so lonely. I have to do all the kitchen work myself. I felt terribly sorry for my younger brother when I caught him looking enviously at our neighbor's boy who had something good to eat. He is so innocent. Why should he suffer for the wrongs of others?

Mieko Hara
12th grade girl (6th grade at the time)

The atom bomb! The atom bomb! No, I do not want to think about it! I hate to think about it! Still, it is a name I will never forget. The cruelty of it! The atom bomb! The atom bomb! I cannot stand it! Why am I living in this world? This forlorn and dismal world? This is Mieko's attempt to put into words a story of sorrow that should never be repeated. I was not in Hiroshima when the atom bomb was dropped but the shock I received from the atom bombing was huge. The Mieko that I am today, without any hopes for the future, was once under the care of two warm and loving parents. The Mieko of today is completely different from the Mieko of the past.

It was when the Pacific War was at its height. Even we in Hiroshima began to hear the cry of, "Air raid! Air raid!" We children were made to evacuate the city in groups and go to live in rural communities far from our parents. Life there was hard for me. I was an only child and though I was in the sixth grade I was still a baby at heart. Group living was almost impossible for me to bear. I would cry and my teacher would tell me off. In the evening, I would go out to the garden and sob for my mother while gazing at the stars. On August 6, a day none of us will ever forget, we were working by a beautiful stream near Mibu Primary School in Yamagata County. There was a bright flash in the sky that was followed by distant thunder. Everyone looked up in excitement. A strange looking cloud mushroomed up. A beautiful cloud! An ironic cloud!

When I heard that Hiroshima had been reduced to ashes, I was frantic. I could only think of my father and mother. No one came to see me from Hiroshima. I was so lonely and anxious that I had nightmares every night. I must have seemed to be out of my mind. My high-strung temperament could not take it. My parents, about whom I was so worried, were no longer here on earth. Nevertheless, I waited each day for them to come and get me.

The sorrow and pain that I suffered when I first learned that they were dead were beyond words. I could not believe it. Mieko had lost everything she possessed in the world. I did not want to go on living. The war ended. I had dreams, many bad dreams. My sorrow grew.

When one of the neighbors told me what my mother's last words had been, I broke down crying. I did not care if anyone saw me. I cannot write any more about it.

The smiling faces of my father and mother would momentarily appear before my eyes. I was told about my father, too, but I do not want to write about that, either.

The scene of my mother being helplessly burned to death is engraved in my mind. Many were the nights that I cried myself to sleep. A large family in a country village had me stay with them. Life with so many people was not easy. Mieko would sit down on the straw and cry when people were not looking. I could not study as I wished in the country, and I was criticized because I was no good at farm work. I was not able to relate to the life. The Mieko who had to bear such a life became depressed, a cold person who almost never smiled. The sunset in the country was beautiful. Everything there was fresh and new. I cried when I saw beautiful things. Mieko was starved for affection.

Death. The thought of death lingered in my mind. I was in sixth grade preparing for girls' high school. My parents had wanted me to go to the First Prefectural Girls' High School. I had dreamed of going there. I went to stay with my aunt in Hiroshima to take the entrance examination. Fortunately I was accepted by the school, but it did not make me feel pleased at all.

The sight of Hiroshima in ruins shocked me. There were pieces of broken china and bottles where my house used to be. Tears began to trickle down my cheeks and a vision of my mother loomed up before me.

I hate war! I hate war! The thought of such a big house coming down on top of my mother who had never had a day's illness! I do not want to talk about it any more. My sorrow only increases as time goes by. What people say about forgetting is not true. It is not as if my parents died of illness.

Oh! It was so cruel! I do not want to tell other people about it. I want to keep it a secret from everyone. The atom bomb was dropped on Hiroshima. And it was dropped on Mieko's heart, too. It hurt me so much that, though I try to live a happy, beneficial life, I cannot. I get more and more depressed.

Kenji Takeuchi
12th grade boy (6th grade at the time)

It has been six years since the end of the war. Even now, I can vividly recall the things that happened then. I shall not forget the day the atom bomb was dropped as long as I live. I lost my mother and big brother because of the atom bomb. It took away the precious lives of five of my relatives in all. The rest of us were in a state of shock when the war ended. Especially my father, who had lost both his wife and a son in an instant, had no desire to live any longer. Nonetheless, he could not bear to think of my sister and I wandering the streets as war orphans. Wiping the tears from his cheeks, he bravely started over again. My sister and I helped him. Together, we have managed to stay alive until today. We would not have been able to do it if my mother and brother had not been watching over us.

I was in sixth grade at Misasa Primary School, but on March 29, 1945, I was evacuated to some relatives' in Gono Village, Takata County. My brother, who was always good to me, got everything ready for my trip and took me to the bus terminal at Kamiya-cho. As the bus started moving, I stretched my arm out of the window and waved to him. He waved back. We went on waving until we could not see each other. That was our last farewell.

I started school in the country. We had almost no school lessons. Instead, we worked in the fields from morning until night, weeding or harvesting wheat, working for the victory of our country. People, who came to the village from Hiroshima City, told us that it was strange that Hiroshima had not been bombed, when all of the other major cities had been attacked.

On that cursed day, August 6, we had gone out into the hills to gather wood in the early morning. When we were about halfway up a hill, we saw three parachutes come falling away from two B-29s. The parachutes came closer to earth and disappeared behind the mountains. The two bombers suddenly turned, one going toward the sea, the other coming in our direction. Suddenly, there was a terrific flash and the blue sky turned white. We threw ourselves to the ground. After a pause, there was the sound of a huge explosion that shook our very bones. A strange looking white cloud came up from behind the mountains in the distance. We could see it moving rapidly; its center was bright red, and convection currents raged around. We raced down the hill to the village, where everyone was worried and rumors were spreading. A bus arrived at the village just after lunch time. The driver said that a large bomb had been dropped over the Yokogawa area. He had turned the bus around and started back at Kabe. I was a little worried, because my house was in Kusunoki-machi, near Yokogawa. About five that afternoon, a truck brought a load of injured people to the Yoshida Hospital. They were groaning in pain and were in a miserable state, and they had some kind of white ointment on their faces, arms, legs, chests and backs.

We had gotten terribly worried by the time my uncle, who had gone off on his three-wheeler to take some machines to Hiroshima that morning, showed up loaded on a truck. His shirt was burned to shreds. He got off the truck and sat down on the ground, crying bitterly. "Chiyoko (my mother), Toshio (my brother), Matsuo (my uncle's brother), Asako (my uncle's sister), and Sadako (Aunt Asako's daughter) are all dead!"

This was so sudden that I could not understand what he meant. I could not believe that my mother, brother, uncle and aunt, who had all been perfectly healthy, could have died in such a short time. As he went on with his story, though, I began to realize that it must be true and sat down on the ground. Tears came streaming down my cheeks and I could not say anything. I was twelve years old at the time and there was no way that I could stay calm in the face of such terrible news. I rolled around on the ground, crying, shouting in my heart that it was not true. It could not be true! As the story went on, I knew that it must be true.

My uncle was always fond of jokes and so I hoped wildly that it was just another one of his jokes. But no one on earth could tell a joke like this. The uncle and aunt who heard the news with me could not even find words to try to console me. They merely looked at me, aghast.

My father and sister visited me on the eleventh and I heard the details of the deaths of my mother and brother for the first time.

My sister said that my mother, father, and she were sitting

down to breakfast after having finished cleaning the house when a bright, white light, like burning magnesium, lit up the skylight of the room. Something shining brightly seemed to have fallen into the garden. As the three of them went running into the six-mat room, there was a crash (my father said it was not very loud) and the second story of the house came down on top of them. My mother ran to the left, my father and sister, to the right. (My two other sisters had already left home for work.) It rained plaster, beams and pieces of glass. My sister automatically crouched down with her hands to her head. A five- or six-inch beam fell on her leg and a nail in it stuck into her. She pulled it out somehow and crawled out of the wreckage into the light. All of the houses for as far as she could see had been leveled. Women and children were screaming. Smoke began to rise in the vicinity of Ohshiba which was due north of our house. In a matter of minutes, the entire area was in flames. My father finally crawled out and started calling for my mother. Her voice came from the very bottom of the wreckage, "My legs are caught under the bureau." My father and sister cleared away some of the rubble but there were a lot of big beams on top of the bureau, so they could not budge it. My father sent my sister to Ohshiba Park for safety. Then he got four or five of the neighbors to help him try to move the beams, using long pieces of wood as levers, but they were too heavy for them. Meanwhile, the fire was spreading, and the neighbors all left. Sparks came flying near Father. Mother put her hand out through a small gap and said in a sad voice, "It's no use. You can't save me now. Just go away and save yourself."

"What are you saying, dear? How can I leave you here alone? If I can't save you, I will die here with you," Father said, trying desperately to move the beams. My mother pleaded, "What will the children do if you die, too? Please!

Go away now!"

At that moment, about twenty soldiers lead by an officer came running by. "My wife is pinned under some beams. Please save her!" he begged on his knees. The officer went on without even answering. The house caught fire; there was the crackling sound of burning wood. It was hopeless. Father felt that he should die with Mother but he remembered her last words, "for the sake of the children, for the sake of the children."

He left her, crying loudly. When he looked back after going a little way, there was white smoke all around the house and flames were leaping out of it. He went back to the house again, but could not stay there when he remembered what she had said, and left again. Undecided, he went back and forth in front of the house many times but finally went to Ohshiba Park where my sister was waiting for him. The park was crowded with injured people, who were lying on the ground groaning and calling out for water. Their skin had blistered and the blisters had opened to expose the red tissue underneath. My sister told me they looked like red devils from hell.

My father promptly went to Tokaichi-machi where my brother had been sent for labor service. He walked around the Tokaichi and Koi areas searching for him, praying for his safety. Thousands of dying people were writhing on the ground. Some of them were burned black; some had faces swollen up like balloons. He finally found my brother in an evacuation center in Takasu on the evening of the seventh. He was in a room full of groaning people. My father later often told me how, when he first went into the room, he was not able to tell who my brother was. His face was swollen up like a balloon, just like all of the other people there. Once he had found him, he said, "Toshio! Toshio! This is your father. Can you hear me?"

Toshio nodded and replied, "Yes, yes," in a low but happy

voice.

My father talked to him quietly about Mother's death and the house. He only nodded. Then he said, "Father, please bring me a glass of water."

When he opened his mouth for Father to give him some water, Father saw that his mouth was swollen on the inside and his tongue was white. Little by little, my brother told Father what had happened. He had just taken his shirt off to work when the bomb exploded. The skin was burned off all parts of his body which had not been covered by his clothes, so he was all red and raw. Perhaps knowing that Father was there made him feel secure, and he fell asleep four or five minutes after he finished talking, never to wake again.

On the second day after my brother's death, my father and sister went back to the burned remains of our house with his ashes. It was such a sight they could not speak. They dug Mother's bones out of the ashes and spent that night there in the open. On the following morning, they were still in tears.

For sure, everyone who was in Hiroshima then and lived through the tragedy remembers it as clearly as if it were only yesterday. How many of them lost their dear ones, their houses, even the desire to go on living. The people of Hiroshima were left standing dazed in front of the burned ruins of their houses, their dirty cheeks wet with tears, the ashes of their loved ones in their hands. Gone were their parents, brothers, sisters, relatives and homes all because of the ambitions and ideology of a small group of people. How would you feel if you could see them standing there? All wars end in this way. Even a person with a heart of stone would have to avert his eyes from the sight. No words of consolation, no deeds of any kind could have possibly dried the tears running down the cheeks of those who had lost their families.

The people who took refuge in Ohshiba Park, moaning and

twisting their raw, burned bodies, calling for water through burned lips, died, praying that their children, brothers and sisters who outlived them would be able to live in peace.

It has been six years since then. The seventh annual service for my mother and brother is coming up. What are the souls of our loved ones who rest under the Atom Bomb Memorial praying for now? And my dear mother who was burned to death under our collapsed house after entreating Father to look after us children, what prayers does she say for us?

Yuriko Sakurai
12th grade girl (6th grade at the time)

Everyone in the farming village was very kind. They were a group of sincere, earnest, hard-working people. The melodious song of the people weeding the rice fields could be heard on the crisp, dry air. Apart from the dissatisfaction I felt from being separated from my family, my life in the country, where I was evacuated, was interesting and satisfying, surrounded by the trim, picturesque beauty of nature. However, one day, a sudden stroke of fate completely changed my entire world. It was a splendid morning. The sky was beautiful and the hills stood out so lovely. The girls were playing jackstones. Suddenly a pink and violet cloud, shaped like a parachute, rose in the clear blue sky. I had never seen such a cloud before. It just suddenly appeared, like out of a dream. How was I to know that it was the sneer of a cruel devil?

Two days after that, I arrived in Hiroshima. I had been happy that I would be able to see my mother but had been trying not to show it. But what did I see in Hiroshima? Bloated bodies were floating in its seven, once beautiful, rivers. The air of the razed delta city was thick with the stench of burned bodies. My high spirits were cruelly dashed. But even worse was to see the terrible change in my mother. She was wrapped up in rough cloth from the neck up, with only her eyes, nose and mouth showing. I was frightened to death. Her eyes seemed to be pleading with me, but I avoided them, and by her saw my big brother lying there looking like a bug. I wondered what my grandfather, who was in his seventies, must be thinking as he watched his daughter and grandson lying there unable to speak or move.

The following days of privation and struggle changed me. I had been spoiled and pampered because I was the youngest child in my family, but from then on, I had to work ceaselessly from morning to night, caring for, and cooking for, my sick family. On one of these days, we heard a special news program on the radio, that had lasted through everything: the voice of the Emperor himself, announcing the end of the war. Our faces became tense, and even the blank eyes of my mother showed a gleam of emotion. In the midst of all this anxiety and confusion, it was decided I was to take my ailing brother back to where I had been staying in the country. There were no longer smiles on the faces of the people there. They had suffered, too. My sister's husband was as seriously hurt as my brother. People, who had gone to Hiroshima to work in the house clearance program, returned only to die, one after the other. A deep air of gloom settled over the entire community. The people seemed to have lost even their will to work.

One hot summer day, my sister and I were walking quietly along a country lane, pulling a small cart with my brother on it. The midsummer sun was searingly hot. Suddenly the image of my mother's injured face flashed vividly through my mind, like an ill omen, and my little heart went cold. I did not have the courage to tell my sister about it. Suddenly, my brother began to sing a song. For all his effort, though, he could make only a strange, faint sound with his twisted mouth.

My mother dead—my whole world came crashing down. My mind was a dry, whirling emptiness, my emotions were paralyzed, my reason stopped working. Why had I walked for miles on a hot day to hear such terrible news? Fate did not spare this eleven-year-old girl its cruelty. I could not believe it. I did not want to believe it. What I wanted was so different from the reality . . . tears poured down my cheeks. The days of despair and unrest went on, regardless of me. Every night I would think of my mother, of her touch, her love, and the thought that she would never return tormented me. I knew I was changing. I became melancholy and gloomy, unlike other girls my age. My uncle and sister were concerned and arranged for me to enter a girls' high school in the town, starting in March the following year. My love for Mother turned into hatred of war. I devoted myself to study, to forget my torment.

A battle for existence on the scorched earth began for my grandfather, brother and myself. And I found something strange, the strength of the will to live, possessed by people who had been tormented and crushed. As the little housewife, I had to use all of my limited time to the fullest extent, cooking, washing and cleaning for the family, as well as studying. Since my grandfather passed away last summer, the three of us left, my brother and sister and I, have been praying for our mother and the thousands of other people who lost their lives for peace. The desire for everlasting peace is always with us.

When the twilight draws nigh and lies about me, I feel as if those terrible days were only yesterday, and I join those others in the world, who aspire for world peace, in a solemn prayer that such a sorrowful event is never repeated in this world of ours.

Megumi Sera
12th grade girl (6th grade at the time)

O ld Mrs. T., one of our neighbors, had come over to bor-row our stone mortar. My mother was talking to her on the veranda, holding the top of the mortar. I was in the living room, leaning against a post and folding things out of paper for my three-year-old brother. I had roasted some beans for my brother that morning, and he was eating them, one by one, out of a dish. He saw our neighbor sitting on the veranda, and went over to her, holding the dish out and saying, "Have some beans."

The bomb was dropped at that very moment. The paper sliding doors began to burn. I automatically thought, 'Water!' and ran to the kitchen. That instant, I was knocked down by the ceiling boards, plaster, pictures and things that came falling down. By the time I could get up, the fire had already been put out by the blast following the flash.

There were a few minutes of ominous silence.

"Megumi-chan! Megumi-chan!" I came to my senses at the sound of my mother's voice and rushed into the air-raid shelter in the back garden. My mother, brother, old Mrs. T., the old lady from next door, and her daughter-in-law, were there.

My mother put her arms around me and cried. I saw that my mother, brother and Mrs. T. had all been burned so badly on the right side of their bodies that the burns were blistered and raw looking. I was shocked, and ran back into the house to get some medicine. This was the first time I saw how badly the house had been damaged.

Though our house was about 2½ miles from the center of the explosion, almost nothing but the uprights were left of it. There was a huge hole in the roof, all of the ceiling boards of the sitting room were gone, and the ones in the next room were snapped upward. The sliding doors were blown down, and the plaster had come off the walls. There was a one to 1½-inch layer of broken glass and plaster on the *tatami* floor. The sewing machine, which had been in the hallway, was on its side in the middle of the sitting room. Some bed quilts, which had been hanging out in the sun on one side of the house, had been blown through the two rooms to the kitchen. My mother came nervously following after me. She stopped me from going inside the house. "A bomb fell here. It's dangerous to go in."

At the time, each of us believed that our house had received a direct hit. But I wanted to treat my brother's burns as soon as possible, so I went inside, moving cautiously, picking my way from the threshold. I could not see a bomb anywhere. Fortunately, the medicine box was undamaged, and there was medicine for burns in it. We put the medicine on everyone's burns.

Shortly after that, we heard loud voices from the street in front of the house, and we all went to see what was happening. There were a lot of people gathered around the neighborhood air-raid shelter. The M.'s house was on fire; about eighty percent of it had already burned down. Mrs. M. was running frantically around her house, shouting, "Mother must still be inside!"

Once we calmed down a little, we started worrying about the people in our family who had gone out to work. Two of my older sisters were working in a company far out in the suburbs of the city, and were sure to be all right, but my father was at the Clothing Depot, and my other big sister was at the Credit Association in Sakan-cho. Since she could get home from there in less than an hour, we knew that something must have happened. Either she had been injured, or not allowed to leave, or...worse.... Fate chose the last. The life of my 19-year-old sister and that of the Credit Association Building ended together.

About six-thirty, we got word that my eldest sister was all right, and my other sister got home around seven o'clock. I asked the people coming by, on their way to a safe place, about the Credit Association Building and the Clothing Depot, but they had no time to be concerned about other people. I could only pray for the safety of my father and sister.

My father got home about ten that evening. I was so happy that I hugged him tight and cried. It was all I could do to say, "Father, Yukiyo hasn't ...."

He must have known already. There were tears running down his cheeks.

That night, we and the neighbors put straw mats on the ground around the air-raid shelter and lay down on them. The stars were out and the sky was beautiful but we were not able to sleep because air-raid sirens kept going off.

The morning of the seventh came. My head was heavy from lack of sleep. My shoulder and thigh hurt badly. Something must have hit them when the house collapsed, but I didn't say anything about it and went out with my father to look for Yukiyo. Only a block from our house, everything had been burned down. We could see the twisted girders of the Industrial Exhibition Hall and the Fukuya Department Store. Here and there, electric power poles were still burning, and trees smoldering. We walked through the heat, around electric wires and burned trees, and finally got to Yokogawa.

We thought that Yukiyo might have returned to the main office. We walked in, but I immediately staggered back, covering my eyes. Was this the meaning of 'hell on earth?' There were burned bodies, eyes lifeless, all over the floor and on the counters. My father walked among them shouting, "Yukiyo, where are you? Is Yukiyo Sera here?" But we could not find her.

From Yokogawa we went on to the Tokaichi area. There were many bodies on the ground that had been burned black. There were the bodies of a soldier and his horse, and of a mother and her baby. But we didn't find any sign of Yukiyo.

We stopped and prayed in front of the Credit Association Building, where we thought perhaps Yukiyo had died. The prayers we had said before, for "victory," had brought us hell.

We learned that the juice of cucumbers was good for burns, but at the time cucumbers were very difficult to get. The local doctors, whose homes and clinics had been destroyed, set up an emergency treatment center at the Ohshiba Primary School. But, of course, none of them knew the best way to treat the bomb sickness, when its true nature was unknown.

Whenever he heard an airplane, my three-year-old brother would run out into the street, his arms and legs all in bandages, and shout, "Bring back my sister! Bring back my sister!"

There was no electricity for many days. When morning came, a newspaper with printing you could hardly read would be delivered. Bodies were cremated every day, in the bamboo grove near the house, on the river bed, or in the corners of fields. It made a horrible smell, and sometimes even the white smoke would come around our house. The burns of my cute little brother took a long time to get better. But even so, he was just like any boy, wanting to go out and play with the other children on the sand-banks. He took a long stick and poked holes in paper doors we had just patched. Other times, he would make us laugh by taking a piece of paper and copying what we were doing, and make gestures and sing something we could not understand.

The food situation got worse. Often we had only pumpkin

from morning to night. Once my brother said, "Mummy, I hate pumpkin," and refused to eat it, and my mother slowly turned away and wiped away her tears.

My brother's burns finally got better, but he began to suffer from diarrhea from the beginning of September. By that time, even we knew that diarrhea was one of the symptoms of radiation sickness, but they only treated him for dysentery at the clinic. He kept getting worse. It was terrible to see him suffer.

Typhoons hit our half-wrecked house. Twice there were floods. My brother, who had always been high-strung, was convinced that terrible things came out of the sky and began to be afraid of looking at the sky.

'The stars are beautiful, look at them,' I would say, but he would never look up. Whenever there were typhoons, or flood waters came near, he would stay in my mother's arms, trembling.

October came and it was cooler in the mornings and evenings, but my brother got worse. He could not get out of bed after the tenth. We went to the country to look for more nutritious food for him, but all we could find were a few eggs. My little brother, who had cursed the airplanes that had taken the life of his loving sister, and who had feared even to look at the sky, died in my mother's arms on October 22, without having known even a single pleasant moment and without a chance to be treated by a doctor. The neighbors cremated him on the river bed. It was done simply and plainly. Just a little bit of white smoke rose up . . . .

The cold winter came, making people living in the galvanized iron make-shifts suffer. The weather seemed even colder because of our empty stomachs. Nevertheless, spring came again. It had been said that for 75 years, nothing would grow on the ground that had been scorched, so when grass started coming up that spring, everyone's spirits revived. Stands selling rice soup overflowed with crowds of unemployed people from morning on. The sound of hammering began to reverberate across the razed city.

Yohko Kuwabara
12th grade girl (7th grade at the time)

Work is steadily going on to rebuild the Hiroshima that was completely destroyed in an instant. Although six years have gone by, thoughts of that day still leave me with a feeling of fierce resentment for the atom bomb which I will never forget.

It was a clear but sultry morning. The midsummer sun was so bright it almost hurt my eyes. I looked at my watch. It was already past seven. 'I'll be late for school!' I started getting ready for school in a hurry. The awful scream of the air-raid siren began to echo across the morning sky, but the all-clear signal was given soon after. I left home and rushed over the dry and dusty asphalt to the Yamaguchi-cho streetcar stop. After I had waited thirty or forty minutes, a streetcar bound for Koi pulled up, already packed. Everyone at the stop moved toward the door at once, pushing and shoving. It looked as if I would not be able to get on, no matter how hard I tried. The streetcar suddenly started off, with someone perched with only one foot on the step. Someone shouted, "Stop! Stop! It's dangerous!" The streetcar came to an abrupt stop after about five yards, and again the people struggled madly to get on. Two or three more people got on, and it started off once more. I was one of the two or three. I pushed my way through until I was standing behind the driver. Through the windshield I looked at the pedestrians hurrying on their way, and soon we got to Hatchobori.

Just then, I was blinded for a moment by a piercing flash of bright light, and the air filled with yellow smoke like poison gas. Momentarily, it got so dark I couldn't see anything. There was a loud, dull, thunderous noise. The inside of my mouth was gritty, as if there were sand in it, and my throat hurt. As it started getting lighter, I desperately tried to pull the door open, but couldn't. In the dim light, I saw an electricity pole, with severed wires dangling from it, lying in front of the streetcar. I turned around and was astonished. There was no one else in the streetcar! Everyone else had already gone out by the rear door. Electric wires lay coiled on the ground like barbed wire entanglements. Red flames were leaping from the windows of the Fukuya Department Store. I picked my way through the rubble and made it out to the main street. I saw a two-year-old child with blood all over him, crying in pain for his mother. I thought of my own mother and of going home. I looked to the east. An undescribable black thunder cloud was rolling upward. 'It's hopeless!' I thought as I stood there dumbfounded for a moment. Then I looked down at myself. Gone was the bag I had been carrying in my hand. Gone were the clogs I had been wearing. All I had left was the first-aid bag on my shoulder. I heard children crying, buildings collapsing, men and women screaming. I saw the bright red of blood and people with dazed expressions on their faces trying to get away. Where should I go? I ran after the other people. I crossed the West Parade Ground and finally found myself on the river bank behind Sentei.

Soon after, the houses on both sides of the river began to burn. I swam across the river to a strip of sand on the other side, and dropped to the ground, exhausted. The wind got stronger, and it started raining something like ink. This strange rain came down hard out of the gray sky, like a thundershower and the drops stung as if I were being hit by pebbles. All through this, sparks kept falling on me. I got up to go to the river, but a gust of wind blew me down. 'I've had it!' I lay down on my stomach with both hands over my face. Hot sparks fell on my bare feet but I could not change position to brush them off because I was afraid of being blown about by the wind. Big sparks like lumps of fire fell like rain. I couldn't take it any longer and stood up, determined to get to the water, but I was knocked down again by the strong, hot wind. How can I ever describe on paper what I went through then? Desperation and despair went through my mind one after the other.

I don't know how many hours passed after that. The hot wind had died away and it was getting dark. I wandered around by myself, looking for a place to sleep. I walked in the direction of Koi, along the street the streetcar had run on, through Hatchobori, and over Aioi Bridge. There were fires on both sides of the street.

I had a long stay in the hospital afterwards, with my parents nursing me. My life was miraculously saved, though I cannot say whether it was for better or worse.

People say that memories of the past are pleasant, but I, whose fate was completely changed by the atom bomb, will never forget the anger I feel for it, no matter how hard I try not to think of it.

What was the cause of this great tragedy? War, of course. No one wants a tragedy like this to occur again, ever, anywhere in the world. It is my hope that by telling the people of the world of the horror of the atom bomb, and the pain it caused, I will have helped in making a new, kind-hearted world, where everyone can live without fear. If such a world full of hope for everyone is to be made through the prayers and efforts of the people of the world, then it is the duty of the people of Hiroshima to have the strength and resolution to lead others in this endeavor. In closing, I want to call out, 'People of the world, do not let what Hiroshima has experienced ever be repeated!'

Yoshiko Uchimura
12th grade girl (6th grade at the time)

We heard less news about the warfronts after the spring of 1945, but the air raids increased in intensity, day and night. We were all in a terrible state of anxiety.

I was in the sixth grade. I had been going to Takeya Primary School in Hiroshima City, but all of us were evacuated en masse to Togochi-cho in Yamagata County. We were able to forget about the air raids there. We spent three happy months in the quiet countryside, until the atom bomb was dropped on August 6.

That dreadful atom bomb was dropped over Hiroshima, our home. The sky which had been perfectly clear where we were in the country that day turned dark; the sun, which had been shining brightly, became orange, and seemed to be suspended in the gray sky. We all immediately sensed that Hiroshima had been bombed.

At the time, my father, grandmother and elder sister were still living in our house (in Tanaka-machi, Hiroshima). My mother, and my younger sister and brother had been evacuated to Ku Village, Asa County, but they had returned to Hiroshima late on the fifth, only to be bombed on the sixth. My grandmother and brother were never found. My parents and sisters were trapped under the wreckage, but fortunately there was a fire station across from our house, and two or three firemen came and got them out. The firemen, who ignored their own bloody injuries while saving my family, all gave their precious lives within the next few days.

My parents and sisters managed to escape to Hijiyama that day. My mother's and elder sister's backs had been cut all over by broken glass, but my father and younger sister had escaped without a scratch. On the following day, they moved to Ku Village and rested there. My little sister's hair started falling out on August 20, and red spots appeared all over her body. She was in terrible pain, and passed away a week later.

During this time, my father went out to search for my grandmother and brother in the scorched remains of the city, every day, for ten days. Though he was getting weaker himself, he would go to the evacuation center in the east one day, and to the one in the west, the next. But he never found either of them.

My father got worse then, and he, my mother and big sister had to stay in bed. The condition of my father and sister deteriorated; it seemed to be only a matter of time now. When I got home from the country with my aunt, my father was too weak to speak. He passed away the night there were strong winds and heavy rain. I didn't know what to do, also because whenever my mother or big sister combed her hair, a lot of it came out. They had both inhaled the poison gas and had sustained many cuts, but perhaps the cuts did them good. They got better day by day, and their hair began to grow back, though it was a little kinky at first.

My mother had a total of thirty-two cuts and abrasions . . . she literally had cuts all over her body.

It will soon be the sixth anniversary of the atom bombing. Now, with war clouds looming over the thirty-eighth parallel, I hold fast to the "Prayer for Peace" in my heart. That there shall be 'No more Hiroshimas.' We have had enough war.

We must never forget Hiroshima's sixth of August, the day

of the atom bomb.

Just as the hydrogen bomb has been developed to follow on from the atom bomb, the destructiveness of wars will increase with the progress of the civilization of the world.

In the right hand, we have penicillin and streptomycin; in the left hand the atom bomb and the hydrogen bomb. Now is the time for the people of the world to consider more rationally this contradiction.

Atsuko Tsujioka
Student, Hiroshima Women's Junior College

It happened instantaneously. I felt as if my back had been struck with a big hammer, and then as if I had been thrown into boiling oil. I was unconscious for a while. When I regained my senses, the whole area was covered with black smoke. It seemed as if it were a bad dream or something. I felt stifled, I could hardly breathe. I thought I was going to die! I lay on the ground with my arms pressed against my chest, and called for help, again and again: "Mother! Mother! Father!"

But, of course, neither Mother nor Father answered me. As I was lying there quietly, accepting now the thought of death, an image of the smiling face of my little sister, who is no longer alive, came into my mind. Oh! Now I was really conscious! I could hear the other girls shouting for their mothers in the hellish darkness, and I sensed that they were getting away. I got up and just ran after them desperately. Near Tsurumi Bridge, a red hot electric wire got wrapped around my ankles. I pulled free of it somehow, without thinking, and ran to the foot of the Tsurumi Bridge. By that time, there was white smoke everywhere. I had been working in a place called

Tanaka-cho, about 600 yards from the blast center. I seemed to have been blown quite a bit north and had to take a completely different route to the bridge, which would have been straight ahead of me if I was where I should have been.

There was a large cistern at the foot of the bridge. In the tank were some mothers, one holding her naked, burned baby above her head, and another crying and trying to give her baby milk from her burned breast. Also in the tank were schoolchildren, with only their heads, and their hands clasped in prayer, above the surface of the water. They were sobbing for their parents, but everyone had been hurt, so there was no one to help them. People's hair was white with dust, and scorched; they did not look human. 'Surely not me,' I thought, and I looked down at my own hands. They were bloody and what looked like rags hung from my arms, and inside was fresh-looking flesh, all red, white and black. I was shocked and reached for the handkerchief I carried in the pocket of my trousers, but there was no handkerchief or pocket. The lower part of the trousers had been burned away. I could feel my face swelling up, but there was nothing I could do about it. I and some friends decided to try to get back to our houses in the suburbs. Houses were blazing on both sides of the street as we walked along, and my back started hurting worse.

We heard people calling for help inside wrecked buildings, and then saw the same buildings go up in flames. A boy of about six, covered in blood, was jumping up and down in front of one of the burning houses, holding a cooking pot in his hands and yelling something we could not understand. It was as much as I could do to take care of myself, so I had to go on by without offering any help. I wonder what happened to those people? And the ones trapped in the buildings. In our rush to get home quickly, the four of us were proceeding toward the center of the atomic explosion, in the opposite direction from everyone else. However, when we reached Inari-machi, we could not go any further because the bridge had been destroyed, so we headed for Futaba Hill, instead. My legs gave out near Futaba, and I almost crawled the last part of the way to the foot of the hill, saying, "Wait for me! Please wait for me!"

Luckily for us, we met some kind soldiers in white coats there, who took us to a place we could lie down and rest, and treated our wounds. They dug around and told me that they had removed pieces of tile from the back of my head. They bandaged my head for me and tried to console us by saying, "Rest here now. Your teacher is bound to come and get you soon."

However, no teacher came. (All of the teachers were seriously injured. Some died on the afternoon of the sixth, and all of the others were dead in a few days.)

The soldiers couldn't wait any longer and carried us down on their backs to their barracks at the foot of the hill. There was a Red Cross flag on the building. They took us inside and asked that we be treated immediately, but the building was already full of injured people, and we had to wait a long time for our turn. I was so weak that I could not stand in line. We were finally treated and spent the night there. The big buildings in the city were still burning. The barracks was bedlam that night, with some people calling out for mats to sleep on, and others rolling over onto burned people.

That first night ended. There were cries for water from early morning. I was terribly thirsty. There was a puddle in the middle of the barracks. I realized that the water was filthy, but I scooped up some of it with my shoe and drank it. It looked like coffee with milk. I had always been very healthy. Perhaps that was the reason why I was still in possession of all of my senses, although I had been badly injured.

I found out that there was a river just behind the barracks and went out with my shoes and drank to my heart's content. After that, I went back and forth many times to get water for those lying near me, and for the injured soldiers. My underpants got soaking wet each time, but they soon dried out in the hot sun. Mercurochrome had been painted on my burns once, and they got black and sticky. I tried to dry them out in the sun. My friends and the other people were no longer able to move. The skin had peeled off of their burned arms, legs and backs. I wanted to move them, but there was no place on their bodies that I could touch. Some people came around noon on the second day and gave us some rice balls. Our faces were burned and swollen so badly that we could hardly open our mouths, so we got very little of the rice into them. My eyes had swollen up by the third day, and I could not move around. I lay down in the barracks with my friends. I remember being in a kind of dream world, talking on and on with my delirious friends. Another time, I must have been dreaming: I thought that my father and sister were coming up the hill to get me. I was so glad that I forced my eyes open with my fingers to see, but it was dark and I could not see anything. People who came to the barracks would call out the names and addresses of the people they were looking for. My father and four or five of our neighbors had been searching for me since the bombing. They found me in a corner of the barracks at the foot of Futaba Hill, on the evening of the third day. They were able to find me because the wooden name tag my father had written for me was on my chest. The writing on the tag had been burned all the way through it, as if it had been etched.

"Atsuko! This is your father!"

I was so happy I couldn't speak. I only nodded my head. My eyes were swollen closed. I could not see my father, but I was saved.

I still have the scars from that day; on my head, face, arms, legs and chest. There are reddish black scars on my arms and the face that I see in the mirror does not look as if it belongs to me. It always saddens me to think that I will never look the way I used to. I lost all hope at first. I was obsessed with the idea that I had become a freak and did not want to be seen by anyone. I cried constantly for my good friends and kind teachers who had died in such a terrible way.

My way of thinking became warped and pessimistic. Even my beautiful voice, that my friends had envied, had turned weak and hoarse. When I think of the way it was then, I feel as if I were being strangled. But I have been able to take comfort in the thought that physical beauty is not everything, that a beautiful spirit can do away with physical ugliness. This has given me new hope for the future. I am going to study hard and develop my mind and body, to become someone with culture and inner beauty.

Science. What is science after all? The atom bomb was a product of science. Can science be said to be truly advanced through the production of things that can take away hundreds of thousands of lives at once? Science should be something that works toward the betterment of civilization. Its purpose should be to raise the standard of living. It should never be used to take away human lives. Atomic energy, also, should not be used to take lives, but to advance civilization. I hope that the disaster of Hiroshima will never be repeated, and that atomic energy will be used to create world peace. I believe that this type of dreadful experience is wholly unnecessary for mankind.

Kumiko Tamesada
12th grade girl (6th grade at the time)

In an instant, the atom bomb shattered the happiness of my family—it was when I was in the sixth grade of primary school.

I was safe because I had been moved away from my family to my grandmother's house in the country. We were told that my grandfather must have been trapped under the wreckage of the house in the city. Not even his bones were found. My brother was missing, too. We had no idea if he was alive or dead. And my dearest mother also died.

I stayed with my grandmother for a year, in the tiny house in the country where she had been living alone until then. There were three other families, all relatives of ours, living in the same house with us. Whenever I saw my cousins enjoying themselves with their parents, I would remember my dear mother and become very sad. To avoid seeing my cousins' family together, I would go off by myself, out of the back door, and into the hills behind the house. I would run around there as fast as I could. When my teacher took my class out for long walks, my friends were happy to go along but I told my grandmother that I did not want to go, and stayed inside alone. My cousins started avoiding me. But after that one hard year, I was able to live with my own family again. My father, who had escaped without injury, remarried, and so my brother and I were able to live together. I was able to smile again.

My father would tell us about the "hell on earth" after the bomb was dropped. There was a mother who was all bloody, with her dead baby in her arms. There were people whose skin had been stripped off their arms from the shoulders and was hanging from their finger tips. There were people on the ground that had been burned so badly it was impossible to tell whether they were lying on their stomachs or on their backs. There were school girls who were crying because they had pieces of glass stuck all over their backs. Everyone was trying to get out of the city to the suburbs. Those who could not walk further dropped by the side of the road or in the fields. Between gasps for breath, they screamed for water. Children with pale faces were looking for their parents and babies crying for milk clung to the dead bodies of their mothers or fathers.

Peace came at last. One evening after supper, my father, my new mother, my brother and I were listening to the radio. A preview of the movie, *The Beginning or the End?* came on. "The aircraft is approaching Hiroshima," the commentator said in a tense voice, to the sound of airplane engines. As the metallic roar of the engines got louder, the atmosphere in the room became stifling and our faces turned pale. "Stop!" my father suddenly shouted. His face was tense and white. I knew very well how my father felt then.

Now that the world is at peace, my heart feels as if it will break when I think of my mother, who died saying, "I hate America and England." We have had enough of wars.

Meisaku Ohkawa
12th grade boy (6th grade at the time)

For a long time, there was the uncomfortable mass-evacuation life, like something hanging over my head. I didn't know what to do to keep my life going. In the end, I collapsed with the work of tilling fields at the place I was evacuated to. And the two days of nursing I got from the matron in the main hall of the temple was more like a dream. My father, who hurried there and looked quite confident, took my young sister and me back to our home in Hiroshima. After we returned, my sisters and brother would never leave our side until they went to bed.

But those air-raid warnings went on without a stop. I had a sense of danger particularly on the night of August 5. I couldn't sleep until dawn and was very tired. We had breakfast at seven and my oldest sister caught the train before the one she usually took to the factory where she had been drafted to work. The next oldest sister should have gone to Zakoba-cho to do building clearance work, but instead she stayed at home because she had a headache.

It was about eight in the morning. The time of the instantaneous flash that tried to obliterate the eight members of my family from the surface of the earth had come. At that instant, all I could hear was my father shouting "Shut your eyes!" But his voice disappeared in the terrible noise of the house collapsing. Minutes or hours passed in pitch darkness, with one feeling as if his whole body was being squeezed. From their breathing, I was aware that three or four living people were near me. Over my head, there were crashing sounds as someone struggled with obstructions. Finally, my father managed to break through the roofing boards and I could see his figure climbing up as he made his way out through a bright escape hole. It was the path from death to life. I also got out and was followed up onto the roof by my young brother. My father was bleeding heavily from his head. As the three of us got out, we heard the voice of my big sister from the courtyard: "It's Father!" My mother and baby brother appeared, and then one of my young sisters. They had been in the four-and-a-half mat room directly under the second-floor room we'd been in, but there was no sign of my other little sister who'd been in the second-floor room with us. Father went back in through the escape hole.

"Michiko! Michiko!"

"It hurts . . ." a voice said faintly. We fell to digging out my sister who was completely buried. Over the face of my sister, who'd fallen face upwards, was a round, heavy post, pressing down across her face. It was heavy and didn't budge. Father used a nearby beam to try to lever the post up, but it didn't move even a fraction.

My father shouted, "A saw, quick, quick; isn't there a saw?" We all frantically pushed beams and debris aside, looking for a saw. Then my sister shouted she'd found one, near the back entrance, and came running with it. It was a charcoal saw, and father started sawing away with it—one minute, two minutes. Smoke was rising from the roof of the house three doors away, and beyond that fires were already burning brightly. The post under the lever everyone was supporting was being cut as one minute, two minutes passed, but it wasn't going very fast. Everyone's mouth was dry and our breath rasped painfully. Finally, there was a splintering sound and we all peered into the hole to see father holding my sister, who was covered with fresh blood.

Mother and all of us gasped when we saw my sister's face. It was terrible: her face was cut completely in two, from above the left eyebrow down across her nose to below the right side of her mouth. Thinking back on it, it looked like a slashed pomegranate. No hope, I thought. As Father handed her over to Mother he said, with tears in his eyes, "It may be hopeless. You must realize that just getting her out may be all we could do. Everyone got out safely, there's nothing to regret here."

"Saved, all saved. We don't need anything else; let's get away to Ohshiba Park as fast as we can."

The group of us hurried over the top of our flattened home to the road, where we found people lying around, moaning. Standing nearby, as if keeping watch on all this, was a policeman, badly burned and naked except for the tattered remnants of trousers. He was just like a sleepwalker. We managed to reach the river embankment. Almost all our neighborhood was in flames.

There were so many badly wounded on the embankment that it was difficult to move. When we got to Ohshiba Park, my father carefully explained the escape route to my mother, then he went off to his work at the first-aid station. As we reached Hazama Bridge in Nagatsuka Village, we heard a roar as two or three planes came and began circling overhead. Everyone dived into the fields. Suddenly, I found myself clinging to a large pumpkin.

When we finally got to the house of the mayor of Nagatsuka Village and received their kind hospitality, I felt most keenly that kindness is something of true value for people. In particular, I can never forget the balls of silvery rice we got.

When we reached the farmhouse, in Yasu Village, designated as our emergency refuge area, deep in the mountains, it was about eight o'clock, and dusk had settled. It was then that I first noticed my mother had cuts all over her back. I had burns on both arms and cuts on my head and back. My second oldest sister had a big wound on her back and the bleeding had dyed her shirt bright red. My young brother had countless cuts nearly all over his body and the younger sister who'd been evacuated with me had many cuts on her back and arms. The wounds of the sister we'd rescued together were horrible, terrifying even to look at.

Although he had an eight-inch gash on his head, Father came to have a look at our place but left again after less than thirty minutes.

At about nine o'clock on the night of the eighth, an air-raid warning was sounded, and Father came back on a bicycle. Saying we didn't want to die separated from each other, we lined our pillows in a row, lay down and breathlessly listened to Father's story. First and second year students of Sutoku Middle School who'd been out working at Hakushima were burned over the whole upper half of their bodies, and their eyes were so badly swollen that no matter how hard one looked they didn't look like part of a human face. Unable to see and staggering around like sleepwalkers, two or three collided with each other and fell over: the scene was like hell on earth, my father said. And he told of how out of 271 members of one part of Higashihara Village who were working in the hypocenter area, 268 never returned, so only women and children were left in that part of the village. And how on the night of the sixth in the sandpit of Ohshiba Park there was no space to walk because of the badly wounded, groaning; and how toward dawn, about five o'clock, two-thirds were dead. My father's voice faded away . . . .

Although my father said that he had written a note at the razed remains of our house, saying that we were safe and were at the refuge place in Yasu Village, my oldest sister hadn't come even by the evening of the ninth. It seems my mother didn't sleep a wink the previous night, because of her anxiety for my sister. The color of my mother's face was not that of a living human being. I thought that that is what happens when parents worry about their children, and I was grateful. At ten on the morning of the tenth, when we went to Yasu Primary School with Mother, we met my sister nearby. We were so happy we all cried.

Early in the morning of August 11, it was decided we were finally to be moved to the second place of refuge, Kanon Village in Saeki Country. On the way, we were pursued by Grummans. Mother carried my badly injured sister on her back, and we trudged along, with our various hurts and injuries, and finally reached Kanon Village. We couldn't help feeling somehow that we'd found a peaceful place to live. Mother and us seven children stayed in the house of the N.'s, a very nice, elderly couple.

Father came back for the first time on the night of the sixteenth. He looked in very low spirits, and after telling us to get in touch with him at Yokogawa Station if there was an emergency, he went straight out again.

On August 31, the work at the first-aid station settled down somewhat and Father came back home. On the first of September, he was going out to deliver the last patients, so my mother made a particularly nice packed lunch for him. He said it was the first time in a long while that he'd had a lunch fit for a human being, and he went out in good spirits. But, by about four in the afternoon, he had lost all his energy, and came staggering home. Seeing the worried look on Mother's face, we just milled around, not knowing what to do. After delivering the last thirteen patients and Ohshiba First Aid Station by truck to Honkawa, and finishing up some paperwork, Father had eaten about half of the lunch he was so proud of, and was having a rest.

Just then, when a friendly nurse offered him a glass of milk and he saw a stream of flies come out of the shallow kettle, he suddenly got a stifling feeling in his chest and made his way home in a daze.

From then on until the middle of October, Father was in agony from what was called 'atomic sickness.' There was no medicine, only some pills called 'Red Wave' recommended by the Prefectural Health Department. First nourish him, they said, so three times a day we gave him *sashimi,* roast beef and chicken soup, and kept on with this. Sometimes, we got hold of some late tomatoes. It was really at that time, though, that the number of people in our house suffering from atomic sickness grew: first my second oldest sister, then my second oldest brother, followed by my third brother, my mother and myself, so it ended up with six of us laid up in bed. Father was told by the first-aid station that the most effective treatment was injections of dextrose and Ringer's solution. This treatment had probably not been tried much in Japan. Japanese military personnel as well as doctors were surprisingly unprepared for atom bombings. Why had no treatment been announced yet? My father's motive for trying it was unexpected. Patients found that one bottle of Ringer's stopped their hair falling out. But if no pain was felt at the time the Ringer's was injected, it was too late to save that person. Of the eighty-six patients confined there, thirty-three died and fifty made a complete recovery and left hospital. The final thirteen that were transferred showed unusually good results. And my family too, by persisting with Father's treatment and nourishment, saw health return to our faces a month and a half later, in mid-October. My sister Michiko had cuts from pieces of glass in a total of 38 places, and even now the scars remain. The two brothers lost nearly all their hair, with my second brother being particularly badly affected. Since the atom bomb, his development has been retarded, and this had been a worry to the whole family.

The memories of those times are really nightmarish, and I'll never be able to forget them. Also, I must always pray to God that such a thing will not happen again.

Yoshiaki Sasai
12th grade boy (6th grade at the time)

A Letter To M

Greetings, how have you been? Six years have already gone by since we parted in Tokyo. I was very glad that you moved to Kyoto right after that, and spent your days without ever having to undergo the experience of an air raid. I experienced that atom bombing of Hiroshima just shortly after I returned there. I've told you from time to time about the days of suffering which followed. It has been six whole years since that day and another August 6 is here. Today I've decided to tell you about that day, that day I have always avoided talking about.

As you know, my family had been evacuated to the mountainous part of Takata County, and we were working hard at the job of cultivating and farming, which was unfamiliar work for all of us. I finally became ill, perhaps because the work was too strenuous. It was August 2 when I returned to our home in Hiroshima so I could be examined at the Red Cross Hospital. It almost seems as if I went there just for the atom bombing, doesn't it?

It was the morning of August 6. I had just left home with my mother on the way to the Red Cross Hospital, when we heard the sound of airplanes. We looked up, thinking how strange that there were planes when there had been no air-raid warning. The sun was shining brightly and the sky was so clear it was almost eerie. Three B-29s flew over reflecting the sun against the background of the clear blue summer sky. It was just about the time we reached the railroad crossing near Yokogawa Station that there was a blaze of light and we were thrown to the ground by the blast.

When I opened my eyes and looked around, it was hazy and dark because of the clouds of dust filling the air, so it looked as if it were close to sundown. Pieces of wood and all kinds of fragments were falling onto our heads. A large ox which had been pulling a loaded cart just a moment ago was now writhing about, and all the houses which lined the streets were crushed. Then I saw the streetcar. Passengers covered with blood were fighting their way off the streetcar, and I could hear the cries of children and the groans of adults.

Suddenly, we became concerned for the safety of the three members of our family back at home, my grandmother, younger sister and brother, and so we both started running back to our house. The voices crying for help from under the crushed houses seemed to pursue us. The bus garage had collapsed; the two-storied fire station was flattened and the four fire trucks were a sorry sight. We became more and more anxious as we rushed back toward our house, but street after street was blocked by collapsed houses and those on the verge of collapse. Given no other choice, we ran over the roofs of the crushed houses. I felt as if my heart was being torn apart as I kept running on in spite of the sounds coming from below, the sounds of crying children and their parents yelling for help, but we finally made it back to our house.

What a sight greeted us when we stepped into our house. The straw mats were heaved around and turned every which way. The windows had been blown out and furniture was scattered all around. I heard the sobbing voice of my six-year-old sister crying, "Mama, help!" She was buried underneath one of the mats. When I got the mat off of her, I found her covered with blood from the cuts on her head and face from glass fragments. I can picture that heart-rending scene even now as if it were right in front of my eyes.

My three-year-old brother was wailing loudly, buried, together with grandma who was holding him, under a pile of furniture and sliding doors. He was also bloody from a cut on his head, and Grandma seemed to be in pain from her back where she must have been hit by the blast. My mother and I put mercurochrome on the cuts of my brother and sister and bandaged them, but the white bandages became soaked with blood in no time.

It was then that we heard the voices of the firemen who were themselves injured and bleeding all over. They strained painfully to shout out their message in short blurts: "This area is about to be overtaken by fire. Everybody evacuate to Yasu Village, the designated safety area. Quickly! Hurry! Hurry!"

Mom carried my sister on her back and led grandma by the hand, and I carried my brother on my back. Both Mom and I wore air-raid hoods and short coats to cover the children on our backs. We hurried toward the designated safety area with some neighbors.

In the beginning, I had thought that the area around Yokogawa Station was the only place hit by the bomb but no matter how far we went, every house in sight was demolished. Fires had started up in the houses all around and the road, which was about fifty feet across, was engulfed in flames. We stopped and soaked our air-raid hoods and short coats with the water in the tanks provided for fires, and continued on our escape. Our clothes became bone dry in just two or three minutes so we had to stop and wet our clothes over and over again. I was thirsty and my head was throbbing with such pain that it felt like it was going to split open.

We somehow made it through this blazing inferno and finally reached the bamboo grove in Mitaki, where we let out a sigh of relief. From there, we continued further to the designated safety area, and it was dark by the time we reached our final destination, Yasu Village. I have no words to describe our feeling as we watched the city of Hiroshima burning like the fires of hell, far to the south. I'll leave that to your imagination.

In this way, the conclusion of the Pacific War was sped up by the first atom bomb dropped on Hiroshima, the Russian declaration of war on August 8, and the second detonation of an atom bomb over the city of Nagasaki; and the Great Empire of Japan collapsed completely. That flash of light, which mankind had never before experienced, reduced to ashes the city of Hiroshima on the delta of the Ohta River with its seven clear streams, once lush with green willow trees. The lives of some two hundred odd thousand innocent people came to a lamentable end.

The cry that rose up out of this antithesis of world peace was 'Don't ever let this happen again.' It was the last plea welling up from deep in the hearts of those people who lost their lives. Is it not then the duty of us young people to take up the cry of these two hundred and some thousands who died so miserably, and, making it into a plea for world peace, to begin a movement to make the date of the tragedy, August 6, a memorial day for world peace? Isn't making Hiroshima the last city to suffer from the atom bomb and bringing permanent world peace the very least we can do for those two hundred thousand victims? We must get all the people of the world to choose the path toward complete world peace, and not the road to total destruction by a Third World War. If this isn't done, it would mean that all of those two hundred thousand people died for no reason at all. We must shoulder the burden and the noble duty of seeing to it that the deaths of our mothers and fathers, brothers and sisters and grandparents are not in vain.

We, the youth of Hiroshima, experienced the tragedy of the

atom bomb with our own bodies. The atom bomb destroys the happiness and hopes of all mankind, and further, is leading mankind down the path toward destruction. Those of us who think like this continue to pray for the day when peace will reign throughout the world and all mankind can join hands and live in happiness. When the last cry of the dying citizens of Hiroshima, the plea to 'never repeat the tragedy of Hiroshima,' at last becomes the basis of a lasting world peace, then, and only then, may our deceased loved ones finally rest in peace. Vowing to work for world peace, and praying that the victims of the atom bomb rest in peace, I put down my pen.

I've rambled on quite a bit but I've not been able to say even half of what I feel. I'm sure that you are well and working hard at your studies. I pray for your brilliant success in the college entrance examinations next spring.

Yours truly,

Tohru Hara
12th grade boy (6th grade at the time)

We could not have been expected to hear that engine drone just after the all-clear that morning. The air-raid alarm had been on all night long. It was superb timing for that extra-high flying B-29. The sky over Hiroshima was perfectly clear. There could have been no better conditions for dropping the first atom bomb. Came 8:15.

Nobody had any idea that it was an atom bomb. 'Don't know what was dropped. Probably some new kind of bomb,' was what the people in the suburbs, who were spared the disaster of the direct hit, said that evening. But at that time, the conflagration was at its height in the city. Pitifully disfigured bodies of men and women, young and old, were floating in its seven rivers. The few who found themselves alive fled the city they had known for a place of refuge, leaving their names scratched on the water tanks provided for coping with fires from air raids, but which had proved to be useless for the purpose. Some had left their families behind, inside burning houses. Some had gone without heeding the cries for help that they heard coming from the wreckage of their neighbors' houses. They went, carrying with them their grief at being able to do nothing. But those cries for help are branded on our hearts, and will never leave us. After the flames of that day and night went out, Hiroshima was a city of death. What was left there was hell. Dying people lay down with their heads on train tracks. There were rows of white skeletons inside the steel frame of a streetcar. There were bones of the legs of the people who had tried to escape, sticking out of the doors.

There were junior high school children of twelve or thirteen, who had been mobilized for the Building Clearance Program, who were still barely alive, and calling out for their mothers, fathers, brothers and sisters in faint voices, without knowing that they would soon be dead. Yet others went to the rivers to cool their bodies that had been burned by the radiation of the bomb, and they died there.

For days after, smoke from the burning of the bodies drifted in the sky of Hiroshima. The sight of smoke wafting up from here and there along the river banks was enough to cause one's spirits to sink to the depths of hell. People who had forgotten even their sense of sorrow stood, watching the smoke rise, as if in a daze. And as it faded into the August sky, new grief would burst forth from their hearts. The tears they shed fell on the burned soil of Hiroshima, and were absorbed by it.

Following this period of grief, a new terror came over the people who had narrowly escaped death: radiation sickness. The radioactivity of the uranium of the bomb had penetrated the bodies of those who appeared to be uninjured, even to the marrows of their bones. Their hair fell out, their gums bled, eventually purple spots showed up all over their bodies, and they died one after the other.

The atom bomb brought death to Hiroshima. The city became a desert of white ashes. The priceless lives of three hundred thousand innocent people were claimed by heaven. That day will come again this year. Six years have gone by. The sky over Hiroshima is clear. When I look at it, I am reminded of that day. The blue of the sky seems to be reflecting the endless pain of those of us who were in Hiroshima that August 6.

There was a time when the words democracy and liberty, and also peace, were on the lips of everyone. Is it possible to call the 'peace' of Japan today, real peace? To be more specific what about that of Hiroshima? Is there true peace in Hiroshima?

There are peace campaigns, peace exhibitions, and there is that festival called Peace Day every August 6 that exploits the three hundred thousand atom bomb deaths. Who is behind them? Where were they on August 6, 1945?

As things are now, it is impossible to refute the charge that Hiroshima's title, that of "Peace Memorial City," was only meant to attract tourists. Should a "Peace Memorial City" be a mere sightseeing spot? Is it right that those pathetic keloid-stricken people be made exhibits in a show booth? Or guinea pigs in a laboratory? You visitors to the Peace Dome by the Motoyasu River! Remember that you are not looking at a side show.

The talk of dedicating Hiroshima as the Mecca of Peace died

away as soon as that City Bill was passed, and has not been heard since. Perhaps it was just as well for the three hundred thousand dead and their families, since the intention behind the plan was all too clear. It showed the whole thing up for what it was. The surviving members of the families of those who were killed by the bomb lost fathers and mothers, or sons and daughters who would have supported them. Their health is poor. And they have been left alone, without aid, these six years.

There are people who say that those three hundred thousand were sacrificed to give us peace. Have we got anything worth such a high price in return? We sought true peace. Were we not given something false in its place? Now is the time for all of us to forge true peace. First, we must create true peace, little by little, here in Hiroshima.

Six years have passed. The seventh anniversary of those killed by the atom bomb is coming. Let us meet his day solemnly and reverently. Let us pray to those three hundred thousand souls that we will achieve true peace in Hiroshima. Let us build the real City of Peace, Hiroshima, not the side-show attraction, Hiroshima, the City Destroyed by the Atom Bomb.

Once that is done, Hiroshima will have taken her first step toward becoming the Mecca of Peace.

Sumie Kuramoto
Student, Hiroshima Women's Junior College

S ince November, 1944, I had been working as a mobilized student with a certain unit stationed south of Hiroshima. The jobs we students were assigned to had become almost the same as farm work and our faces and hands were getting deeply tanned. We, girls, disliked this and each morning we would stand before the mirror in the washroom putting on our towels and straw hats. On the morning of August 6, I stood in front of the mirror looking at myself as usual when . . . .

It was just after eight in the morning, a moment I will never forget. There was a reverberant boom like an exploding shell and at the same moment a flash of orangish-yellow light came through the bullet-proof glass in the ceiling.

"A bomb!" someone screeched, and instinctively, as if by reflex, I turned to join my classmates at the rest house. It became as dark as night. A blast of wind threw me through the air and smashed me down on the flat stones. The pain of this was still shooting through me when bricks began to tumble about me. It was just like the air-raid scenes in newsreels I had seen. 'Oh, don't let anything fall on my head,' I prayed, sorry now that I hadn't put on my padded air-raid hood. As when the fog lifts, my field of vision grew gradually larger. It was an indescribably long time of pain and terror.

"Run for cover," a soldier was shouting.

Everyone ran and I ran after them. It was difficult for me to breathe and my wobbly legs wouldn't do as they were told. Finally by grabbing on to someone's back, I made it into the air-raid shelter. Soldiers, factory workers and students all sat about on chairs, their faces pale, and tried to imagine what might have happened.

Five or six of my friends arrived a little later, the color drained from their faces. Their streetcar had arrived at their stop and they were just getting off when this strange thing happened. One had her glasses blown off, another had a bundle containing her work clothes and lunch blown away by the blast, another had burns all over her face, another had burns only on one side of her face and still another had the strings burned off her first aid kit. A chill went through me when I realized that

I would have met the same fate if I had caught one streetcar later.

Back at the rest house, everyone talked about what had happened and nothing else. The ones who were unhurt were telling each other that the flash had been red, or blue, or yellow . . . . About half had burns or cuts from flying glass. My big toe was hurt and it was hard for me to walk.

"The rescue squad is going to make some rice balls so those who weren't hurt, come and help."

This was one of the many orders that were being shouted out.

A first aid station was hastily set up and injured people started coming in, both members of our squad and outsiders. Some came running in, stripped of their clothing and crying. Some had puffed-up, bloody faces. Some had burned skin dangling from their arms and legs. People who had been wearing hats had hair left only where their hats had been, making them look like river imps. All were desperate to keep their hold on life. I was disappointed because I wasn't included among the injured.

The fire truck was quickly converted into an ambulance and was racing about rescuing people.

As my excitement subsided, I began to worry about my family. In the morning, Mother had set out for voluntary labor, my big brother had gone to school and I had left for mobilized student labor, leaving my grandmother and two little brothers at home. One of my little brothers was a middle school student and went to school every other day. Today was his day off.

I was the last one to leave the house. I cheerfully said goodbye to my sleepy-eyed brothers as I went out and, throwing my first aid kit over my shoulder, ran off to the streetcar stop. I had walked about a hundred yards, when I noticed one of my brothers, the smallest one, walking after me.

"Where are you going?" I asked.

"To the shrine."

"What for?"

"To see Mommy . . . ."

"Mommy has to work today," I told him, "so you can't go to the shrine."

"No, Mommy went to the shrine," he insisted.

"You listen to what I say or you'll get caught in an air raid. You're a good boy. You'll go on home now, won't you?"

At last, he turned back and I went on to the streetcar stop just in front of the shrine. This was our family's tutelary shrine. And since my father had gone away to war, my mother had for seven whole years, come rain or snow, visited this shrine every day to pray for his well-being and victory in the war. That's why my little brother, who always tried to monopolize Mother's attention, was so sure that Mother had gone to the shrine today, too. The streetcar came and, luckily, I was able to get on. From inside the streetcar, I looked out at the groups of people who had gathered for clean-up work in connection with the building clearance program. My eyes flitted about looking over the banners and faces, wondering whether my mother had arrived yet and, before I knew it, I was at my destination.

I thought of my family, and their faces floated before my eyes one by one. 'I hope everyone is all right,' I said to myself. 'Of course, they are all right. I'll have to get home as quickly as I can and tell them about my sore toe and how I was blown ten yards by the blast. I'll make a big story of it so they will all feel sorry for me.'

But then news of the bombing started coming in. The city was a sea of flames and all traffic was stopped. The city was in total confusion. My house was probably burning, too, but it would be dangerous to try to go home since none of the roads were open. So I had to stay where I was till evening. As if they were not satisfied even with the great catastrophe they had already created, American planes passed menacingly overhead again and again. After we had waited for a long time, gripped by fear and anxiety, we were at last given permission to return home.

As we were leaving, our commander said, "If your house has burned and you can't find your family, come back right away. Bring family members with you if you want. We have plenty of food and space. Please be careful on your way."

Thankful for his words, I rushed out into the burning, sultry night and with my classmates raced toward home.

The heat that came up through the bottoms of my canvas shoes seemed about to set me afire. The electric light poles had been knocked over and were smoldering. Burned houses stood ready to collapse. Light wires were down. A bridge had fallen down and twenty or thirty injured people were lying about on straw mats near the approach to the bridge. Some people who had already died had straw mats laid over them. People who had come back home looking for their loved ones were shouting out in crazed, hoarse voices. The streetcar rails radiated an eerie light. I went to our shrine since it had been designated as the place we were supposed to meet in case of a disaster. The large *torii* gate and the stonewall looked the same as when I had caught the streetcar in the morning but the shrine itself was gone and all that remained were some smoldering electric light poles. Who could have imagined that this would happen? I was dumbfounded. In the shrine grounds, there were people lying one over another like so many lepers fallen by the wayside. Some people still breathed; others had stopped. People cried for water from here and there. It was nothing other than hell. Though I felt uneasy and anxious at not finding my family, there was still a chance that they were safe, so I told myself that I had to be brave and began walking around. Before long, I ran into my big brother and then, with him, at last made it to where the rest of our family was. With my arrival, all six members of the family had come together.

The hopes I had had about my family were in vain. Mother was lying face down near the entrance to the hillside air-raid shelter and one of my little brothers lay still without even enough strength to cry. They looked little different from the other injured people lying by the sides of the road. I was dazed and could find no words to go with the tears that flowed down my cheeks. Next to my mother and brother, who were both almost unrecognizable, was my youngest brother with a blood-stained towel wrapped about his head. He seemed to have broken his leg and was crying from the pain.

Because of their burns, Mother and my brother kept asking for water, which was a problem for the rest of us because the soldiers kept issuing orders that those with burns were not to be given any water. My big brother got some wine from the burn squad and tried to get my little brother to drink it, but he wouldn't take so much as a swallow and kept pleading for water.

"You're not supposed to drink any water, my boy," my brother kept telling him, but even as he did, he would give him a small amount at a time from the cover of his canteen.

Ominous reddish purple clouds that seemed to foretell of death covered the sky, making us feel uneasy and helpless as the night drew on. We had almost nothing with us. Mother had got one blanket and two first aid kits out of the house and we had been given a large quilt by a friend. The heat of the fires seemed to be kept from reaching the hill by the dense overgrowth of trees and summer grass so that instead of being too hot, we were in fact kept awake by the chilly air. I prayed that dawn would come soon and put an end to the unpleasant night. That the six of us had been able to get together was our only good fortune during this disaster. My toe, which had been so painful, was suddenly better.

"Teach me some English, won't you, huh?" my little brother suddenly said to our big brother.

My little brother had been studying hard for an entrance test to the military preparatory school.

"Can I go to the South Seas? . . . Uncle!" he said a little later.

Then he dropped off into what seemed to be a quiet sleep but really was death. He died peacefully without a struggle.

My big brother's anguished voice echoed through the air-raid shelter as he called to his motionless brother. The body of our brother was still warm but his soul had already left him. He died quietly and in peace.

His face, as I saw it peering through the darkness, was beautiful. My mother's brother died instantly near the blast center so that explains his final word, "Uncle!" And when he asked, "Can I go to the South Seas?" I wonder if he was going to see our father at the front?

I went to my mother's family's village to the east of Hiroshima and, learning that it had escaped the flames, though just barely, I borrowed a pushcart in the neighborhood and, together with a distant relative, returned to the air-raid shelter. When we arrived at the shrine grounds, some staff officers were just holding a conference. As we left the shrine, we prayed for the souls of the many unfortunate people who would go on sleeping again tonight.

After we had gone about three hundred yards, a soldier came out of a first-aid station and asked us where we were going.

"These are not ordinary burns," he said, "You can't treat

292 Children of Hiroshima

them at home. They're poisoned and will start rotting, and you'll die from them. You'd best go along to the emergency treatment center."

It was kind of him to give us this advice, and we were so worried by his warning that we went straight off to the center.

Fortunately, the center wasn't full yet and we were able to choose an area and settle in. The Grummans continued to attack in waves. Where a window had been there was a gaping hole about six feet square.

"All but the seriously injured to the air-raid shelter!" the soldiers were shouting.

We got ready to make a dash for a shelter but then discovered that Mother was now too weak to move. So, telling ourselves that it would be better for all of us to die together than for one of us to be killed alone, we decided not to go to an air-raid shelter at all. I and my big brother sat by the window with our air-raid hoods on. All five of us were trembling. Up to this time, my feelings had been so numbed that the B-29s and Grummans hadn't frightened me in the least no matter how many times they came over. But now, feelings, fierce feelings, awoke within me. Suddenly, I was filled with hatred and bitter resentment. Those American planes—they had injured and killed so many people and turned the whole city into a sea of flames, but they still attacked in raid after raid, plunging the people deeper and deeper into fear. Would they never be satisfied? Oh, how hateful and inhuman. It wasn't so bad for the uninjured but for those who could only lie gasping for breath, the shouts of 'Air-raid! Air-raid! Run for cover!' were like death sentences and they made the sick even sicker. Day after day, victims of the bomb passed away and more helpless injured came to join us.

Those who had no relatives to care for them would call to the soldiers again and again for water. The soldiers themselves had bandages wrapped about their heads, arms and legs. What could be more unselfish, more self-sacrificing, more admirable than what these soldiers were doing? They made me feel secure and the respect I showed for them came from the bottom of my heart.

There was nothing that a mere human could do against those nights of death, those nights of fear. Each morning, one would awake to find that someone had died on this side of him or that, over here, over there. You could sense the terror of the badly injured who, as they lay there, knew that the next morning it might be them. Those close to death nearly went mad with their suffering and ranted constantly.

The seriously injured were served rice porridge and those who were fairly well got rice balls. But both were too horrible tasting to eat so I went to Grandmother's house every day to get us food.

On the eleventh, five days after the bombing, Mother said that she wanted to go to Grandmother's house because it was so unpleasant at the center that she thought she was going to die. We arrived at Grandmother's house about eleven that evening. Really, if a person had to stay at the emergency center, he might be driven to death just by the unpleasantness of the place even though he wasn't so sick that he would die otherwise.

As all of our relatives lived in the city, their families were either wiped out completely or at least two or three of them were killed or injured. Still, I think that we suffered more than any of the rest. We, children, had had only our mother to depend on and it was terribly hard on us to have her confined to bed. At night, my five-year-old brother would start crying vigorously for Mother because of the pain from his leg and his burns and bruises. It was impossible for Mother to take him in her arms so she would just hold his hand.

Every day, I carried my brother to the emergency center

and to a bone setter just outside the city, but his injuries wouldn't heal and his whole body shriveled up till he looked like a prune.

We applied oil to my mother's burns and, every half hour, we removed the pus and applied fresh cloths that we chilled with well water. I got almost no sleep.

On August 15, about ten o'clock, we heard the sound of the National Anthem coming from the school across the street. Though it was an unusual hour for the National Anthem, we didn't take any particular notice of it at the time. But then about noon, one of our relatives stopped by to tell us that Japan had unconditionally surrendered.

"Unconditionally surrendered? Impossible!" was our response as we rejected the idea completely, but we finally had to accept it as true since it had been announced over the radio by the Emperor himself.

My astonishment and deep sadness at that moment cannot be expressed in words.

It may not have been the same with all Japanese but I think the atom bombing had even further roused the determination of the people of Hiroshima to totally destroy the Americans and the British and win victory for Japan. And in spite of this, the government was the first to knuckle under. Usually, a war comes to an end when the people give up, but with Japan it was completely the other way around.

The arrival of the occupying forces . . . . Tojo's unsuccessful attempt to kill himself with a pistol . . . .

I have no love for war but, still, I feel a real sense of injustice when I think of our young heroes, those who died in the war and those took their own lives because of the war, our young heroes who faced death with such gallantry and manliness.

One day as I was sitting on the verandah with my big

brother, I gave his hair a tug to see how easily it would come out. It came out with hardly a pull. So did mine. We were shocked by this symptom of radiation sickness. Before long, my brother was confined to bed. At the time, Mother was already suffering from radiation sickness. She had two doctors looking after her but, nevertheless, she got worse and worse. My brother's condition became critical and we thought he might die but, probably because he was young, he recovered in about a month.

Mother grew weaker day by day and her arms and legs became swollen. We, children, were so disobedient and impudent that some in the house began to grumble that we should remember that we were the guests, not they.

The time came to observe the forty-ninth day from the death of my uncle, aunt and little brother. The smoke kept rising from the crematory. There was about one death per family in the neighborhood.

School started. My big brother went back but I decided to stay home. As Mother weakened, she began to suffer from various symptoms. We got still another doctor to come by.

One of the doctors finally told us: "She'll never recover. Just let her eat whatever she wants."

"You quack!" my big brother screeched at him, and then ran out into the back yard and cried.

Only the lonely stars twinkling in the sky seemed to be our friends.

We all began to feel that there was no hope of our Mother's recovering. I felt so terribly sorry for her. I became rebellious and started taking out my feelings on everyone.

"No matter what happens, I'm not going to die before your father comes home," Mother said, contradicting the words of the doctor.

My brother who had been evacuated to the country together with his fourth grade class came home about the time, and the hundredth day from my little brother's death came around.

That same day, as though God was angry with me for resisting so long, I suddenly fainted. By evening though, I could, with great effort, lift up my head.

The priest from the temple had come and I could hear my mother's feeble voice telling him that she was still unable to get up. This was the fourth ceremony for the dead that she observed without being able to get out of bed.

It was just one week later, on the twenty-first of November, that Mother passed away—quietly, without a parting word, as though she had died a natural death. Mother had lived only for her children; she never thought of death and was certain that she would go on living. And she had so often spoken of what she was going to do when she got better . . . .

Still, the flame of life had flickered out in her and heaven's angels had come to fetch her away.

They say that a mother's love for her child outshines the child's love for his mother, and this was certainly true of our mother.

On the day the bomb fell, Mother came rushing home, putting her concern for her children above that for her own severe injuries. On her way, she came across my little brother, crying and with a towel wrapped about his head. Then, when she got home, she discovered my big brother, the one who was in middle school, standing at our gate shouting for someone to come and help. Entering the house, she found our grandmother buried under the fallen roof tiles and, after digging her out, she led the three of them to safety. If Mother had not returned to the house, these three would certainly have died and we would have probably not even been able to identify their bones.

The older of my two younger brothers had just stepped out

on the verandah to see the airplane when he was burned by the flash and then blown out onto the street by the blast. Miraculously, he was not killed, possibly because he was quite athletic. He jumped into the water tank to extinguish his burning underpants and then set about rescuing his grandmother. After he had removed two or three of the tiles, though, he realized that the job was too much for him alone and went out to the gate and shouted for help. No one came, however, since all but the children and the sick were away at voluntary labor. The fire was closing in from all directions and my brother was getting very worried. It was just then that Mother made it back.

Mother, driven by her maternal love and with complete disregard for her own safety, had made it back to the house, a feat that was all but humanly impossible. And now, so simply it seemed, she was gone from our world.

As Father had been in China ever since the China Incident, we children were especially attached to our mother. Mother stayed alive as long as she did out of the responsibility she felt toward us children. Seen objectively, it was a wonder she did not die much earlier. We, children, had been so blinded to reality as to think that it was absolutely impossible for her to die.

The priest from the temple came again. And he had the gall to tell us that he knew from the appearance of her face the last time he saw her that she was near the end.

The amount of smoke issuing from the crematory finally began to diminish from about the time Mother died. The cushions Mother had rested on were stained with oil, so we decided to burn them. In the flames, we thought we could see our mother's image and this illusion made us feel all the sadder.

The moon shone coldly through a crack in the wall.

Two days after Mother died, her sister returned from Korea. As we watched, our aunt bowed and crying before our mother's

298 Children of Hiroshima

ashes, the grief that we had been repressing at last overwhelmed us and tears flowed endlessly.

From shortly before Mother's death, there had been talk of our building a temporary house where our old one had stood and waiting there for our father to return. Thus, my big brother set out for the site of our burned down house even while he was still grieving the loss of our mother. About ten days later, the remaining three of us joined him.

We pulled logs and boards from the air-raid shelters at Hiji-yama and somehow or other put together a shack that we could live in. A man who had been one of our father's subordinates gave us five straw mats to use as a floor. It was only after we had settled into our new house that it really came home to us that we were just a group of parentless children. We were at wit's end. The family's deposit book had been burned together with the house and, because of the unsettled state we were in, we had never received any of the things that were due to us as war victims. When we thought of the small amount of money we had left, all we could do was sigh.

We got various reports concerning our father. People would cheer us up by telling us that he was well and that he would be back before long.

Grandmother seemed to have lost her resistance to infection. A scrape she had received at the time of the bombing had still not healed. She said she was ready to die as soon as she had seen our father's face. It was a hundred days after the bombing when my little brother was able to get on his feet. He had a limp though, and the burn on his head had not responded to any kind of treatment and gave off a bad smell.

Father finally made it back from the South Seas in the middle of January. His safe return from an area from which so few came back alive was the one bit of good luck among all our many misfortunes.

Feeling his responsibility as commanding officer, Father had obtained a bible by pretending to be a Christian and then kept memos concerning his subordinates in the margins. In this way, he was able to bring back the remains of over seventy dead soldiers. Although the jacket, trousers and poncho he received at Uraga were his only possessions, Father felt cold so he came home also wearing two POW uniforms that he had put on inside out. What with the way Father had changed and we had grown, it was difficult to tell that he was our father or we his children. Father had lost much weight and neither his face nor his bearing was like that we remembered. If anything, the glint that remained in his eyes made him look like a black marketeer. We were ecstatic at being able to be back with our father for the first time in four years. How I pitied our poor father though, a defeated soldier coming home to a dead wife and dead children.

Grandmother went to her final resting place at the end of February, weakened by her radiation sickness which she no longer saw the need to resist.

I returned to school for a month and received my diploma. My graduation, which should have been one of the happy moments of my life, left me feeling nothing at all. The hope of going on to high school that I had been harboring since the third year had now completely disappeared, gone like the morning mist. When I was disqualified as a member of the group that would be taking the entrance test, I and the other girls who met the same fate threw our arms around one another and cried.

Father's life in the 'match boxes' of the South Pacific had ruined his health. His body swelled up from malnutrition and he had symptoms of kidney trouble. But somehow he came through it and recovered.

We brought back the few items that we had taken to the

country for safekeeping during the war and these made our house feel a little more like a home.

About that time, the families of men who had been under my father in the army started coming around to ask what had become of their husbands and fathers. In every case, the person they were asking after had died.

They all asked the same questions: How did he die? You were short of food, weren't you? He didn't starve to death, did he?

Father's face always clouded over when he heard the word 'starve.'

Though those who had got back the ashes of their menfolk were more fortunate than the rest, I felt very sorry for all of them. For about a half year, our shack-like house was shrouded with the gloom these visitors brought with them.

For us, who had lost three of our family within half a year, the days passed bleakly. The razed area surrounding us was studded with artificial mounds and ponds, the remnants of previous gardens, and with wells, pumps and bathtubs. Occasionally, some friends who had gone on to high school would stop by, reminding me of my ill fortune. Sorrowed by not being able to continue my studies, I grew more resentful about the bomb and began to curse life itself. In the end, I even felt resentment toward my friends. Our conversations when we met became little more than empty exchanges of words.

From that time on, August 6 came to be known as Peace Day among the people of Hiroshima. For those who amassed wealth as a result of the war and its aftermath, a 'Peace Day' it may well be. And I don't deny that it might be a day for some to really sing in praise of peace. As for me, however, I feel empty at the very mention of Peace Day events and it is certainly beyond me to get into a festive mood. I pass the day in anguish.

Those who celebrate the day make no attempt to fathom the sorrow and shock of the bomb's victims, and so many of them seem, in their shallow-minded way, to think only of having a good time, even if at someone else's expense. If to celebrate Peace Day means to gorge and giggle and dance in the streets, I wish they would hold it on some other day than August 6. The sixth should be spent quietly and piously, for only in this way will those in their graves be consoled.

This was begun from 1950. As evidence of an awakening from decadence, it is to be welcomed. My little brother and all those other children with atom bomb symbols on their caps— they are growing up most satisfactorily, but I wonder about their spiritual growth.

Even leaving the matter of war aside, my convictions concerning the atom bomb will be with me till the day I die. I am repulsed by phrases like 'Hiroshima, a city cleansed by the bomb' or 'No more Hiroshimas.' The atom bomb is a more vile thing than even poisonous gas. Still, two have been dropped. And now all the preaching of God the missionaries might do will not help. It is meaningless to repeat phrases like 'No more . . . .'

What we must ask first is why people did not love their enemy.

Talk of massacres by Japanese soldiers . . . . There were exceptions on both sides and I don't think either was faultless. During the war, when I listened to news about the prisoner exchange boats on the radio, I would almost cry at the cruel treatment the Japanese had received. The Japanese themselves would all be the most warm-hearted of gentlemen. Today, those Japanese who have come to see so much in America are making much of this and using it to criticize Japan.

What nonsense! What has happened cannot be changed and the significance of it all comes solely from the participation of everyone in the war. If America had not dropped the bomb, this might have been appraised more highly, I think.

About the time that Orion began to show forth brightly, General Tojo and the other war criminals were executed. Though he had once been active as a master of blitz-like attacks, after the war he became to be despised as the central figure in a war of aggression. I can't help wondering how he felt himself, this once-great man who met such an inglorious end. I myself was angered by Tojo's death. It was only a convenient yard-stick made by human beings.

Although I never once attended the memorial service for those killed by the atom bomb, some of my friends who had still not been able to build a temporary house in the city would spend a whole day coming in from far out in the country just to attend the memorial service and pray for the members of their families who had died. That there are Japanese with such pure hearts as this is something that neither the Japanese nor the Americans should forget. A person who sticks to the path that he knows best regardless of what blows life may rain upon him is a person with a beautiful spirit. I am afraid that beauty of this kind does not exist in my own heart.

But I did have my dream, a dream that was destroyed in an instant. I have said goodbye forever to that beautiful dream, a dream that can never return, and have turned to loneliness, deliberately avoiding both the Buddhist altar and the graves of those I lost.

Now six years after that day, I still cannot totally erase the memory from my mind and I seem to be escaping into the mist of my past dream. But what is the past? What is a dream? What good is it for me to live in my past dream?

A Japanese should try to develop, using those good qualities which are special to Japanese. He should always take pride in being a Japanese and advance through life steadily and quietly, without resorting to false shows of courage. I truly believe that if we all live with the single word 'Japanese' engraved into our hearts as a guiding symbol, that then we will be able to know a utopia that rises above all suffering.

Osamu Kataoka
12th grade boy (7th grade at the time)

S ix years have gone by since the atom bomb was dropped; but six years does not seem like such a long time; it would be impossible for me to recount all of the things that we have learned, and the 'invaluable' experiences we have had. Somehow the people in my family managed to survive the inflation that took hold of Japan after we lost the war, but at one go the atom bomb took two members of our once-happy family away from us.

There is no one who does not want happiness, who does not want a peaceful life. I am certain that the one thing that everyone wishes for is everlasting world peace, and that the world never again be drawn into the terror of war, which is the way of doom. There is no such thing as rose-colored glory where there is war. The war itself ended six years ago; now that it is over, I do not want to recall any of its horrors. The tragedy brought about by the utterly inhumane atom bomb is something that cannot be recorded in ink. Those who, witnessed how the priceless lives of hundreds of thousands of people were cruelly taken away and the city of Hiroshima laid waste in an instant, have only one thing to say: "May there never be war again!"

In those days, we were already out in the schoolyard by 7:30, puttees on tight and shovels on our shoulders. After roll call, the whole school would proceed to the building clearance site. We almost never had classroom lessons, or even opened our textbooks. That was the situation at the prestigious high school we had been so proud to enter.

Students from the second year up were sent out to work at a factory in accordance with the Student Labor Project, so we freshmen were the only ones remaining at school. That day we gathered as usual in the schoolyard at 7:30 for the morning assembly. Lt. Col. So-and-so, the military officer attached to the school, instructed us on the last-ditch defense of the mainland. After that, our six classes were divided into two shifts, and work began. The odd numbered classes were sent out to the site at Zakoba-cho first, while the even numbered ones waited their turn in the classrooms. As we were doing physical labor in the hot sun, the shift was changed every half hour.

I was in an even numbered class, so I went to my classroom and started talking with my friends after the assembly. In retrospect, everyone in those days was on the verge of collapse, both physically and mentally. Hardly a night passed that was not interrupted by air raids. Most of each day was spent in some kind of heavy physical labor. With the food shortage on top of that, merely keeping alive from day to day was the most that an imperial subject of the time could manage. We had lost the energy to fool around in the classroom like ordinary high school boys. I opened my English vocabulary, but my eyes glazed over and I started looking off into space. My desk was the one closest to the window: I hunched over it, gazing at the branches of the willows in the schoolyard swaying gently in the August breeze.

Hiroshima had been on alert from midnight to some time around four in the morning on the sixth of August. We had heard B-29s many times, coming from all directions; each time, we had had to drag ourselves to the shelter. Even now, I can remember that ominous droning sound, like the engine of a car, that the B-29s made.

Father was working in the Social Welfare Section of the city government. It was the office that would be busiest in the event of an air attack, because it was responsible for the relief of attack victims. He spent most of each day at the office and had been spending more and more nights there, too. It was my job, as the youngest member of the family, to take his meals to him at the office.

After the all-clear had been given on the morning of the sixth, Father had a quick breakfast and left home for the office. I think that he was really on the shift that started at noon, but he left home at the same time as usual, a little before I went to school that morning. That was the last time we saw him.

How many people are there who had the same thing happen to them? One bomb ruthlessly claimed the lives of more than two hundred thousand people. I suspect that there are people who think, even today, that another war would be welcome. In my opinion, anyone who thinks that has unconditionally relinquished his own right to live.

It was a little after eight o'clock. Through the window, we saw the colonel returning from the work site. He was tall and thin and he walked into the teachers' room with his peculiar military gait, flicking an arrow about like a pointer. I thought that it would be our turn soon, and started getting ready, relacing my shoes and re-wrapping my puttees. I had my canteen, shovel, towel, etc.

In the meantime, a four-engined B-29, with the usual trail of white cloud, was brazenly circling above us. The all-clear had already been given and the sight of the huge B-29s was part of the daily routine in those days, so we paid no particular attention to it. There were a few boys looking up at it from the hall windows with blank expressions on their faces. But we had become so accustomed to seeing the B-29s, enemy planes though they were, that our sense of fear had diminished. No matter what came over, B-29s or Grummans, it was unlikely that a single fighter plane would go up to meet them.

I shifted my gaze from the willows to the poorly lit, dingy classroom.

A brilliant flash of light! That instant my eyes were blinded by vermilion light. I do not know how to describe it—it was as if a giant lump of celluloid had burst into flames. The building was already down. I felt clay, roof tiles and beams come falling on my head, my shoulders and my back. There was the smell of old clay, mingled with a strange, offensive odor.

I do not know how much time went by then. My breathing gradually became labored. There was a terrific stench, it almost choked me. I was buried under the school building. A direct hit! Fire! That's right! I must get out of here! I did not feel frightened. 'All right, boy!' I tried to wriggle myself loose from the things that held me by the shoulders and waist. I struggled to find a place that was light, or a gap.

Man is capable of tremendous strength when his life depends on it. The power of his will is marvelous. I could never summon that much energy again.

'I'll smother if I don't get out from under the building.' I noticed a faint shaft of light above me and thrust myself up. I broke through the building's thick ceiling boards and out into the air.

I stood on the ground of the schoolyard. Strangely, it was dark there, too. There was an acrid smell. I wet the towel I had in my belt and put it over my mouth. O., I., K., and M. came out on all fours, as I had. We stood under the willow trees, that were leaning to one side, and without thinking started reciting the Imperial Military Precept: "One. Soldiers, hold loyalty as your paramount duty. Two. Soldiers, be correct in matters of courtesy. Three. Soldiers, esteem valor." Soon, we were singing the song of our Alma Mater:

"The evening rain is white
Over Hiroshima Castle.
Faded is the flower
That was at its height.
Spring leaves with the flowing Misasa,
But . . . . "

It was a pathetic chorus, low and hoarse, and it disappeared in the black smoke and dust, and the din of the building falling apart.

In those days, we boys were taught the Imperial Military Precept instead of mathematical formulas and English words. Was the Imperial Military Precept and a shout of "Long live the Emperor!" enough consolation for our classmates who could be heard but not seen, or the friend who was burned to death because one of his legs was caught between timbers that the five or six of us could not move?

Were the friends thus burned to death consoled and happy, receiving such gifts from militarists who knew nothing about human love? The young men of the Special Attack Force volunteered to plunge to their deaths for the sake of the Emperor and the Fatherland. Did they really die contented, with smiles on their lips?

We ran to the swimming pool, dragging a classmate whose legs had been injured, and eyes blinded. What I saw there! There was already one dead in the water. He must have fallen in, blinded because of the burns all over his body. Another was trying to put out someone else's burning clothes with the blood that was gushing from his own wound. Yet another jumped into the water with his clothes on fire and drowned there, unable to move his burned body. Another was beyond recognition, with his face swollen to two or three times normal size. They could not even move any longer. I cannot forget one of them who, even then, was looking up at the sky and shouting, "Damn! Damn!" The sight is branded on my mind. What did he mean? What did he want me to do?

Our gymnastics teacher, who had been at the work site, came up to the poolside. He was swollen with burns and wearing a pair of trousers burned to rags, but his spirit was not broken.

The sight of him released our pent up emotions and we burst into tears. He encouraged us on in his strong voice, and we left the school, carrying the blind and wounded on our shoulders. The building was starting to burn. Some of our fellows who were unable to move were left behind. There may have been more trapped inside the building. Were we deserting them? No, certainly not! What else could we have done?

At that time, we were under the impression that our building had received a direct hit. So, there was bound to be a relief station nearby, and we would have them send the rescue squad to the school. But everything was on fire, no matter how far we went. There was brutally smashed house after house, all burning. There were figures that hardly looked human in the midst of it. A long line of people filled the wide road that runs from Takano Bridge to Hijiyama Bridge, moving eastward.

Two of my friends, who had been working at Zakoba-cho hung on to my arms. The surface of their bodies had been burned all over, and their skin had peeled off and was dangling loose from their elbows like the sleeves of a kimono. Their bodies slippery and red, they clung to my weak body. Their eyes were gone, and they could not see anything. They trusted me and believed that I would take them to safety and to medical care. I could not desert those two, but there were also the many others who were still at the school, believing that rescue was coming. I wondered what I should do.

Fortunately, I had not been burned, because I had been

inside of the building. (Although many who were inside were also burned.) My wounds and injuries were neglible, but perhaps because I had breathed in the fumes as I struggled to get out of the wreckage, I could not stop vomiting. My energy was completely gone. It was all that I could do to walk along, holding the other two up. From time to time, I had to sit down with my two friends and rest in the street.

We had fallen far behind the big crowd heading for Hijiyama. A mother, her child clasped to her bosom, ran by us, screaming as if she had gone mad. She was stark naked and burned and swollen all over. Her baby had already died of burns and injuries. There were schoolchildren and women who had died; their dark-purple, bloated bodies floated in the water in the ditches and water tanks by the road. There were people with only their heads sticking out of the wreckage of houses, calling for help.

I knew then what the thing called war was. It was not the world we live in, but hell. Perhaps what I saw there was worse than war on a battlefield: it was utterly cruel and horrid. Priceless human bodies were no different from the sardines' heads scattered around a fishmonger's. This horror was the greatest gift that war could give inherently decent, peace-loving people.

A rescue squad truck picked us up at the bridge at Hijiyama. I kept on vomiting as the truck swayed. I vomited until there was nothing left in my stomach, and I could not move anymore.

By the time the truck had reached the Cooperative Hospital, (the present Prefectural Hospital), in front of Koryo High School, I could not even stand up. My two friends, N. and T., were taken to the ward for burn patients. That was the last that we saw of each other. I had T.'s towel with me. I still keep it to remember him by.

I had no visible burns or wounds, and I was handled as if I were a sack of something, (which could not be helped, since

there were crowds of victims at the hospital). I was put into a suf-
focatingly hot underground shelter. In the shelter, people much
worse off than I was had been lined up haphazardly, as if they
were so many pieces of wood, with no room to move at all.

There was a man, still alive, with his abdomen ripped open,
and pinkish and yellowish intestines bulging out. He groaned
and writhed, pressing the wound with his hands, probably to
keep the rest from spilling out. There was the body of a woman
who must have died after she had been brought in (there was no
one in the shelter who could move, much less leave without
assistance, so there was no one to take the bodies away). There
was the corpse of a small child, too. Both of these bodies had
already started stinking. I had been put next to them.

I was an unusual sight in the shelter, as I had both trousers
and a shirt on, though they were torn in many places, and had
no visible wounds. I felt embarrassed just being there.

I spent a few hours there and then went out and walked
through the burning city. I cooled my body in the water tanks
on the way again and again. I went across the Takano Bridge to
Koi, and finally got to the house in Rakuraku-en that my grandmother had evacuated to. It was almost 10 o'clock at night.

I would not like to think about those days any further, they
were all too tragic and cruel. There was the instantaneous death
of my father, my radiation sickness . . . the hair coming out, the
spots all over my body. There was my elder brother's death.

In closing, I would like to quote Teiyu Amano and Al-
eksandr Gertsen. Amano says, "It is my opinion that although
the majority of the people do not want war, there is a minority,
that, while not desiring war for itself, causes war to attain a
purpose. Whether that minority be the state, a clan, or an
individual, its ultimate purpose is profit, and the killing itself,
the means to attain that purpose. Any man, who desires men to
kill one another, is no longer a man, but a devil." (*The Road to*

Live By, Hosokawa Publishing House, p. 47)

What I have related here was not concerned with the state, clan, or individual, whose "ultimate purpose is profit." It was not about the "minority," the "devil," who caused the war "to attain that purpose."

"Standing where I am, I mourn for nobody but those victims. I love nobody but those who suffer [from war]. I adore nobody but those who have been executed [by the damnable wars . . .]," Gertsen.

I have written about those, as Gertsen put it, who were victimized by the war, suffered because of it, and were executed by it. I have written about the people Gertsen "adored," the schoolboys of only 12 or 13, the housewives and respectable fathers, who were sent out to work at the building clearance site at Zakoba-cho, in the Labor Volunteer Corps and so forth, and were burned to death in that hellish flash of light; about my friend who jumped into the pool to put out his burning clothes, and died there; of another one, who yelled, "Damn! Damn!" at the sky, as he died of his burns; and the others, who were "executed," roasted, inside the collapsed school building. I have written about the mother that Gertsen "loved," who screamed as she held her innocent baby, already dead from the burns it had "suffered," to her bosom, and about the child, whose death Gertsen "mourned," who died alone in the shelter in front of Koryo High School.

Although they had lost the physical strength to appeal to us, they were clearly speaking out. What was it that they were appealing to us for? What did they want? What were they demanding?

I cannot write anymore. I cannot hold my pen any longer. I will not even read this over myself, unfinished though it is.

Mitsukuni Akiyama
12th grade boy (6th grade at the time)

A Distant Yet Clear Memory

"Remember that any parting may be the last!"

8:15 a.m. August 6, 1945. In this instant which made its mark in the endless flow of time, world history underwent a drastic change, and mankind, struck with awe, was given no other choice than to accept a new view of life. If it were possible for us to see even one second into the future, such a tragedy would have never occurred. It was a sad moment.

The weather was fantastically clear and the morning brought a deep sense of serenity with its stillness. I stretched out on the back porch and thought about all that had happened up till that time. About the two big air raids in Osaka, that metropolis which was transformed into an expanse of charred earth overnight. About those air-raid sirens which haunted us night after night until finally one night, I just lay in bed and listened to the sirens, thinking, 'why not die, as long as we can die together?' There was a moment in which our family of five held each other, huddled together in desperation at the sound of the bombs exploding nearby.

'But compared with that, what a peaceful town this is,' I thought. 'It hasn't yet once been hit by the ravages of war, and it still lies beneath this blue sky no different than before. Still it seems somewhat odd. Isn't America planning to raze Hiroshima?'

I leaned up against a post and made myself comfortable, picking up the book which I had set beside me. I opened the book. Was it this very moment? Looking back on it, I feel fairly certain that it was that very instant. Suddenly an eerie silence overtook me. My surroundings seemed to have become washed over with a gray color. It felt like sound, color, and time all came to a sudden stop. Following a sharp hiss, "Flash!" The whole yard lit up in a blaze of light. How can I describe this light, the rays of which penetrated every corner of my body and even my mind as if to say, "Take that!" The light seemed to be pure white, or rather, more like shining silver. Mother said it was red and my sister said it was golden.

They say a long row of points makes a line. Perhaps time is also made up of an endless extension of such frozen moments. If this is true, then I can say that I actually saw a frozen instant of time. I can't be sure whether the eerie silence came before or after the blinding flash. All I can say is that, within just a fraction of a thousandth of a second, an unimaginable number of incidents took place.

"Oh! A bomb! Run!" My mother cried. "Wowww . . . ," my sisters shouted. I probably gave a cry of astonishment my-self but I can't even recall the sound of my own voice. The lintel just above my head came floating down as in a slow motion movie. Not only the posts and furniture in the house, but the whole house was caving in, ever so slowly. This is actually how it happened. I saw this with my very own eyes. The posts fell down inside the gray background, and clouds of dust and dirt wafted gently upward. I feel like saying that it was all a lie, and yet it was all true.

How much time elapsed I can't say. I was sitting in the entrance way and my mother was just in front of me, while my sister was sitting inside the small three-mat room. None of us said a word. If everything up until now was just a nightmare, everything from now on was real life. This 'real life,' however, made me want to cry out, 'Please let this all be a bad dream.'

The town which was so peaceful just a few minutes before was nowhere to be found. There was nothing left of our new house which we had just moved into. My mother and I stared at each other dumbfounded. We must have temporarily been turned into complete idiots by the violent change which had just taken place. I can't even remember what our first words were when we finally did speak.

I verified this later, but there were at least three rooms between the back porch where I was first sitting, and the entrance way where I again became conscious of what was happening. This means that I went through three rooms, eight, six and three mats in size. I don't recall at all how I ran through the falling uprights and toppling furniture. Even now it makes me tremble to recall the scene.

I stood outside with my mother and two sisters. I had only a pair of undershorts on, and my mother and sisters were wearing clothes that were torn to shreds. By intention or by coincidence, I don't know which, all the people in our neighborhood gathered together in one place. We were all just staring at the most astonishing spectacle before us. "What on earth happened?" "What could be going on?" Such words, spoken by no one in particular, brought us back to the present.

"That's what I'd like to know!"

"What do you think could have happened?"

Such voices gradually became louder. But no one could answer any of these questions.

Crying lips and flailing arms and legs were gradually breaking out with the effects of burns. Masses of flesh were turning red, swelling and starting to crack. I could stand no more and I started running. I ran back to the ruins of our house and pulled a pair of my mother's work pants out of a fallen dresser. Hoping to get away from this dreadful place as fast as I could, I had just set out walking with my sisters, who were by now both covered with blood. Just as we started walking, I came across my accordion. The instrument, which I was very fond of, had been somehow thrown out into the street. I picked it up and held it tightly to me as we walked along, tears that I could not explain rolling from my eyes. We headed toward the Gion section where our elder brother lived.

I received burns on both legs in this tragedy and my older sister was burned on the face. Our aunt who lived in Nakahiro-cho was crushed to death. Her baby died crying for milk in its father's arms. Our next-door neighbor, an interesting and humorous man who had dropped in to talk to us just the day before and even that same morning, also became one of those we would never see again. As I gaze upon my ugly scars from these burns, the faces of these people appear and disappear again and again in front of my eyes, and before I know it, I find myself in tears.

We must not let such a thing happen again—such a dreadful moment which takes away the precious lives God has given and imprints an unforgettable phantom of horror. God has taught us how to forget, but how could I possibly forget that instant, that spectacle. Some people say that the only things we actually remember are nostalgic memories. I wonder whether enough years could ever pass for me to be able to look back and recall that event with nostalgia.

Hiroshi Yoshioka
University student (8th grade boy at the time)

The atom bomb brought me a burden of sorrow and grief in an instant, in accordance with a script in which I had no say. I have lived with my burden ever since. A scene out

of hell unfolded before me with that flash of light. A new,
empty and lonely life, the likes of which I had only read about
in books, began for me at 8:15 on August 6, 1945. I was a
second year student at the Prefectural Middle School. My class
was doing plowing work for cultivation at the East Parade
Ground under the Student Labor Service Program. My elder
sister, who was a fourth year student at the Prefectural Girls'
High School, was working at Toyo Industries at Mukainada,
under the Student Labor Mobilization Program. My mother
and younger sister, a fifth grader at Hirose Primary School, were
at home in Yokobori. My father had been transferred to Osaka,
and was living there alone. One of our elder brothers was at
Haiko and the other one at Seoul.

There was a flash of light and I was knocked down on to
the grass. My cap and lunch box were blown away. The grass
around me seemed to have burst into flame; I instinctively
crouched down and waited. The sheet of fire retreated; by that
time flames were shooting out of the houses. My body felt as if
it had been stung, and I discovered that the side of my face and
both hands were blistered. Fluid collected under the skin, and
the burns swelled up rapidly. I decided to go home right away
and started walking toward Hiroshima Station. There were
people so badly burned that their skin was hanging loose.
There was a woman dragging the body of what must have been
her child; it was impossible to tell if it had been a boy or a girl.
A young man with both of his legs cut off came crawling along.
I cannot imagine what state of mind I was in—to see all of those
horrors without feeling shocked or frightened, to feel nothing at
all. The entire city was on fire and I could not make it home
that day. My house was close to the center of the explosion,
and thinking about it later, it must have been blown to pieces
the moment the bomb exploded, anyway.

Early the next morning, I and two of my classmates went

into the city, getting some rice balls at an emergency food stall on the way. We walked along the streetcar tracks. Both sides of the street were lined with houses that had been leveled and were still smoldering. There were dead bodies all the way along. Arms and legs were dangling from the windows of burned out streetcars. Bodies of schoolchildren were piled up in the community water tanks, and burned bodies were floating on the Ohta River like lumps of charred flesh, with no way of telling which was the front and which the back; the air was thick with the smell of burned flesh. We walked in silence, the three of us, dragging our ragged sandals. Hatchobori and Kamiya-cho, that had been packed with houses and shops, had vanished without a trace. The railings of Aioi Bridge were down. We could see the hills of Koi from there; they looked so close it seemed as if we could almost reach out and touch them. When we got to Toka-ichi, we could see all the way to the banks of the Tenma River. We said goodbye there.

Naturally, my house had been razed. There were some crushed pans, the iron part of the mask guard of my fencing outfit and a lump of burned salt. The roof tiles were still hot enough to burn the bottoms of my sandals. I thought that my mother and younger sister had probably died in the wreckage of the house. I lifted up the roof tiles and looked for their bones, but I could not find anything. I did not know whether there was any hope for them or not. It was too much for a 15-year-old to take, but I could not even cry; I seemed to have forgotten how to. I was sure that my father would come back from Osaka, and that my elder sister was all right. I made up my mind to look for my mother, but I did not have any idea of where she might be. Every day, I walked from one receiving center to another in vain; each night, I felt almost crushed by despair and anxiety. My only thought being to keep alive, I spurred myself on. I weighed the walking, the stink, the misery, the straw mats I had to sleep on, the fatigue, against the joy I would feel when I finally found Mother, and went on searching for her.

One day, I ran into my father at Yokogawa Bridge. I was so happy to hear that both my mother and elder sister were at Toyo Industries at Mukainada, and that though they were slightly injured, neither of them had been burned. It was the happiest moment of my life. But my joy was short-lived. Though my mother's surface wounds healed, she died twenty days later from radiation sickness. What a cruel fate it was that had clutched me and would not let me go until it had sucked the marrow from my bones! I cursed all medicine, all doctors, all living things. From that time on, I began to oppose everything and be a rebel. As my mother got weaker, Japan was heading for defeat. There had been no hope for my little sister from the beginning. My mother said that she was playing with a ball outside when it happened. We still do not know what became of her, though it will soon be the seventh anniversary of that day.

The days went on without meaning. We were disconsolate. All of us children have tremendous respect and gratitude for Father, who courageously started out again and sent all three of us boys to college. We feel that we must repay him for all that he has done for us.

My elder sister acted as a mother to us three boys while we were going to school. I have many memories of the days when we four children lived together in Fukuoka. There was the special way in which people regarded motherless children; that they were disturbed because of the experiences they had had; that they were emotionally rigid; that they were precocious and impudent; that they were hard-boiled and clever at fooling people; that they were untrusting, like old people. It was hard to bear their prejudice. There is no worse childhood than having to grow up with people gazing at you with curiosity, pity, sympathy, contempt, suspicion. "No, sir! We won't be second to somebody with a mother!" was our motto those days. Looking back on those days, we can see that, though we may not have turned out as well as our mother would have wished, we have all become people with the strength to keep our spirits up no matter what, and to stay alive under any conditions.

'The dead will never return. What is left for the living to do?' This is the question for which we must find the answer. The atom bomb turned to cinders everything that was living and everything that was lifeless, but it cannot burn away the souls of us who survived and live.

Tetsuo Miyata
University student

I

Eight o'clock on the morning of August 6, 1945. I was serving as an assistant teacher in Kakogawa Village Primary School in Hiroshima Prefecture's Asa County, although I had only just left middle school; I lodged in the school. I was conscious of the fatigue caused by the long periods of air-raid alerts the previous night, but as I stood in the school playground I felt relieved that Hiroshima had not been attacked.

With the increasingly heavy incendiary bombings by the B-29s since March, Japan's cities, first one, then the next, were being reduced to ashes. How many times it happened that halfway through the night the warning would be given, and as we tightened our leggings and helmets we would think: Tonight it will be Hiroshima. At that time, Hiroshima was Japan's seventh largest city with a population of 400,000, and even amidst the tense atmosphere it was bustling and lively. With smaller cities being hit one after the other, why had Hiroshima been spared? This question that came to the mind of everyone living there appeared together with a kind of desperate irritation, a feeling of 'If it's going to happen, let it come quickly'; or there were the wishful rumors it gave rise to that Hiroshima would absolutely not be attacked by the ravages of war because its gods were giving it special protection. But when one's dreams were shattered in the night by the chill sound of the air-raid siren and we stared up into the black sky, such feelings of irritation and complacent credulity dwindled and disappeared.

The start of morning roll-call. The summer sun was already burning down, and the white-shirted figures of the lines of children dazzled the eye. The number of children evacuated to this village since spring had passed two hundred. It was certain that they and local children seated beside them had a nameless sense of foreboding. And in addition to that, what were the feelings of the children who'd been evacuated? It was already three months since they had streamed off the train at the village station, rucksack on back, holding their small roll of bedding bound with reeds, looking around at everything, as if it were all so strange to them. Even they, who during the day played happily, gathering herbs, would all gaze toward the southern sky, toward where their parents lived, as twilight came over the mountains and fields and lamps flickered on in the farm houses. The child who slipped away in the night and ran twelve miles over mountain roads back to his parents stands here today; and with their feet in sandals and burned black by the sun, the town children cannot be distinguished from the country children.

Suddenly far overhead in the sky, the roar of B-29 engines! Probably just one, or maybe two. The alarm hasn't sounded; no need to worry. It had probably just come to check on the effect of last night's air-raid. Thus were we so used to B-29 re-connaissance flights that we didn't think much about it at first. Suddenly, though, the roar changed to a high howl and we looked up without thinking. A single B-29, its huge fuselage gleaming in the direct rays of the midsummer sun, was turning sharply and tearing up into the blue, leaving a trail of vapor in the sky. Thinking about it now, everything was already over at that instant. It was at that time. A flash like lightning—no, a much more intense flash. I covered my eyes and dived onto the ground. And how much time passed then? An immense, earth-shaking, thunderous explosion. 'We've been hit! This village, this school is done for! The white shirts were too noticeable!'

"Escape!"

The children fled into the bamboo groves, scattering like so many young spiders.

It was only when I saw the bright red mushroom-shaped cloud billowing up into the azure sky way off to the south that I became conscious that we were safe. Beneath that red cloud was Hiroshima. Hiroshima had already had it. But what had been dropped? Ordinary bombs, or incendiaries? But no, it seems to have been something bigger than that. And what had happened to my sister, Fusae, under that red cloud? Had my father already reached his office? And what of my brother and his wife? My mother was supposed to be on a trip to Shikoku, so she at least was all right, but . . . I stood there alone on the exercise ground, absent-mindedly thinking all this.

II

It was in the evening of that day that the first train carrying people from Hiroshima arrived. The figure of a woman, dressed in a tattered utility suit and with a nominal strip of blood-stain-ed bandage, trudging along wearily on bare feet, but still firmly holding the hand of a wailing child. A man limping along, wounds all over his body and carrying on his back a child whose whole face was so blistered from burns that it could not see. An old woman came by, a small parcel cradled in one arm and using a hand to keep wiping away the sweat, stained brown from the blood and dust, that threatened to enter her eyes. She was wearing odd clogs she must have found somewhere and was mumbling something as she walked along, but suddenly she staggered and sat down heavily on the ground, clawed at the earth, looked up at the sky and started crying noisily, like a baby. The parcel, covered with a gray *furoshiki* cloth, was dropped and went rolling along the ground. A man, arm in a sling and looking like a laborer; inside a haversack hung carelessly from a shoulder, some rags could be seen: he was behind the old woman but went on, stepping around her and her parcel with nothing more than a quick glance.

The pitiful line of victims continued to stream toward the school. It was an eerily silent procession, a scene of wretched humanity, people who, even while in pain and trembling before a callous fate, were trying to somehow carry on living. They had no objective; all they could think of was to automatically keep following the person in front. As to where the resting place was that would receive them, or what kind of place they were heading for—such things probably never entered their mind. Even if one of those at the front had made a mistake and lost his way on a mountain road, the others would probably just have followed along without a word, gasping for breath.

The victims the school accommodated that day numbered several hundreds. It was made into a temporary first-aid station, with thin mats spread over the classroom floors. There were some—though very few—uninjured people who, with blood-shot eyes and a high, excited color to their faces, bustled back and forth along the corridors, giving shrill shouts and cries. A girl student, her face so swollen by burns it looked like she had mumps, came in, her mother leading her by the hand. When I asked them, it turned out that she'd been in school when the bomb fell, and although she'd been caught in the flames she'd walked the two miles to her home barefooted. As she lay on the matting, gripping her mother's hand, she asked in a faint voice where she was. The poor girl couldn't see. Suddenly I thought of Fusae—I hoped that she was safe somewhere . . . .

"This is the Kako River."

"I see. What's-her-name at school comes from here."

The girl, breathing so feebly, was yet in full command of her senses. Her mother just kept gripping her hand tightly. With burns over half of her body and no medicine, what could be done? To leave her fate to heaven? Was this a time to pray only to God? No, perhaps it was more true to say that no urge to pray to God arose. From the figure of the mother, who was dithering around as if possessed, no attitude of piety could be discerned.

By next morning the girl was a corpse. Except that there was a white cloth over her face, she seemed the same as before, lying there beside the other wounded and injured.

"The tears won't come. It's strange," was all her mother said.

III

I set out on foot for Hiroshima, holding a bag of rice-balls. The weather was very fine that day, too. Along the way I got a lift from a passing truck. As the truck rolled along the road to Hiroshima, raising a trail of white dust, what was I thinking and worrying about? Oddly enough, I can't recall how I felt at that time. All I can remember is that as I felt the blood racing around my body and a stifling pressure in my chest, the blood in my head would be sucked away somewhere, and this kept on happening.

There were lines of injured people along both sides of the road, and they kept on wearily trudging north, always to the north. Old people being moved on carts; children being led by the hand; a soldier hunched in the shade of a tree. The eyes of all were blank and vacant. They were like people who were not seeking anything, or who were filled with limitless desires.

Kitayama was still burning and we circled it to the right, whereupon before our eyes we saw Hiroshima—but how changed it was! In the midst of a plain of rubble stood trees and power poles, charred black by the flames; the skeletons of concrete buildings burning here and there presented a lurid spectacle. Overhead, a lone B-29 was circling, but soon after disappeared toward the south. Oh, B-29! What did you find? This field of rubble? That scorched mountain? Were you able to see the figure of the young girl near me, her whole body burned and swollen, lying as if dead, with no protection from the sizzling heat of the sun? Were you able to hear her call faintly yet clearly for her mother, her dying cry?

The unpleasant odor of bodies being burned filled my nostrils.

Picking my way between piles of rubble and dangling electricity wires, using Hijiyama Hill to orient myself, I reached home about midday. Luckily, my house was in the shadow of Hijiyama so it hadn't been burned, but it seemed so badly damaged it didn't look like somewhere you could live. My brother and his wife had just come back from one of the designated safe areas, but there was no sign of my father or Fusae.

I said the first thing that came to mind: "Father and Fusae have probably had it," though in my heart I hoped, no, I was certain, that they were all right.

We quickly left the house and went back along the road to search for the two who had not come home. The men and women who were lying by the side of the road were so burned and injured that it hard to tell them apart. I searched among them, peering into each face. I tried enquiring at two or three schools on the outskirts. They were all packed full of the injured, who overflowed into the exercise ground; but we couldn't see anyone among them who looked like the two we were looking for.

Where were Father and Fusae? Had they really had it? Or were they in some safe area somewhere we hadn't thought of. I forced myself to hang on to this vague hope; driving away the despair that threatened to overcome me, I took another mouthful of food.

When I arrived at the school the sun had already set.

IV

The second time I visited Hiroshima was on August 13, six days later. What had I been doing at the school for five whole days? And if I was looking for Father and Fusae, why hadn't I even tried to tread the soil of Hiroshima? It was a state of mind hard even for me myself to understand, now. But anyway, in the end there was nothing to do but shake off any weakness. While I was taking care of people in the school, if the two of them were alive they would probably have returned home within four or five days; if they were not back yet, I decided it meant there was no hope. Until the door of fate opened for me of its own accord, on 'life' or 'death' as the case might be, I wanted to leave it untouched. I remember the day the middle school entrance exam results were announced and I deliberately came an hour late, sneaking in to see by myself, trying to control the pounding of my heart. But while this kind of individual characteristic of mine is a thing of the past, it is a fact that my thinking at that time regarding people's deaths was different from what it is now. Of the disaster victims who had brought themselves to this school, five died yesterday and ten today. I just watched them, as if emptied of feeling. It is the evanescence of inanimate nature, as seen in the red-ripe wild persimmons which, as if drawn by something, drop one by one, in the autumn, to the earth. What a miserable death for a human being.

As I stepped inside the half-wrecked house that smelled peculiar to burns came to my nostrils. I went through into the living room with a foreboding of something bad. There was my father lying down, breathing painfully, completely transformed by the burns which covered half his face and his limbs.

The first words to leave my lips were, "What about Fusae?" "Look, over there," my mother said, then broke down crying. A single small urn wrapped in a white cloth was standing there.

"Oh, I see," I said, pretending as hard as possible to be calm, and I moved shakily into the next room, as I couldn't bear to stay there any more. Fusae's desk was there. Two or three of the girls' novels she used to like reading were scattered carelessly around. Inside a drawer were her notebooks and school texts and her diary, containing the dreams of a sweet, innocent girl, all just as she left them. It was then, for the first time, that it came home to me that I'd lost someone. My choking gasps changed to wracking sobs.

"Fusae, Fusae; you're not here any more. No matter where I go in the world, I can never meet you again."

She was a thin, sickly girl, always catching colds and having to miss school. And she was nervous, too, susceptible, but she also had a wild side. It may have been because she was the youngest. My next brother was a full six years older than me, and when I was in the fourth grade of primary school he went to school in Tokyo, so after that it was just the two of us, Fusae and myself. We used to play a lot, but we also used to fight a lot. She liked to win, and seldom screamed about a little hit, but when she did cry it was in such a loud voice that I'd shut up. After she entered girls' school, she suddenly became a bit precocious; but even then, in those pure eyes there was always a touch of playfulness, and that never changed. One day, I remember, we went to Grandmother's place to play. I was a rather bashful boy and was somehow embarrassed walking together with her, so I couldn't help issuing a 'categorical imperative'—"You must walk five yards behind me." Commendably, perhaps because she understood the feelings of this poor middle-school student, she followed along disconsolately, never saying anything about it being unfair.

When she became a third-year student this spring, she was drafted under the Student Mobilization Program to work on the communications staff of the Hiroshima division general headquarters.

Fusae had died. Her life had ended when she was fourteen years and some months old. Thinking about it, the last time we'd met was August 4. That was a Saturday so I'd returned home for the first time in some days. She was wearing her work trousers and busily helping with the dinner.

"Oh, welcome home, Tetsuo," she said, turning around, with that special smile of hers. Her black hair round her shoulders and neatly tied looked so adult.

"Got my salary. I'll give you ten yen." I drew a ten-yen note from my forty-five yen pay packet and thrust it in front of her eyes. She protested that she didn't need it, but I forced it into her pocket. That ten-yen note probably stayed in her pocket right to the end. On Sunday, the next day, while I was still in bed, she went out in high spirits for a 24-hour work stint. Behind her, she left the home she could never return to. It was while she was on standby in the underground communications room that she was bathed in that attack. Fortunately, she did not receive any injury and she quickly tried to crawl out of the underground room through the escape hatch, but the flames were already everywhere. As the flames came nearer, she and her friends were forced to jump into the river at the back, but she was a sickly girl and didn't know how to swim. Somewhere, though, she'd picked up a wooden bucket and was clutching it. But how cruel fate is, for she let go of that bucket which meant life to her. She called frantically for help, but there was no one to extend a helping hand.

Thus it was that she drowned.

On the morning of the eighth, a first-aid worker recovered her body downstream, where it had fetched up against a support of Yanagi Bridge; she was promptly cremated.

My mother came back to Hiroshima that day and without pausing for rest wandered aimlessly through the scorched plain, calling Fusae's name. And, perhaps through her determination, she discovered Fusae's remains just after cremation was completed. The only clue was the name, Miyata Fusae, written on some underwear.

V

On that day, Father breathed his last, watched over by everyone in the house. After the hardships he'd had as the father of seven children, he'd entered the peaceful life of old age only to suddenly have to finish his life at the age of sixty. He was moved in a coffin made of boards from the collapsed ceiling.

"Please put up with this." My mother's words were heart-breaking, spoken as if to a living person. On Hijiyama, it seemed that many cremations had already taken place, with here and there dug-out depressions in which scattered wooden embers disturbed the white ash.

The coffin flared into flame; inside it my father was stretched out quietly, hands pressed together. The kind, gentle father of bygone days. My brother and I, gripping the wooden pokers, dazedly sat down on a rock. The purple smoke swirled around two or three times, then was lifted into the sky by a wind from somewhere.

VI

Already six years have passed since then. The atomic desert, on which it is said nothing would grow for seventy years, was quickly cleared up, and the shacks with their rusting tin roofs were replaced by new homes smelling of fresh wood, and by reinforced concrete apartments. Where immediately after the war tents were set up on the rubble and a few objects arranged to sell to the people passing by, now there are shopping streets lit by neon lamps, with young men and women jostling after the latest fashions.

Just as weeds send forth shoots no matter how much they are trampled or kicked, so the savage desire to live can never be removed as long as it is rooted in man's true nature.

There is no sign now of that memorable place where my father was cremated; now there is only thick green grass everywhere.

On the clear waters of the Ohta, boats now float, and as I idly gaze up at the white clouds in the blue sky, I cannot believe that this was the stream which swallowed up that poor young girl, as she gave her death cries. But if I stare at the blue waters I feel that her figure is going to appear, rising up from the depths, smiling. And isn't the gentle sound of the waves lapping against the side of the boat the soft murmur of her voice?

Day by day, such sad recollections fade from a person's memory. However, maybe even the power of time cannot heal such blows that have pierced to the marrow of our being. In the blood that flows through me there is a black undercurrent that ebbs and flows, sometimes with great pressure, sometimes gougingly, but never can I control it. Rather, as time passes, it becomes more distinct, more intense.

compiler's letter to the writers

The following letter was sent to each of those who contributed compositions. It is reprinted here for reference.

I would like to thank you for the account of your experiences of the atom bombing. I am deeply grateful for your cooperation with my troublesome request. First, on reading your manuscript, I was once again astonished and grieved at how deep a wound the tragedy had inflicted on the human soul, and also at the candid and forceful style of your writing. Your clear account of such painful scenes often made my eyes blur with tears, though I have gone through many things in my sixty years of life.

At that time, I myself was hospitalized in the compound of the Clothing Depot, and the doctors had said that I would die. But after remaining in critical condition for over four months, I very fortunately got better.

Since then, I have been actively engaged in peace education movements, such as the Japan Culture and Peace Association, UNESCO, the Peace Center movement, and others. It is my ambition to devote the rest of my life to the peace movement, through education.

I would like to make it my responsibility to preserve the invaluable record of your experiences in my room at the Education Seminar of the Faculty of Education, Hiroshima University, as an everlasting spiritual memorial in the history of the world.

You have your future before you. By way of thanking you, I pray for your health, and I hope that you study hard, and help make our country a fine, independent state. I also hope that you eventually contribute to the happiness of mankind and to the peace of the world.

The seventh anniversary of the death of the victims of the atom bomb is this year. While you were writing your account, you must have been remembering the faces of the dead and talking to them in your heart. I think that this is a kind of memorial service for those lost through the atom bomb. Besides preserving these manuscripts for peace education studies, we also want to publish at least some of them in Japan and abroad. I think that it would please those who died, if, through their publication, these manuscripts became a lasting monument to peace in the hearts of people in Japan and in other countries. I am sure that not only the people of Hiroshima, but good people on other parts of Japan and the world, will earnestly pray at the spiritual monument you have built. Monuments made of clay or bronze crumble and decay after thousands of years, but the spiritual monument for the people who died because of the atom bomb, the monument that you have built will last as long as mankind does.

Last, I pray for the repose of the souls of the grandfathers and grandmothers, fathers and mothers, elder brothers, elder sisters, sweet younger brothers and sisters, and all other relatives, who died.

name index

index

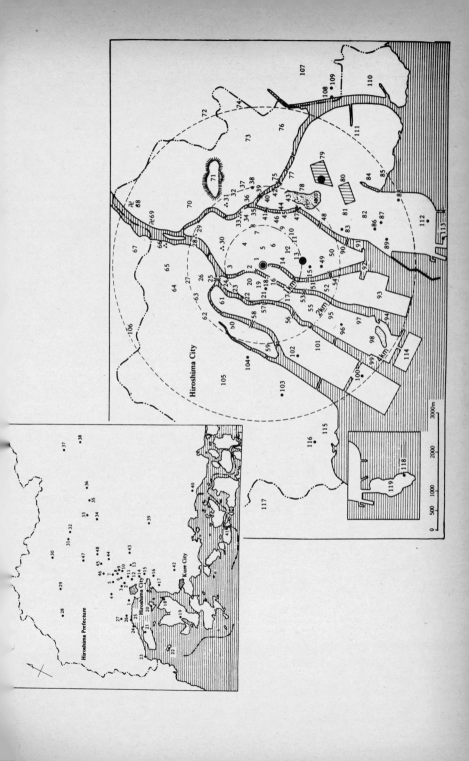

Hiroshima City

Hiroshima Prefecture

Kure City

107
108
109
110
111
72
74
76
73
79
80
84
85
71
75
77
78
8
32
37
38
31
36
39
40
33
34
35
41
46
43
81
82
87
86
89
112
113
70
68
69
30
29
28
33
35
41
46
45
47
48
42
49
50
90
91
92
93
94
95
96
97
98
99
100
114
1
2
3
4
5
6
7
8
9
10
11
12
13
14
15
16
17
18
19
20
21
22
23
24
25
26
27
51
52
53
54
55
56
57
58
59
60
61
62
63
64
65
66
67
101
102
103
104
105
106
115
116
117
118
119

2km
4km

0   500   1000   2000   3000m